VOLUME 574

MARCH 2001

THE ANNALS

of The American Academy *of* Political
and Social Science

ALAN W. HESTON, *Editor*
NEIL A. WEINER, *Assistant Editor*

THE SUPREME COURT'S FEDERALISM: REAL OR IMAGINED?

Special Editor of this Volume

FRANK GOODMAN
University of Pennsylvania Law School
Philadelphia

 Sage Publications, Inc. *THOUSAND OAKS LONDON NEW DELHI*

Origin and Purpose. The Academy was organized December 14, 1889, to promote the progress of political and social science, especially through publications and meetings. The Academy does not take sides in controverted questions, but seeks to gather and present reliable information to assist the public in forming an intelligent and accurate judgment.

Meetings. The Academy occasionally holds a meeting in the spring extending over two days.

Publications. THE ANNALS of the American Academy of Political and Social Science is the bimonthly publication of The Academy. Each issue contains articles on some prominent social or political problem, written at the invitation of the editors. Also, monographs are published from time to time, numbers of which are distributed to pertinent professional organizations. These volumes constitute important reference works on the topics with which they deal, and they are extensively cited by authorities throughout the United States and abroad. The papers presented at the meetings of The Academy are included in THE ANNALS.

Membership. Each member of The Academy receives THE ANNALS and may attend the meetings of The Academy. Membership is open only to individuals. Annual dues: $65.00 for the regular paperbound edition (clothbound, $100.00). For members outside the U.S.A., add $12.00 (surface mail) or $24.00 (air mail) for shipping of your subscription. Members may also purchase single issues of THE ANNALS for $20.00 each (clothbound, $30.00).

Subscriptions. THE ANNALS of the American Academy of Political and Social Science (ISSN 0002-7162) is published six times annually—in January, March, May, July, September, and November. Institutions may subscribe to THE ANNALS at the annual rate: $375.00 (clothbound, $425.00). Add $12.00 per year for subscriptions outside the U.S.A. Institutional rates for single issues: $70.00 each (clothbound, $75.00).

Periodicals postage paid at Thousand Oaks, California, and at additional mailing offices.

Single issues of THE ANNALS may be obtained by individuals who are not members of The Academy for $30.00 each (clothbound, $40.00). Single issues of THE ANNALS have proven to be excellent supplementary texts for classroom use. Direct inquiries regarding adoptions to THE ANNALS c/o Sage Publications (address below).

All correspondence concerning membership in The Academy, dues renewals, inquiries about membership status, and/or purchase of single issues of THE ANNALS should be sent to THE ANNALS c/o Sage Publications, Inc., 2455 Teller Road, Thousand Oaks, CA 91320. Telephone: (805) 499-9774; FAX/Order line: (805) 375-1700. *Please note that orders under $30 must be prepaid.* Sage affiliates in London and India will assist institutional subscribers abroad with regard to orders, claims, and inquiries for both subscriptions and single issues.

Printed on recycled, acid-free paper

THE ANNALS

Editorial Office: Annenberg School for Communication, 3620 Walnut Street, Rm. 232, Philadelphia, PA 19104-6220.

For information about membership* (individuals only) and subscriptions (institutions), address:

SAGE PUBLICATIONS, INC.
2455 Teller Road
Thousand Oaks, CA 91320

Sage Production Staff: MARIA NOTARANGELO, KATE PETERSON, and ROSE TYLAK

From India and South Asia, write to:
SAGE PUBLICATIONS INDIA Pvt. Ltd
P.O. Box 4215
New Delhi 110 048
INDIA

From Europe, the Middle East, and Africa, write to:
SAGE PUBLICATIONS LTD
6 Bonhill Street
London EC2A 4PU
UNITED KINGDOM

**Please note that members of The Academy receive THE ANNALS with their membership.*
International Standard Serial Number ISSN 0002-7162
International Standard Book Number ISBN 0-7619-2440-x (Vol. 574, 2001 paper)
International Standard Book Number ISBN 0-7619-2439-6 (Vol. 574, 2001 cloth)
Manufactured in the United States of America. First printing, March 2001.

The articles appearing in THE ANNALS are abstracted or indexed in *Academic Abstracts, Academic Search, America: History and Life, Asia Pacific Database, Book Review Index, CAB Abstracts Database, Central Asia: Abstracts & Index, Communication Abstracts, Corporate ResourceNET, Criminal Justice Abstracts, Current Citations Express, Current Contents: Social & Behavioral Sciences, e-JEL, EconLit, Expanded Academic Index, Guide to Social Science & Religion in Periodical Literature, Health Business FullTEXT, HealthSTAR FullTEXT, Historical Abstracts, International Bibliography of the Social Sciences, International Political Science Abstracts, ISI Basic Social Sciences Index, Journal of Economic Literature on CD, LEXIS-NEXIS, MasterFILE FullTEXT, Middle East: Abstracts & Index, North Africa: Abstracts & Index, PAIS International, Periodical Abstracts, Political Science Abstracts, Sage Public Administration Abstracts, Social Science Source, Social Sciences Citation Index, Social Sciences Index Full Text, Social Services Abstracts, Social Work Abstracts, Sociological Abstracts, Southeast Asia: Abstracts & Index, Standard Periodical Directory (SPD), TOPICsearch, Wilson OmniFile V,* and *Wilson Social Sciences Index/Abstracts,* and are available on microfilm from University Microfilms, Ann Arbor, Michigan.

Information about membership rates, institutional subscriptions, and back issue prices may be found on the facing page.

Advertising. Current rates and specifications may be obtained by writing to THE ANNALS Advertising and Promotion Manager at the Thousand Oaks office (address above).

Claims. Claims for undelivered copies must be made no later than six months following month of publication. The publisher will supply missing copies when losses have been sustained in transit and when the reserve stock will permit.

Change of Address. Six weeks advance notice must be given when notifying of change of address to ensure proper identification. Please specify name of journal. **POSTMASTER:** Send address changes to: THE ANNALS of the American Academy of Political and Social Science, c/o Sage Publications, Inc., 2455 Teller Road, Thousand Oaks, CA 91320.

#4595660I

THE ANNALS

of The American Academy *of* Political *and* Social Science

ALAN W. HESTON, *Editor*
NEIL A. WEINER, *Assistant Editor*

――――――――――― **FORTHCOMING** ―――――――――――

CHILDREN'S RIGHTS
Special Editor: Jude L. Fernando
Volume 575   May 2001

COURTHOUSE VIOLENCE:
PROTECTING THE JUDICIAL WORKPLACE
Special Editors: Victor Flango
and Don Hardenbergh
Volume 576   July 2001

REFORMING WELFARE, REDEFINING POVERTY
Special Editors: Randy Albelda
and Ann Withorn
Volume 577   September 2001

See page 2 for information on Academy membership and
purchase of single volumes of **The Annals.**

CONTENTS

BOOK DEPARTMENT CONTENTS

INTERNATIONAL RELATIONS AND POLITICS

AFRICA, ASIA, AND LATIN AMERICA

ECONOMICS

PREFACE

In the last decade, the Supreme Court has handed down a remarkable series of decisions invalidating congressional legislation in the name of federalism or states' rights. Most of these were decided by a razor-thin majority of five justices—the Court's conservative quintet of Chief Justice William Rehnquist and Justices Sandra Day O'Connor, Antonin Scalia, Anthony Kennedy, and Clarence Thomas. The cases fall into four categories.

First, the Court reaffirmed and expanded the principle of state sovereign immunity. In *Seminole Tribe of Florida v. Florida*[1] and *Alden v. Maine*,[2] it held that Congress cannot subject an unconsenting state to suit in either federal or (its own) state court, whether the suit is brought by a citizen or noncitizen of that state, and whether it is based on federal law or state law. The four dissenters in *Seminole* argued that the states' constitutional immunity is confined within the four corners of the Eleventh Amendment, which rules out of federal court only suits against a state by "citizens of another state." The majority, however, concluded that the immunity is inherent in the concept of state sovereignty, rests upon a structural principle of the Constitution that is presupposed by but not limited to the text of the Eleventh, and extends even to suits by the state's own citizens for violation of federal law. Three years later, *Alden* further extended this nontextual constitutional immunity to suits in the state's own courts.

In a second pair of cases, the Court held that state governments (other than their courts) cannot be "commandeered" by Congress to assist in the enforcement of federal law. State legislatures cannot be required to regulate in accordance with congressional instructions,[3] nor can state executive offices be forced to perform federal tasks.[4] This aspect of state sovereignty, like immunity from suit, was attributed by the Court to the intentions of the Founders. Both immunities—from suit and from commandeering—can be waived by consent, and consent made a condition of eligibility for federal grants or privileges.

Third, for the first time since the early New Deal, the Court, by the familiar 5-4 margin, invalidated a federal statute enacted pursuant to the interstate commerce clause. For nearly 60 years, the reigning principle of that clause has been that even local activities are reachable by Congress if they have "substantial effects" on interstate commerce.[5] In 1995, however, *United States v. Lopez*[6] declared unconstitutional a law banning possession of guns within 1000 feet of a school, despite the aggregate impact of the regulated activity on the national economy through its effects on education and crime. The Court declared that to accept such remote effects as justification for

NOTE: The author owes many thanks to Jarett Epstein both for his splendid assistance in the editing of this volume and for his useful comments on the preface.

federal regulation would virtually obliterate all limits on congressional power; but it also stressed the noneconomic character of the regulated activity, a fact that distinguished *Lopez* from all previous cases sustaining legislation on the "substantial effects" rationale. Any doubt as to the importance of this latter factor was removed last term in *United States v. Morrison*[7] in which the same narrowly divided Court struck down a provision of the Violence Against Women Act (VAWA) creating a federal civil remedy against the perpetrators of gender-motivated crimes of violence. Again the Court stressed the noneconomic nature of the regulated activity, stopping just short of a categorical rule placing such activity beyond congressional power.

Finally, the Court adopted a new, and extremely demanding, standard of review for congressional action under Section 5 of the Fourteenth Amendment, which empowers Congress to "enforce" the amendment "by appropriate legislation." That standard—which requires that prophylactic legislation under Section 5 must have "congruence and proportionality" to the evil Congress seeks to remedy—was laid down only four years ago in *City of Boerne v. Flores*[8] but has already resulted in the invalidation of four congressional statutes.[9] What makes this lethal standard particularly important from the standpoint of federalism is that *valid* legislation under Section 5 trumps all of the other limitations on congressional power discussed previously in this preface. Acting validly pursuant to Section 5, Congress can subject a state to involuntary suit in either federal or state courts, can commandeer state cooperation in the enforcement of federal law, and, of course, can regulate local noneconomic activities regardless of their effect on interstate commerce. "Congruence and proportionality" thus constitute a multidimensional red light.

A PREVIEW OF THE ARTICLES

The 13 articles in this volume deal with various aspects of the Supreme Court's federalist revival and the principles underlying it. The first 3 articles discuss these principles in comprehensive terms. Steven Calabresi argues that federalism serves important values highly deserving of constitutional protection; that the political branches of the federal government cannot be trusted to police the boundaries of federalism on their own; and that judicial review by the Supreme Court is no less vital a safeguard for the rights of the states than for the rights of the individual.

In contrast, Edward Rubin is a nonadmirer of federalism and, beyond that, a nonbeliever in its reality. He contends that contemporary America is, and long has been, a unitary national polity, with the states as branch offices; that the lip service we pay to federalism is a nostalgic hangover from our formative years, a mere "puppy federalism" related to the authentic one as puppy love is to the real thing. The Supreme Court's recent decisions in this area, though incorrect, are essentially harmless and will go no further than our popular national commitment to centralized government allows them to.

Robert Nagel, on middle ground, sees both powerful centralizing and potentially radical decentralizing tendencies in our current cultural and social situation and is uncertain which of these tendencies will prevail. He is convinced, however, that the Supreme Court and the mechanisms of judicial review will do little to foster attitudes of defiance and dissent at the local level that are necessary for an effective decentralization movement. The justices themselves are too little committed to federalism, and the constitutional text too little supportive of it, to be an effective barrier to centralized national power. Indeed, those who favor greater decentralization may well conclude that judicial review—with its concentration of power in a single national tribunal not notably shy about exercising it—is part of the problem, rather than the solution.

Each of the next three articles focuses on a particular aspect of the federalism principle or its judicial enforcement. One of the most prominent arguments for federalism is its claimed contribution to individual liberty. Seth Kreimer evaluates this claim in depth. He argues, among other things, that some states are more protective and others less protective of individual liberty than is the federal government, so that displacement of the states by a unitary national government would enhance the liberty of some citizens while reducing that of others. A further implication of his analysis is that the mutual ability of the state and federal levels of government to check one another's excesses makes them jointly more protective of liberty than either level alone would be. A particularly important conclusion is that the greatest contribution of federalism to freedom is the court-enforced right of every citizen to exit his or her own state and find sanctuary in another, notwithstanding the laws of either, and to be treated as an equal in the state of refuge. By thus guaranteeing interstate mobility, constitutional federalism enables each citizen to choose the kind of liberty he or she prefers, an option unavailable under either a unitary national government or a multiplicity of independent, fully sovereign states.

Evan Caminker explores whether the "dignitary" interests of the state—the "respect due them as members of the federation"—provide a plausible justification for the Court's sovereign immunity jurisprudence rather than merely a rhetorical embellishment. He concludes that the idea of the states as coequal sovereigns is anachronistic and that the constitutional rule giving the states immunity from suit as an expression of respect for their dignity as sovereigns is in conflict with a competing expressive norm of respect for the dignity of the individual.

A number of eminent scholars have argued that judicial enforcement of federalism is both unnecessary and undesirable because the political process—chiefly, the influence of the state governments upon Congress—can be relied upon to protect the states from excessive interference by the federal government. Marci Hamilton disputes this claim, invoking both historical arguments—the understanding of the Framers and ratifiers of the Constitution—and contemporary empirical evidence for the proposition that judicial enforcement is an essential safeguard of states' rights and that politics alone will not suffice.

The ability of Congress to escape the constitutional limitations of federalism by means of conditional grants under the spending clause has led some commentators to conclude that these limitations are toothless formalities and should be abandoned. Lynn Baker argues, to the contrary, that it is the spending clause itself that should be brought into conformity with constitutional restrictions on congressional regulatory power. Congress, that is, should not be permitted to condition the grant of funds to the states (beyond reimbursing their cost of compliance) upon actions that Congress would be powerless to command.

The next three articles point up alternative themes, purposes, or agendas in the Court's federalism decisions. In a fiercely critical article, Herman Schwartz argues that the states'-rights rhetoric of the conservative justices is merely a cover, a "fig leaf," for their true agenda: an attack on the New Deal, on civil rights, and on the racial and economic groups that have benefited from them. The conservative members of the Court, he claims, are interested in protecting the states from Congress only when they approve of what the states are doing and disapprove of what Congress is doing.

Unlike Schwartz, Ann Althouse is generally sympathetic to the Court's federalism decisions, but she, too, believes that more is going on in them than meets the eye. *Lopez* and *Morrison*, she contends, reflect in addition the Court's disapproval of the congressional tendency to load federal courts with ordinary criminal and tort cases that properly belong in state courts. Protection of the federal judiciary, no less than protection of the states, she argues, is the underlying concern in those cases.

Both Althouse and Vicki Jackson draw attention to the theme of judicial supremacy that runs parallel with federalism in many of the Court's decisions. As Jackson puts it, the Court may be driven "at least as much [by] concern for its own role vis-à-vis the political branches as for federalism." Jackson also suggests ways in which Congress might craft its legislation with a view to improving its chances for judicial survival.

The articles by Matthew Adler and by Daniel Halberstam and Roderick Hills, Jr., both focus on the anti-commandeering issue but place that issue in a broader context—Adler in a general analysis of the "state sovereignty" concept, Halberstam and Hills in a comparison of the American and German models of "cooperative federalism." Adler concludes that the categorical rule announced in the *New York* and *Printz* cases is mistaken but not clearly so; that the danger of excessive intrusion by Congress upon the structure and operations of state government is a legitimate concern; and that alternative approaches to that problem, narrower and perhaps less rigid than the one the Court has adopted, are worth serious consideration.

Halberstam and Hills compare German and American federalism with particular reference to the constitutional mechanisms by which the states (or *Länder*, in Germany) can be required to participate in the implementation of federal law, enabled to resist such conscriptions if they so choose (either through a collective veto as in Germany or an individual veto as in the United States), or bypassed by federal agencies as in the United States if they exercise such a veto. They conclude that the German model is more protective of state autonomy because of the collective veto and the absence of federal bypass but that Germany pays a price for this in reduced opportunities for flexible and efficient cooperation between the state and federal authorities in the implementation of national law.

Finally, Jordan Steiker illuminates, from several perspectives, the four-year-old federal habeas corpus statute (the Anti-Terrorism and Effective Death Penalty Act). Steiker observes that for students of federalism, this statute presents an "enormous puzzle," enlarging the size and power of the federal law enforcement bureaucracy while at the same time seeming "to honor the finality concerns of state criminal justice systems and the comity of state courts." He explains this apparent "schizophrenic attitude toward federalism" by noting that the political debate about the scope of federal habeas has more to do with the death penalty than with federalism.

BUSH V. GORE: THE WORLD TURNED UPSIDE DOWN

The Supreme Court's recent decision in *Bush v. Gore*[10]—issued shortly before this volume went to press—dramatically subverts the federalist principles that are the subject of our inquiry. The Court, as most politically sentient Americans know, reversed the decision of the Florida Supreme Court, ordering a statewide manual recount of the "undervotes" in the presidential election, the ballots registered as nonvotes by the machines that did the initial counting and recounting. In an unsigned *per curiam* decision by the five conservative justices, over fierce dissents by the four more liberal justices, the Court held that the absence of uniform statewide standards for determining how to count these ballots, and the marked disparities from county to county (and even within counties) in the standards actually used, violated the equal protection clause of the federal Constitution, but that this problem could not be corrected by the Florida Supreme Court within the time allotted by Florida law. Both sides of this Scylla and Charybdis—the federal-law holding of equal protection violations and the state-law conclusion that time had run out— have generated a blizzard of criticism, much of it characterizing the *per curiam* decision as a grievous self-inflicted wound that threatens to diminish public respect for the Court.

Although the equal protection issue is not immediately germane to this volume, its centrality to the case demands comment. Local disparities in voting mechanisms and procedures are pandemic in the United States and certainly were in Florida. The most conspicuous and consequential of these was the use of voting machines in some counties, while others settled for punch card equipment that made it much more difficult for voters accurately to register their choice. This inequity tended to cut along class, racial, and political party lines. Counting *all* of the unperforated but clearly legible punch card ballots as legal votes would have partially, but not entirely, redressed this larger technological inequality. Without commenting on this enormous reality, seven justices found fatal constitutional defects within the category of punch card balloters at the manual recount stage. For example, ballots with "dimpled chads" (those having an indentation but no perforation in the space for presidential electors) would be counted as legal votes in some counties but not in others. Although the Court could do nothing about the technological disparity in voting equipment (no party having formally challenged its constitutionality either before or after the election), its very existence should have dissuaded the Court from making its doctrinally audacious and politically momentous constitutional assault upon the mini-disparity between punch card voters and, more narrowly still, chad dimplers. The remedy urged by Justices Breyer and Souter—to allow the Florida Supreme Court to repair the constitutional flaws by adopting a uniform statewide standard—might not have reduced the larger inequality but would not greatly have increased it. In contrast, the remedy adopted by the *per curiam* five—once-and-forever disqualification of all ballots not sufficiently perforated to be read by a machine—significantly widened the disparity of treatment between the machine-equipped and punch-card-equipped voters, while paying lip service to the principle of equal protection.

It is arguable, to be sure, that voters who break the rules—by failing to perforate their ballots as instructed by signs at the polls—do not *deserve* to be treated as well as those who follow the rules. However that might be as a policy matter, it is doubtful that a majority of the Court would have been prepared to invalidate, on federal constitutional grounds, a statewide rule (whether legislatively or judicially prescribed) requiring that unperforated but legible ballots be counted as legal votes.

For purposes of this volume, the more relevant feature of the Court's *per curiam* decision was its holding that it was too late under state law for the Florida Supreme Court, upon remand, to correct the equal protection flaws by adopting uniform statewide standards for the manual recounts. Here the U.S. Supreme Court appeared to be second-guessing the Florida court on a question of state law, a federal intrusion upon state autonomy more drastic than any of the congressional intrusions nullified by the Court in the decisions discussed in this volume. The *per curiam* opinion concluded that the Florida legislature intended that all of the counting be completed, the contests resolved, and the presidential electors certified by 12 December—the safe-harbor date specified by 3 U.S.C. § 5. Given that the Florida statute makes no mention of this or any other deadline for completing the contest process, and no mention of the federal constitutional or statutory provisions relating to presidential elections, the attribution of that drop-dead date to the legislature seems a clear usurpation of the interpretative authority of the Florida Supreme Court. One would have expected the five conservative justices to be the first, not the last, to adhere to the well-established principle that a state supreme court is the final authority on the meaning of state law. Moreover, after the criticism some of the justices leveled at the Florida Court for reading a deadline *out* of the election statute (at the earlier "protest" phase of the post-election proceedings), it was particularly inappropriate for the federal Court itself to read such a deadline *into* the statute.

The justification offered by the *per curiam* opinion was that "the Florida Supreme Court has already said that the Florida Legislature intended to obtain the safe-harbor benefits of 3 U.S.C. § 5" and that the state's electors should be able to "participate fully in the federal election process." In other words, the federal Supreme Court was not itself interpreting Florida law but merely acting upon the ready-made interpretation of the Florida Supreme Court. This reading of the state court's opinion, however, was a gross distortion. Suffice it to say that the Florida Supreme Court came nowhere near attributing to the Florida legislature an intent to achieve the safe-harbor of 3 U.S.C. § 5 come hell or high water, even if it meant that thousands of contested machine-rejected ballots—many clearly indicating voter intent—would remain uninspected by human eyes. In the contest phase, as in the protest phase, the task of reconciling conflicting legislative objectives properly belonged to the court in Tallahassee, not the one in Washington, D.C.

Against all this, it might be replied that the Supreme Court's disrespect for the Florida judiciary ought not be equated with disrespect for the state of Florida, its legislature, or its citizens. On the contrary, it was necessary to overrule the state supreme court precisely in order to effectuate the decisions and protect the role of the elected legislature. Indeed, three members of the federal Supreme Court majority—Rehnquist, Scalia, and Thomas—joined in a concurring opinion[11] interpreting Article II of the federal Constitution as a grant of authority to the state legislature to direct the manner of choosing presidential electors without judicial review by the Florida courts. The conservative justices, however, have repeatedly invoked the principle of judicial supremacy over the legislature in the interpretation of federal law,[12] faithful to Marshall's famous declaration in *Marbury v. Madison*[13] that "it is emphatically the province and duty of the judicial department to say what the law is." It is ironic that these same justices should be the ones to reach out for a textually unnecessary interpretation of Article II that strips the Florida Supreme Court of its normal responsibility for resolving ambiguities and contradictions in what the legislature has done. One might have expected that sticklers for judicial supremacy would have read Article II, the Florida election statute, or both as taking judicial review for granted.

Perhaps the best justification for the Court's action is not legal but political. The majority justices—or some of them—may have looked down the road and seen a constitutional catastrophe in the making: a Gore victory in the manual recount; two competing slates of electors placed before Congress, both bearing the Florida governor's signature; a conflict between the two houses (neither Gore nor Lieberman having recused himself); and absolutely no legal basis for resolving that conflict. In bypassing the political process, the Court may have saved the process from itself. Unfortunately, there is also a less benign explanation: one or more of the justices may have reached the conclusion that if the presidential outcome were going to be determined by an act of judicial will, it would be their will, not that of the Florida Supreme Court.

I conclude this preface with some observations on two discrete topics. The first is the federalism-based limitations the Court has placed, chiefly in *Lopez* and *Morrison*, on the grants of congressional power in the commerce clause and Section 5 of the Fourteenth Amendment. The second is the "sovereign immunity" of the states from suit, a subject little treated in the articles that follow.

LIMITATIONS ON THE GRANTED CONGRESSIONAL POWERS

In *Lopez* and *Morrison*, the Court was struggling with, and against, the legacy of two similarly named Warren Court decisions of the mid-1960s: *Katzenbach v. McClung*[14] and *Katzenbach v. Morgan*.[15] In *McClung*, the Court upheld, under the commerce clause, provisions of the Civil Rights Act of 1964 prohibiting racial discrimination in "places of public accommodation" (restaurants, theaters, hotels, and so on). Although the world was aware that the purpose of this legislation was moral and social, not economic, the Court nevertheless sustained it on the ground that racial discrimination had substantial effects on interstate commerce, including macro-effects on the locational decisions of skilled professionals and new businesses. Two years later, in *Morgan*, the Court upheld a provision of the Voting Rights Act of 1965 that barred the use of state English literacy tests to deny the vote to persons with a grade-school education in Puerto Rico. Although it was clear that such literacy tests were not themselves unconstitutional under the equal protection clause, and that Section 5 did not authorize Congress to enlarge the substantive scope of that clause, the Court nevertheless upheld the statute as a "prophylactic" measure, protecting the Puerto Rican community against other potential state actions that would be unconstitutional (for example, discrimination in public services or racially motivated voting qualifications). Taken together, *McClung*'s macro-effects theory of the commerce clause and *Morgan*'s prophylactic theory of Section 5 seemed to throw open all doors to Congress, promising (or threatening) to remove all limitations on the two great affirmative grants of congressional power. *Lopez* and *Morrison* can be understood as the current Court's refusal to permit this erasure of boundaries. Both decisions expressed deep skepticism about the acceptability of aggregating instances, and then piling up inferences, to demonstrate remote macro-effects on the national economy, and *Morrison* continued to cut back on the "prophylactic" use of Section 5.

The commerce clause: Lopez *and* Morrison

If one accepts the premise that the basic architecture of the Constitution requires meaningful limits on the power of Congress to regulate interstate commerce, the line between economic and noneconomic activity is not a bad one. First, it has an arguable footing in the constitutional text: "Commerce among the several states" must, at least, be "commerce" before we start wrestling with the rest of the phrase. Second, it is consistent with prior cases, at least at the factual level. Third, the activities it would place beyond congressional power are, for the most part, activities that concern Congress mainly for reasons other than their effects upon interstate commerce. Admittedly, the economic-noneconomic distinction presents some problems. Not all activities can easily be classified in this way. Moreover, if it is the effects on commerce that bring an activity within the reach of Congress, the nature of that activity would seem irrelevant.

Other possible ways of limiting Congress might, however, present even greater problems. First, the Court could be more demanding in its assessment of the substantiality of an activity's effects on interstate commerce, but this approach would be indefinite, often unrealistic, and disrespectful of established precedents and principles. Alternatively, the Court could try to build a fence around activities of traditional state concern and competence; but a similar approach proved unworkable when the Court tried to use "traditional state functions" in defining which activities of the states themselves would be off limits to Congress.[16] Third, a balancing test that weighed the interstate commerce interest against the competing state interests would be more likely to combine the defects than the virtues of the other two methods. Fourth, an inquiry into congressional motives to verify that interstate commerce was truly the animating concern would be unseemly, uncertain, and a major departure from precedent.

The objection to the economic-noneconomic distinction on the ground that it is formalistic ignores the fact that formalism has been a persistent feature of commerce clause case law, often *favoring* congressional power. A century ago, the Court upheld federal statutes prohibiting the interstate transportation of lottery tickets,[17] prostitutes,[18] and adulterated foods,[19] even though everyone knew that the purpose of this legislation was moral and social, not economic; and in the 1960s, it sustained a prohibition against racial discrimination by restaurants receiving a substantial amount of food from interstate sources,[20] even though Congress clearly cared not a whit where the food came from except as a legal front. Indeed, the Court's acknowledgment, both in *Lopez* and *Morrison*, that a "jurisdictional element" (some reference in the statute to interstate commerce) would rescue even regulation of *noneconomic* activities (for example, possession of a gun that has moved in interstate commerce) is a prime example of formalism. Admittedly, a categorical distinction between economic and noneconomic activities would be reminiscent of the distinction between manufacturing and commerce that once, lamentably, helped mark the boundary line of congressional power, but the older distinction made less sense in terms of the text or purposes of the commerce clause and, quite obviously, was vastly more restrictive of congressional power.

Section 5 of the Fourteenth Amendment: Morrison *again*

The Court's new requirement that a federal statute purporting to remedy violations of the Fourteenth Amendment must use means "congruent and proportional" to those violations was unremarkable in its original setting. In *Boerne*, there was virtually no evidence that states had in fact used facially neutral laws to target religion, and the federal statute, supposedly intended as a remedy for this ruse, was thus a transparent effort to expand the substantive scope of the religious freedom guarantee. *Morrison* was quite another matter. The legislative record supporting VAWA contained voluminous evidence of gender-motivated underenforcement of state laws designed to protect women from violence. The congressional response was a civil remedy against the perpetrators of this violence (including persons "acting under color of state law"). The Supreme Court, without disputing either the prevalence of discriminatory enforcement or the possibility of its unconstitutionality, struck down VAWA's civil remedy because it was directed not at the states or their officials but at private actors who could not themselves commit Fourteenth Amendment violations and whose liability would not deter such violations by state actors. Ironically, a federal action against the states—the very remedy that would have been barred by state sovereign immunity had Congress not been acting under the Fourteenth Amendment—might well have been upheld under Section 5.

Morrison was not, in any ordinary sense, a states'-rights decision. Much of the evidence before Congress came from official state reports. Thirty-six state attorneys general submitted an amicus curiae brief to the Supreme Court supporting the federal government's position and defending the congressional remedy as an appropriate complement to the states' own enforcement efforts. *Morrison*, like *Lopez*, and like the immunity and noncomandeering cases, preserved the Court's vision of the constitutional architecture—in this case the distinction between substantive and remedial action by Congress under Section 5, and ultimately, the Court's supremacy over Congress in defining constitutional substance. But neither the states nor their citizens could (or apparently did) take comfort from this brand of federalism.

The use of the "congruence and proportionality" test to raise the bar in Section 5 cases is further ironic—indeed anomalous—in two respects. First, the Court now seems to be judging statutes designed to *protect* basic civil rights with something like the skepticism traditionally reserved for statutes *destructive* of those same rights. Second, it is using in these civil rights cases a standard of review more rigorous than the one traditionally applied in economic regulation cases under the commerce clause. There is a textual, as well as a normative, irony here.

Article I authorizes Congress to make all laws "necessary and proper" for carrying into execution its enumerated powers. This superficially demanding standard was famously watered down by Chief Justice John Marshall in *McCulloch v. Maryland* to mean merely "appropriate."[21] Section 5 of the Fourteenth Amendment adopts this same lenient phraseology, empowering Congress "to enforce, by appropriate legislation," the provisions of the amendment; and the Court, in earlier applications of this language, indicated that "the draftsmen sought to grant to Congress, by a specific provision applicable to the 14th Amendment, the same broad powers expressed in" the *McCulloch* formulation.[22] Now, however, with congruence and proportionality, the Court tracks Marshall in reverse, ratcheting up the permissive textual standard to something approaching "necessary." To be sure, Section 5 gives only the power to "enforce," not substantively redefine, the guarantees of the amendment; but likewise Article I gives only the power to execute, not to enlarge upon, enumerated grants such as the commerce clause. Although Marshall declared that the Court would intervene should Congress, "under the pretext of executing its powers, pass laws for the accomplishment of objects not entrusted to the government,"[23] that promise has largely been honored in the breach. The current Court apparently means to keep that promise in Section 5 cases, using congruence and proportionality as a search engine for pretext.

Even under congruence and proportionality, however, VAWA presented a close case. Congress could reasonably have concluded that the availability of a federal civil remedy would invigorate the states' enforcement of their own laws. A federal judgment against an alleged rapist or abuser might lead state authorities, otherwise skeptical or indifferent, to prosecute and state judges and juries to convict. More generally, the federal regime, if successful, might provide a model for the state, a competitive benchmark against which to measure its own performance, or a source of embarrassing questions from a dissatisfied public. These possibilities might not have played out, but arguably Congress deserved the benefit of the doubt, especially since the alternative remedy apparently approved by the Court—monetary liability imposed on state actors themselves (presumably for their lack of zeal)—seems anything but appropriate.

The *Morrison* majority made no reference to VAWA's possible effects upon the enforcement practices of state authorities, the possibility that VAWA's remedy against private offenders might stiffen state enforcement practices and thus deter constitutional violations. The Court's silence on this score was understandable in that Congress itself made no findings on the subject and there was little or no discussion of it in the extensive legislative record. *Morrison* may well have been a case in which congressional findings would, as envisioned in *Lopez*, have brought to the Court's attention constitutionally critical causal linkages not "visible to the naked eye."[24]

Another possibility, however, is that the majority justices considered and rejected the hypothesis suggested above. They may have believed that the federal remedy, far from inspiring or shaming state authorities to strengthen their enforcement effort, would have the opposite effect, *relieving* those authorities of the political heat they would otherwise encounter. Indeed, the justices might have suspected that the widespread support for VAWA among state attorneys general reflected, consciously or otherwise, a desire to be let off the hook. In this light, *Morrison* might be seen not as a victory for states' rights but as a victory for state responsibility, likewise an important aspect of federalism.

SOVEREIGN IMMUNITY

No one pretends that a state's immunity from suit by its own citizens is supported by the *text* of the Constitution. Under Article III, "the judicial power of the United States" extends, inter alia, to "all cases arising under" the Constitution or laws of the United States and to controversies "between a State and Citizens of another State"; and the Eleventh Amendment excludes only suits against a state "by Citizens of another State." Textually, therefore, the states are subject to federal court jurisdiction either in all federal-question cases or, at the very least, those brought by one of the state's own citizens. Nevertheless, in 1890 the Supreme Court held, in *Hans v. Louisiana*,[25] that Article III was not intended to give federal courts any jurisdiction over unconsenting states and that the Eleventh Amendment confirmed this generally accepted principle in the only situation—a citizen suit under the diversity clause—in which it had been challenged.[26] The Court relied heavily on statements by leading advocates of the Constitution—Hamilton, Madison, and Marshall—during the ratification debates to the effect that, in Hamilton's words, it "is inherent in the nature of sovereignty not to be amenable to the suit of an individual without its consent."[27]

Hans was reaffirmed in 1974[28] and was heavily relied upon in the recent *Seminole* and *Alden* cases. *Seminole*, then, broke no ground. *Alden* did so only superficially. The Eleventh Amendment per se—being concerned only with the "judicial power of the United States"—had no bearing on the immunity question in the states' own courts, not even the limited bearing it had on citizen suits in federal courts. That issue was thus, strictly speaking, a novel one. But the sovereign's immunity from suit in its own courts without consent was the core of the historic doctrine; immunity from suit in *federal* courts was a problematic extension of that doctrinal core. Having approved the extension, the Court could not very well deny the core. *Seminole*, in short, implied *Alden*, but not vice versa.

If the Court had been writing on a clean judicial slate, however, it might have had difficulty justifying these decisions on originalist (and certainly on nonoriginalist) grounds. The letter of the Constitution was clearly against the immunity, and for many originalists (including, now and again, some of the conservative justices themselves) that alone would have been fatal. Other originalists would be prepared to look behind the plain meaning of the text if the evidence of contrary intent on the part of the drafters and ratifiers were sufficiently clear. In the last two decades, however, there has emerged in the scholarly literature a powerful revisionist interpretation both of the Founding debates and of *Hans*—namely, that the assurances of state immunity by Hamilton, Madison, and Marshall, relied on in *Hans*, were intended to apply only to suits based on state law and brought to federal courts under the diversity clause, not to federal-question cases; that the Eleventh Amendment precisely confirmed this limited immunity and nothing more; and that *Hans* was not to the contrary, since the immunity it recognized in federal-question suits by a state's own citizens was merely a *nonconstitutional* immunity that could be, but in *Hans* itself had not been, overridden by Congress. This diversity interpretation of sovereign immunity has never commanded a majority of the Court, but it forms the backbone of the elaborate dissenting opinions in *Seminole* and *Alden*, to which four justices subscribed. Although perhaps inconclusive, the evidence supporting the diversity theory at the very least put the original understanding in doubt. Indeed, in *Seminole*, Chief Justice Rehnquist observed that since the federal courts did not have statutory federal question jurisdiction until 1875, "it seems unlikely that much thought was given [at the time the Eleventh Amendment was passed] to the prospect of federal-question jurisdiction over the States," and it would have been "overly exacting" to expect Marshall, Madison, and Hamilton to have spoken with "greater specificity about a then-dormant jurisdiction."[29] In short, the Framers did not focus specifically on the problem at hand in *Seminole*. What we have, then, is a nontextual—indeed, a countertextual—constitutional immunity for the states, carved out by justices famously opposed to the judicial creation of nontextual constitutional rights, on the basis of a controversial (albeit plausible) reading of the legislative history and on behalf of a state sovereignty principle that has grown progressively weaker in the two centuries since the Founding.

Moreover, the practical importance of the constitutional immunity, either to the states or their adversaries, is doubtful. It is no barrier to suits against local governments, which have never been thought to share the immunity even though they typically have greater financial need of it; suits for *injunctive* relief against state *officials*, even if the costs of compliance fall entirely, and heavily, on state treasuries;[30] suits against *consenting* states, even though the consent may be voluntary in name only, the price of obtaining funds or privileges from Congress that the state can ill afford to pass up; suits by one state against another or by the United States;[31] or suits authorized by Congress pursuant to its power to enforce the Thirteenth, Fourteenth, or Fifteenth Amendment.[32] A determined Congress, therefore, can navigate around the states' constitutional immunity either by purchasing their consent with federal benefits or by authorizing the federal government itself to sue for damages and then pass the proceeds to the wronged private parties. Granted, it would be prohibitively expensive for the federal government to keep track of, and seek redress for, all violations of, say, the federal minimum wage law. But no such comprehensive monitoring would be necessary; Congress could limit government suits to cases in which the injured private parties had already succeeded in obtaining injunctive relief against the appropriate state officials or had otherwise convinced the government of the merits of their claims.

Congress, however, has rarely displayed anything approaching such determination. Indeed, it has not exercised to the full even its undeniable power of abrogation under the Fourteenth Amendment. Although it has long been established that 42 U.S.C § 1983—passed shortly after and pursuant to the Fourteenth Amendment, creating federal civil remedies against persons "acting under color of state law"—was not intended to apply to the states,[33] yet Congress has not amended § 1983 to fill this gap and, what is more, was careful not to make the states liable in its most important recent civil rights statute, VAWA. If it is indeed important that states be financially accountable for federal, and particularly constitutional, wrongdoing, the failure of Congress to act comprehensively within the vital sphere of civil rights, in which it has unquestioned power, may be as regrettable as the peripheral barriers erected by the Supreme Court outside that sphere.

FRANK GOODMAN

Notes

1. 517 U.S. 44 (1996).
2. 527 U.S. 598 (1999).
3. *New York v. United States*, 505 U.S. 144 (1992).
4. *Printz v. United States*, 521 U.S. 898 (1997).
5. See *Wickard v. Filburn*, 317 U.S. 111 (1942); *United States v. Darby*, 312 U.S. 100 (1941).
6. 514 U.S. 549 (1995).
7. 529 U.S. 598 (2000).
8. 521 U.S. 507 (1997).
9. See *United States v. Morrison*, 120 S. Ct. 1740, 1758 (2000) (Violence Against Women Act); *Kimel v. Florida Bd. of Regents*, 528 U.S. 62 (2000) (Age Discrimination in Employment Act); *Florida Prepaid Postsecondary Ed. Expense Bd. v. College Savings Bank*, 527 U.S. 627, 639 (1999) (Patent Remedy Act); *City of Boerne v. Flores*, 521 U.S. 507 (1997) (Religious Freedom Restoration Act).
10. 531 U.S. ____ (2000).
11. Id. at ____.
12. See, for example, *City of Boerne*, 521 U.S. at 529, 536.
13. 1 Cranch (5 U.S.) 137, 177 (1803).
14. 379 U.S. 294 (1964).
15. 384 U.S. 641 (1966).
16. *National League of Cities v. Usery*, 426 U.S. 833 (1976), overruled by *Garcia v. San Antonio Metropolitan Transit Authority*, 469 U.S. 528 (1985).
17. *Champion v. Ames*, 188 U.S. 321 (1903).
18. *Hoke v. United States*, 227 U.S. 308 (1913).
19. *Hipolite Egg Co. v. United States*, 220 U.S. 45 (1911).
20. *Katzenbach v. McClung*, 379 U.S. 294 (1964).
21. 4 Wheat. (17 U.S.) 316 (1819).

22. *Katzenbach v. Morgan*, 384 U.S. 641, 650 (1966); see also *South Carolina v. Katzenbach*, 383 U.S. 301, 326 (1966) (Fifteenth Amendment).

23. *McCulloch v. Maryland*, 4 Wheat. (17 U.S.) 316 (1819).

24. *United States v. Lopez*, 514 U.S. 549 (1995).

25. 134 U.S. 1 (1890).

26. See *Chisholm v. Georgia*, 2 Dall. (2 U.S.) 419 (1973).

27. See *Hans*, 134 U.S. at 13 (quoting Hamilton, Federalist 81). See also quotations from Madison and Marshall, id. at 14.

28. *Edelman v. Jordan*, 414 U.S. 651 (1974).

29. *Seminole Tribe of Florida*, 517 U.S. at 70.

30. *Ex parte Young*, 209 U.S. 123 (1908).

31. *Monaco v. Mississippi*, 292 U.S. 313, 328-29 (1934).

32. *Fitzpatrick v. Bitzer*, 427 U.S. 445 (1976).

33. *Quern v. Jordan*, 440 U.S. 332 (1979).

References

Age Discrimination in Employment Act of 1967. 29 U.S.C. § 621 (1994).

Anti-Terrorism and Effective Death Penalty Act of 1996. Pub. L. No. 104-132. 110 Stat. 1214.

Civil Rights Act of 1964. 42 U.S.C. §§ 2000a to 2000h-6 (1994).

Patent Remedy Act (Patent and Plant Variety Protection Remedy Clarification Act of 1992). 35 U.S.C. §§ 271(h), 296(a) (1994).

Religious Freedom Restoration Act of 1993. 42 U.S.C. §§ 2000bb to 2000bb-4.

Violence Against Women Act of 1994. 42 U.S.C. § 13981 (1994).

Voting Rights Act of 1965. 42 U.S.C. §§ 1971, 1973-1973p (1994).

ANNALS, *AAPSS*, **574**, March 2001

Federalism and the Rehnquist Court: A Normative Defense

By STEVEN G. CALABRESI

ABSTRACT: The revival of federalism limits on national power by the U.S. Supreme Court is a happy development for three reasons. First, judicial review is as beneficial and as needed in federalism cases as it is in Fourteenth Amendment cases, and such judicial review does not raise the problems of the countermajoritarian difficulty. Second, Congress cannot be trusted alone to police the federalism boundaries that limit its own power. Finally, federalism is an incredibly important feature of the American constitutional order. This is indicated by (1) the prominence of federalism concerns in the text of our Constitution; (2) the importance of federalism in other countries around the world today; (3) the fact that the economics of federalism suggest some well-known reasons why constitutionally mandated decentralization is a good thing; and (4) the serious concerns about the dangers of excessive national power implicated by the specific issues that the Supreme Court's federalism case law touches upon.

Steven G. Calabresi is a professor of law at Northwestern University. He served as a law clerk to Justice Antonin Scalia and Judges Robert H. Bork and Ralph K. Winter. From 1985 to 1990, he served in the Reagan and Bush administrations, working both in the White House and in the U.S. Department of Justice. In 1982, he cofounded the Federalist Society, a national organization of conservative lawyers and law students.

P ERHAPS the most striking feature of the Rehnquist Court's jurisprudence has been the revival over the last 5-10 years of doctrines of constitutional federalism. Three major lines of new case law have emerged, each one of which is of first-order importance. First, the Court in *United States v. Lopez,*[1] *City of Boerne v. Flores,*[2] and *United States v. Morrison*[3] has shown that it is willing for the first time since 1937 to police the boundary lines of the congressionally enumerated powers over the regulation of commerce and the enforcement of the Fourteenth Amendment. Second, the Court in *New York v. United States*[4] and *Printz v. United States*[5] has erected a firm Tenth Amendment barrier to congressional efforts to commandeer state legislatures and executive entities. And, third, the Court in *Seminole Tribe v. Florida*[6] and *Alden v. Maine*[7] has expanded the doctrine of sovereign immunity so that it imposes a very high barrier to congressional efforts to expose states to private lawsuits either in federal or in state court. Taken all together, these three lines of case law represent a striking departure from the Court's case law prior to 1992 and seem to be of revolutionary importance. Not since before the New Deal–era constitutional revolution of 1937 have the states received such protection in the U.S. Supreme Court from allegedly burdensome federal statutes (Calabresi 1995, 1998).

One immediate question raised by the Rehnquist Court's federalism jurisprudence is whether the development of this new case law is a good thing. Obviously, the five justices most responsible for the new case law—Chief Justice Rehnquist and Justices O'Connor, Scalia, Kennedy, and Thomas—all think that the states ought to receive more protection from the Court in federal court than they received before 1992. Is this a defensible proposition? Is constitutional federalism enforced by the Supreme Court still of value in the twenty-first century?

I want herein to discuss three major reasons why I think the new federalism case law is a happy development. In part 1 below, I discuss the importance of federalism and explain why its new prominence in the Supreme Court's jurisprudence is justified. In part 2, I discuss arguments of institutional competence and explain why the political institutions of our government cannot be trusted to police the federalism boundaries of their own power. In part 3, I argue that judicial review is just as necessary and beneficial in federalism cases as it is in individual rights cases arising under the Fourteenth Amendment. I will argue here that the Court's federalism case law actually helps to ameliorate the countermajoritarian difficulty that otherwise bedevils judicial review.

In undertaking this discussion, I will focus my attention on defending the *Lopez* and *City of Boerne* line of cases under which the Court reviews congressional exercises of the enumerated powers to see if Congress has exceeded the scope of its authority. These cases have attracted perhaps the most attention and criticism, and they therefore deserve the most enthusiastic defense. While I am also a fan of the Tenth Amendment no-commandeering cases and the sovereign immunity decisions, I will leave their defense for another day.

THE IMPORTANCE OF FEDERALISM

Supreme Court enforcement of the boundaries of the commerce power and of Congress's Section 5 power to enforce the Fourteenth Amendment presupposes that federalism is important. One possible justification for the Supreme Court's refusal to enforce these boundary lines between 1937 and 1995 could be that it was not worth the Court's time to fill its docket with commerce power cases (Calabresi 1995). I submit that constitutional federalism is very important by several measures and that it thus is deserving of the Court's time and attention. In fact, I think federalism is more important to our constitutional order than are many other doctrines that the Court does not hesitate to police and enforce.

Constitutional federalism should seem important to the Supreme Court for at least four different reasons. First, and most obviously, it should seem important because it is a major theme of the constitutional text. The text of the amended Constitution is only several thousand words long, and it is overwhelmingly concerned with federalism boundary line problems (Calabresi 1998). Article I, Section 8, for example, contains 18 clauses enumerating and listing the powers of Congress. Other provisions of the Constitution list and enumerate the powers of the President and the jurisdiction of the federal courts. The original Constitution of 1787 was thus overwhelmingly concerned with federalism problems. The Bill of Rights, as is well known, was added as an afterthought to help secure the enthusiastic ratification of all 13 of the original states. The Framers of the Constitution bequeathed to us a document that is far more concerned with federalism than it is with judicially protected individual rights. To the extent that the text of that document still matters—and constitutional theorists usually concede that the text matters at least to some extent—there is simply no escaping the fact that our constitutional text devotes a lot of attention to federalism boundary line problems. Federalism, thus, mattered to the Framers of our Constitution and for that reason should matter to the present Supreme Court.

Second, federalism should seem important to the justices because it is an important feature of the landscape throughout the contemporary world in which we live. Our world is filled with stories about newly emerging federalisms, both because of the growth of new confederal international trading arrangements like the European Union and the North American Free Trade Agreement and because of the dissolution of once-unitary nation-states into new federalist entities, as is happening in Spain and Great Britain. These two developments suggest that we are living in what could be called an Age of Federalism, in which once-unitary nation-states are increasingly losing importance as some functions like trade and national defense get pushed up into the hands of new confederal decision makers, while other functions, like culture and education, get devolved down to new regional authorities (Calabresi 1995).

This does not, of course, prove that federalism is still important in the United States, but it should predispose a fair-minded observer to the possibility that something that is terribly important in many other contexts might also be important in the context of American politics. We are living in a global Age of Federalism as nation-states increasingly dissolve, and the same economic forces that are producing federalist solutions in other countries remain at work in the United States.

Third, the economics of federalism suggest at least four well-known reasons why constitutionally mandated decentralization is a good thing in the United States, just as it is in Canada, Spain, or Great Britain (Calabresi 1995; Shapiro 1995; McConnell 1987; LeBoeuf 1994).

1. The decentralization of decision making allows for decision makers to be responsive to local tastes and conditions. If one area of a country is filled with smokers, for example, and another area has few smokers, then statewide laws discouraging smoking may make more sense than one national law (McConnell 1987). State laws can be designed to vary with local tastes and conditions, while national laws must be uniform nationwide. The more heterogeneous a nation is, the more desirable decentralization will be. Since the United States is a large, continental-sized

nation with a population of 284 million people, some degree of constitutionally mandated decentralization is likely to be even more important for us than for less populous nations like Spain and Great Britain.

2. Constitutionally mandated decentralization encourages competition between jurisdictions (Tiebout 1956). If local tastes and conditions vary between jurisdictions, and if some degree of decentralization of decision making is required, then jurisdictions will compete with each other to offer optimal laws so that they can attract taxpaying citizens and industries.

3. Constitutionally mandated decentralization encourages experimentation. In a competitive situation, the states must constantly improve the quality of their laws and government programs so that they attract new taxpayers and businesses or they will lose out to their neighbors (Shapiro 1995; LeBoeuf 1994; Epstein 1992). The end result is a race to the top between jurisdictions, with market forces encouraging a constant improvement in the quality of state governmental programs.

4. Constitutionally mandated decentralization keeps government nearer the people, where it can be watched more closely and where it is more likely to have good information about popular preferences as to good policy (LeBoeuf 1994; McConnell 1987). In economic terms, monitoring, agency, and information costs all should be lower at the state level because there is a closer identity of interests between state governments and the governed than is possible at

the national level, where government is inevitably more remote from the citizenry.

These four economic arguments for decentralization are not always dispositive, because there are economic reasons why some measures need to be handled at the national rather than at the state level: for example, because, like national defense or space exploration, they are characterized by increasing economies of scale (Shapiro 1995; McConnell 1987; LeBoeuf 1994); because, like telecommunications regulation, the states would face a collective action problem if they attempted to do the job; because state regulation—of the environment, for example—would generate negative external effects or spillovers (Shapiro 1995; LeBoeuf 1994); or because, as in the case of protection of minorities' civil rights, history suggests that the national government is more sympathetic (Shapiro 1995). Cumulatively, however, what emerges from this economic analysis of federalism is that there is a strong prima facie economic case for constitutionally mandated decentralization, which can be overcome when economies of scale, collective action problems, externalities, or civil rights issues are raised.

A fourth and final reason the justices of the Supreme Court ought to think federalism is important is that the specific issues that the Court's federalism case law touches upon implicate serious concerns about the dangers of overweening national power. *Lopez*, *City of Boerne*, and *Morrison* dealt with the constitu-

tionality, respectively, of the Gun-Free School Zones Act, the Religious Freedom Restoration Act, and the Violence Against Women Act—all federal statutes that sought to expand the reaches of the federal police power. *Lopez*, in particular, involved an attempt by Congress to expand the federal criminal law by outlawing the bringing of a gun within 1000 feet of a school, an action that had already been outlawed by more than 40 states. One issue, thus, which is inescapably raised by *Lopez* is the continuing federalization of the criminal law. This federalization refers to the process by which more and more ordinary state law crimes are relabeled as federal crimes by Congress in its eagerness to show voters that it is tough on crime (Calabresi 1995).

Federalizing ordinary state law crimes transfers power and work from state prosecutors to federal prosecutors, from state police forces to the Federal Bureau of Investigation, and from state courts to federal courts. This process raises valid concerns about the sweeping power of the federal government and implicates genuine issues of that civil liberty which is protected by federalism. It is not too difficult in light of this to see why the Court thought the *Lopez* case was an appropriate one in which to draw a line. Had the Court upheld Congress's statute in *Lopez*, it would have been difficult to imagine any federalization of the criminal law that would not be deemed to pass constitutional muster.

City of Boerne and *Morrison* raise slightly more complicated issues because in those cases, the federal laws struck down involved novel expansions of civil rights. In *City of Boerne*, the Court declined to allow Congress to create a new civil right for protecting religion, which would have trumped ordinary state laws, and in *Morrison* the Court declined to allow Congress to create a new civil right for private acts of violence against women. In both cases, the Court's reason for declining to allow the congressional extension of the federal police power was that the states were already adequately protecting the civil rights of religious people and of women that were in question. In essence, the Court found that there was no ongoing deprivation by the states of civil rights protected by Section 1 of the Fourteenth Amendment that permitted congressional remedial legislation under Section 5 of that amendment.

City of Boerne and *Morrison* thus raise the same problem that *Lopez* raises because they involve congressional efforts to expand the federal police power by regulating traditional state law matters in a situation where the states are already doing a good job. Obviously, Congress cannot be allowed to federalize the law under the guise of expanding civil rights into wholly novel areas. That in essence is what the Court concluded Congress was doing in these two cases and why these portions of the Religious Freedom Restoration Act and the Violence Against Women Act were struck down.

My arguments above about the importance of federalism presuppose that it is important that decen-

tralization be constitutionally mandated. One possible response to the argument thus far might be to concede that decentralization is a good thing but to contend that it ought to be done by Congress as a matter of national grace. Simply proving that decentralization is good, without more, does not establish that constitutionally mandated and judicially enforced federalism is also desirable (Rubin this volume; Rubin and Feeley 1994).

One advantage of constitutionally mandated decentralization is that it is more entrenched and is harder to dispense with than is decentralization done as a matter of national legislative grace. Requiring decentralization in a written constitution makes it more likely that it will actually occur, and that increases the chance that the benefits of decentralization will be experienced. We protect First Amendment freedoms in our written Constitution because we rightly fear that without constitutional and judicial protection, we will not get enough protection of freedom of speech and of the press. The same argument works to justify the need for constitutional and judicial protection of federalism (Calabresi 1995). Without constitutional and judicial protection of the values of decentralization, we will get too much national lawmaking and especially too much federalization of the criminal law. We need decisions like *United States v. Lopez* to counterbalance the enormous pressure that Congress feels to expand the federal criminal law into new areas that had traditionally been regulated by the states.

CONGRESS CANNOT BE TRUSTED TO POLICE ITS OWN POWER

There is a school of thought led by Herbert Wechsler and Jesse Choper that contends that federalism boundary lines should be policed by Congress and the President and not by the federal or state courts (Wechsler 1954; Choper 1980). Wechsler and Choper believe that the states are powerful political actors with great influence in Congress and that they are thus in no need of judicial protection to secure their vital interests. The Wechsler-Choper thesis has enjoyed great success among law professors and was endorsed by a bare five-justice majority of the Supreme Court in *Garcia v. San Antonio Metropolitan Transit Authority*.[8] It clearly holds some appeal for four of the current justices—Justices Stevens, Souter, Ginsburg, and Breyer—who have dissented from most of the Court's recent federalism rulings.

The Wechsler-Choper thesis suffers from several defects, which are fatal in my judgment. To begin with, the thesis is somewhat out of date because the congressional political process is much less protective of federalism today than it was in 1954 when Herbert Wechsler first wrote about the political safeguards of federalism (Calabresi 1995). Since 1954, cloture has become more easily available in the Senate than it used to be and so states'-rights filibusters are less common. Moreover, because of one-person, one-vote decisions, state legislatures have far less redistricting power over incumbent representatives than they did 40 years ago. Taken together, these changes have substantially reduced state power in Congress compared to what it was in 1954.

There are, in addition, three fundamental realities of the modern political process that the Wechsler-Choper thesis overlooks. First, it ignores the influence our campaign finance system has on the political process. The Wechsler-Choper thesis assumes that members of Congress are primarily representatives of particular states or congressional districts. They thus assume that senators and congresspersons will be attuned to federalism problems in pending legislation. In fact, however, senators and congresspersons are heavily focused on the preferences of national political action committees (PACs) because modern media campaigns are very expensive to run (Calabresi 1995). These national PACs are either indifferent to federalism or are opposed to it to the extent that it interferes with their narrowly conceived special interest projects.

A second difficulty with the Wechsler-Choper thesis is that it overlooks the incentive structure that national politicians face. The Wechsler-Choper thesis rightly assumes that members of Congress are interested in promoting the likelihood of their reelection. It errs, however, in assuming that this result is promoted by defending state power. Members of Congress can do more to promote their reelection by expanding national programs and advocating the creation of new national programs than they can accomplish by defending federalism (Calabresi 1995). There are very few votes to be had by defending the proper meaning of the commerce power. In contrast, new national health insurance or education programs can look like surefire winners.

A third weakness of the Wechsler-Choper thesis is that it wrongly assumes that the political power that state and local governments actually have in Congress will be used to defend federalism boundary lines. This hypothesis mistakenly assumes that state and local officials will always resent federal intrusion into state and local government matters. In fact, however, state and local officials may face very complex incentive structures, which may cause them to favor unconstitutional federal expansion under at least some circumstances. For example, state officials may desperately want or need federal funding and may accede to some unconstitutional strings attached to that funding in order to receive an appropriation (Calabresi 1995). Alternatively, state and local officials may under some circumstances want to pass the buck to the national government on some difficult or expensive problem that those officials would prefer not to deal with.

As James Madison observed in the *Federalist Papers*, "No man [should be] allowed to be a judge in his own cause" (Cooke 1961, Federalist 10, 79). For the same reason, it makes little sense to turn Congress into the judge of its own cause, which is the proper scope of federal governmental power.

THE CASE FOR JUDICIAL REVIEW

We have seen so far that federalism is important and is desirable. And we have considered some reasons why Congress cannot be relied upon to enforce federalism guarantees. We are thus faced with the urgent question of whether the courts can protect federalism, at least to some degree, without any serious adverse effects. If so, we would appear to have some prima facie arguments in favor of the judicial policing of federalism boundary lines. If federalism values, like First Amendment values, are important and are underprotected in Congress, then perhaps some modicum of judicial policing of federalism boundary lines would be a good thing. What then of the institutional argument for judicial policing of federalism boundary lines?

To begin with, it is perhaps somewhat surprising that so many modern commentators take the position that the Supreme Court lacks the institutional competence to police federalism boundary lines (Calabresi 1995). For 150 years, from the time of the Founding up through 1937, we had judicial enforcement of federalism boundary lines in well-known and much discussed decisions like *McCulloch v. Maryland*,[9] *Gibbons v. Ogden*,[10] *United States v. E. C. Knight*,[11] *Champion v. Ames*,[12] and *Hammer v. Dagenhart*.[13] It seems a little far-fetched for modern commentators to argue that the Supreme Court is institutionally ill equipped to decide a category of cases that it very visibly handled for the first century and a half of our national existence. This conclusion is, to be sure, a possible one, but it might be more plausible to conclude that the old Court's error was its particular rigidity in *Hammer*—a case that was in my view wrongly decided—rather than its willingness to review federalism matters at all.

The assertion of judicial incompetence in federalism matters seems especially odd because when we look at modern judicial doctrine, we see that the Court protects federalism interests in a whole host of ways (Calabresi 1995; Shapiro 1995). In dormant commerce clause cases, for example, the Court does not hesitate to interpret the scope of the commerce power in order to protect national interests from overly burdensome state laws. In federal diversity cases ever since the *Erie* decision,[14] state law has governed the substantive outcome of the federal case. Consider also such foundational doctrines of federal jurisdiction as the rule of *Murdock v. Memphis*[15] that the state courts are the final arbiters of state law; or the abstention doctrine of *Younger v. Harris*;[16] or the recent narrowing of federal habeas review of collateral state court judgments. In a whole host of ways, the U.S. Supreme Court already considers itself competent to police federalism boundary lines and does so in effect every term (Shapiro 1995). Why should commerce power or Section 5, Fourteenth Amendment cases be any different? Why should the Court have the power to take federalism into account in some cases but not in commerce clause or Section 5 cases?

One possible response is that the line-drawing problems raised by commerce clause and Section 5 cases are unusually difficult and require judgments about the real world that the Supreme Court is ill equipped to make. But many areas of Supreme Court case law raise difficult line-drawing problems, including establishment clause, search and seizure, free speech, and abortion cases (Calabresi 1995). The Supreme Court does not hesitate to expound on the outer limits of the Fourth Amendment merely because hard judgments must be made about events occurring in the real world that are difficult for judges to measure. Similarly, the Court's no-endorsement test in establishment clause cases requires it to speculate on the social meaning of religiously laden speech in ways that produce very difficult line-drawing problems. Under this body of case law, holiday displays that seem mostly secular may be upheld, while holiday displays that are more sectarian may be ruled to fall on the wrong side of the line that the Court has been drawing. Any Court that feels able to draw these sorts of fine lines ought to be able occasionally— in an egregious case—to say that some exercise by Congress of the commerce or Section 5 power exceeds the scope of its constitutional commands.

Foreign constitutional courts interpret and enforce federalism clauses; for example, the Constitutional Court of Germany interprets and enforces the federalism clauses of the German Basic Law or Constitution. Similarly, the High Court of Australia and the Canadian Supreme Court have historically interpreted and enforced the federalism provisions of those countries' constitutions (Calabresi 1995). There is nothing inherent about federalism clauses or enumerated power clauses that makes them hard for constitutional court judges to interpret. These clauses can be applied too aggressively or too passively just like all other constitutional language and thus raise similar issues of judicial activism and restraint.

I fully agree that the Court ought to approach enforcement of the commerce clause and Section 5 power with restraint and that only in cases of egregious overreaching should acts of Congress be struck down. Congressional efforts to enforce the commerce clause or Section 5 deserve to be given the benefit of the doubt both because of Congress's greater information about the real world and because Congress is a coequal interpreter of the Constitution to the Supreme Court. But giving Congress the benefit of the doubt does not mean rubber-stamping everything that Congress has tried to do, as happened from 1937 to 1995. Sometimes in extreme cases, it is valuable for the Court to remind Congress of the constitutional values of federalism, and this is what I think has happened in *Lopez*, *City of Boerne*, and *Morrison*. In each of these cases, Congress was attempting novel federal solutions to problems that a majority of the states seemed to be handling very well. It

was accordingly appropriate for the Court to slow Congress down by forcing it to take a second look at what it had in haste done in each of these areas (Calabresi 1995).

The modern Supreme Court is highly unlikely to overenforce the commerce power or to trigger a modern version of the constitutional crisis of 1937. The justices of the Supreme Court are officers of the national government, whose work is covered and critiqued in the national press and in the elite law reviews of national law schools. The incentive and reward structure of Supreme Court justices is heavily tilted in a nationalist direction, and, for this reason, they are a somewhat biased umpire for state-national disputes (Calabresi 1995). Elsewhere in the present volume, Professor Edward Rubin derides the Rehnquist Court's federalism case law as "puppy federalism" because it is so mild and tame compared with the federalism disputes of bygone days. While I disagree that resisting the federalization of the criminal law or the creation of novel civil rights are trivial matters, I do agree that the Supreme Court is unlikely to pose a serious obstacle to any sustained move by Congress and the President to address some new pressing national problem. What that suggests to me, however, is not that the Rehnquist Court's federalism case law is trivial but rather that it is not dangerous. Far from posing a serious threat of disruption akin to that raised by the old Supreme Court prior to 1937, the new Rehnquist Court federalism is a mild corrective to a half century of steady and sometimes ill-considered expansions of national power.

A critic might wonder at this point how much good, if any, a mild second-look federalism doctrine could accomplish. Is the decision of one or two federalism cases a year by the Supreme Court really likely to make a difference in protecting the values that make federalism an important policy concern? To such critics, cases like *Lopez* are just a sport because the Court cannot and will not follow them up vigorously enough to make a difference. Too few cases will reach the Court and be decided by it to make a practical difference, so judicial enforcement will be arbitrary and sporadic. The resultant "puppy federalism," it could be argued, will foster disrespect for the Court as an institution and an unfortunate divergence between the constitutional law in the *U.S. Reports* and what Congress will actually get away with in real life. Better to end the whole charade and just confess that the structural Constitution has to be enforced politically or not at all.

I think it is reasonable to fear that the Court will do too little in enforcing federalism boundary lines because the Court is a nationalist umpire for national-state disputes. Nevertheless, I still think that the little that the Court does in cases like *Lopez* is better than no federalism enforcement at all. When the Supreme Court decides a big federalism case like *Lopez*, it does a lot more than simply resolve the immediate case and issue at hand. In some fundamental sense, it sets up a symbol for the American people of the importance that is attached to a con-

stitutional value or norm. Symbolism is terribly important in constitutions and in constitutional case law. Symbols help citizens organize their beliefs, reinforce core values, and provide a rallying point for those who believe in them, thus reducing the costs of organization. When powerful symbols issue from the Supreme Court of the United States, those symbols help to set the national agenda, and they affect the flow of our politics. *Lopez*, for example, caused devolution and federalism concerns to become more prominent in Congress than they otherwise might have been. This may well have played into the last Congress's decision to devolve part of the federal welfare entitlement to the states.

The public has always understood that symbolism is terribly important in law, a point that elites often have trouble remembering. It is for this reason that the public has never shared the hostility of intellectuals from John Stuart Mill down to most present-day social scientists to laws creating so-called victimless crimes. Underenforced, but symbolic, laws against drug use, like underenforced, but symbolic, federalism cases, serve important social purposes. They teach the public about the proper hierarchy of norms and values, and in legislative bodies they help to set the agenda for policymaking debates.

One final reason why judicial enforcement of federalism boundaries is desirable is that it helps to ameliorate the countermajoritarian difficulty that otherwise bedevils federal judicial review (Calabresi 1998). When the Supreme Court invalidates state laws under the

Fourteenth Amendment—as it did with the abortion laws of all 50 states in its 1973 decision in *Roe v. Wade*[17]—it acts as a countermajoritarian force in our national political life. All too often in Fourteenth Amendment cases, nine unelected justices displace the outcomes of the democratic process in all 50 states and in Congress by a 5-4 or 6-3 or 7-2 vote.

In contrast, when the Supreme Court decides a federalism boundary line case, like *United States v. Lopez*, the Court does not displace democratic government. Instead, the Court merely rules on which democratic government—federal or state—has the jurisdiction to act. The Supreme Court ought to spend some of its time acting as a constitutional umpire refereeing disputes between Congress and the states (or between Congress and the President) because when it does so it does not act as a countermajoritarian force in our national political life. Rather, it merely perfects the Madisonian constitutional system, which pits differently assembled majorities in different constituencies against each other in the hope that the true popular will will thus emerge and prevail. In *United States v. Lopez*, for example, the Court did not rule that no democratic entity could ban the bringing of a gun within 1000 feet of a school; it ruled merely that the right entity to pass this law was the state of Texas and not the federal government. In contrast, in *Roe v. Wade* the Court's overturning of Texas's abortion law had the effect of nullifying democratic counteraction by all 50 states and the federal government.

In summary, we have seen that judicial review is as beneficial and as needed in federalism cases as it is in Fourteenth Amendment cases and that such judicial review does not raise the problems of the countermajoritarian difficulty that have so beset the Court in its rulings in other areas. Moreover, we have seen that Congress cannot be trusted to police federalism boundary lines that limit its own power. Finally, we have seen that federalism is an important feature of the U.S. Constitution that ought not to be obliterated. We should be grateful to the Rehnquist Court for reviving in a modest and useful way the exercise of the great power of judicial review in federalism cases.

Notes

1. 514 U.S. 549 (1995).
2. 521 U.S. 507 (1997).
3. 120 S. Ct. 1740 (2000).
4. 505 U.S. 144 (1992).
5. 521 U.S. 98 (1997).
6. 517 U.S. 44 (1996).
7. 527 U.S. 706 (1999)
8. 488 U.S. 889 (1988).
9. 17 U.S. (4 Wheat.) 316 (1819).
10. 22 U.S. (9 Wheat.) 1 (1824).
11. 156 U.S. 1 (1895).
12. 188 U.S. 321 (1903).
13. 247 U.S. 251 (1918).
14. *Erie R. Co. v. Tompkins*, 304 U.S. 64 (1938).
15. 87 U.S. (20 Wall.) 590 (1874).
16. 401 U.S. 37 (1971).
17. 410 U.S. 113 (1973).

References

Calabresi, Steven G. 1995. "A Government of Limited and Enumerated Powers": In Defense of United States v. Lopez. *Michigan Law Review* 94:752-831.

————. 1998. Textualism and the Counter-majoritarian Difficulty. *George Washington Law Review* 66:1373-94.

Choper, Jesse H. 1980. *Judicial Review and the National Political Process.* Chicago: University of Chicago Press.

Cooke, Jacob E., ed. 1961. *The Federalist.* Middletown, CT: Wesleyan University Press.

Epstein, Richard A. 1992. Exit Rights Under Federalism. *Law and Contemporary Problems* 55:147-65.

LeBoeuf, Jacques. 1994. The Economics of Federalism and the Proper Scope of the Federal Commerce Power. *San Diego Law Review* 31:555-616.

McConnell, Michael W. 1987. Federalism: Evaluating the Founders' Design. *University of Chicago Law Review* 54:1484-1512.

Rubin, Edward and Malcolm Feeley. 1994. Federalism: Some Notes on a National Neurosis. *UCLA Law Review* 41:903-52.

Shapiro, David. 1995. *Federalism: A Dialogue.* Evanston, IL: Northwestern University Press.

Tiebout, Charles M. 1956. A Pure Theory of Local Expenditures. *Journal of Political Economy* 64:416-24.

Wechsler, Herbert, 1954. The Political Safeguards of Federalism: The Role of the States in the Composition and Selection of the National Government. *Columbia Law Review* 54:543-60.

ANNALS, *AAPSS*, **574**, March 2001

Puppy Federalism and the Blessings of America

By EDWARD L. RUBIN

ABSTRACT: Federalism is a system of governmental organization that grants subunits of a polity definitive rights against the central government. It allows these subunits to maintain different norms, or policies, from those of the central government. Thus it differs from decentralization, which is a strategy that the central government adopts in order to carry out its norms or policies more effectively. Federalism is a useful approach when people in a given area have such basic disagreements that they will not agree to live together in a single polity and be bound by its decisions. The United States is blessed with a sense of national unity that makes federalism unnecessary. This was not the case prior to the Civil War, however, and our continued nostalgia for that period induces us to adopt puppy federalism, which looks like the real thing but isn't. Legal scholars should not allow themselves to be fooled; however, as current legislation by the Republican Congress indicates, real federalism garners no support in our political system.

Edward L. Rubin is professor of law at the University of Pennsylvania Law School. He taught at the University of California, Berkeley (Boalt Hall) from 1982 until 1998 before moving to Penn. He teaches administrative law, commercial law, and law and technology (e-commerce and bioethics). He is the author of Judicial Policy Making and the Modern State: How the Courts Reformed America's Prisons *(1998, with M. Feeley),* The Payment System: Cases, Materials and Issues *(2d ed., 1994, with R. Cooter), and numerous law review articles, as well as the editor of* Minimizing Harm: A New Crime Policy for Modern America *(1998).*

THE United States is a nation that enjoys many blessings. We have vast reserves of petroleum (although we are using them up), magnificent forests (although we are cutting them down), spacious skies, amber waves of grain, lots of coal, and the world's leading supply of molybdenum. We also have wonderful political resources: the English tradition of liberty, well-established representative institutions, a willingness to channel political commitments into two major parties, a deep understanding of law, and a long-standing ability to solve civil conflicts through adjudication.

Perhaps the most valuable of these political resources, however, is our sense of national unity, our belief that we constitute a single people and a single polity. One of the reasons why this is such a great blessing is that it allows us to dispense with federalism. A subsidiary blessing is that it allows us to ignore the political questions that underlie federalism, issues that we would like to ignore because they point to the autocratic origins of all governments, and the impossibility of using democratic principles to constitute a polity.

This fortunate situation did not obtain at the beginning of our history, and we feel a bit guilty about basking in its glow today. Consequently, we have fashioned something for ourselves that can be described as puppy federalism; like puppy love, it looks somewhat authentic but does not reflect the intense desires that give the real thing its inherent meaning. The main purpose of puppy federalism is to convince ourselves that we have not altered the conception of the government that the Framers maintained, when, of course, we have; that we are not a bureaucratized administrative state, when, of course, we are; and that we are a geographically diverse nation, whose regions exhibit interesting differences, when, of course, we are a highly homogenized, commercial, media-driven culture smeared across the width of an entire continent.

This article begins by defining federalism and identifying the purposes it serves. It then discusses the great pleasures of being able to dispense with it. The next section briefly describes the way this fortunate situation evolved in the United States, and the final section explains how that situation is combined with puppy federalism in current legislative policy.

WHAT IS FEDERALISM?

Federalism is a principle of political organization in which a single polity, or nation, has both a central government and separate, geographically defined governments that are subordinate to the central government in certain matters but independent of it in others (Elazar 1984, 2; Leach 1970, 1-10). This partial independence means that there are certain matters in which the separate governments can assert a claim of right against the central government or, alternatively, in which the central government is precluded from issuing commands to these separate governments (Riker 1964, 11; Scheppele 1989). The definition is intentionally broad and may include some approaches that most people would not regard as federalism, such as the existence of partially independent subgovernments in only some parts of the nation. One thing that it does not include, however, is a unitary regime that has decided to decentralize certain governmental functions (Beer 1993, 20-25; Kreimer 1992). Malcolm Feeley and I have discussed this distinction at some length (Feeley and Rubin 1998, 171-203; Rubin and Feeley 1994). Decentralization, or devolution, to use the au courant term, is a decision by the central government authorizing its subordinates, whether geographically or functionally defined, to exercise authority in certain areas. It differs from federalism in that the subunits that have been authorized to act do not possess any claim of right against the central government. That government has given them their authority by some established political or legal mechanism and can take it away by the same means.

Decentralization is a management decision that is intended to implement the policies selected by the central government as effectively as possible (Kochen and Deutsch 1980; Morris 1968). If the government decides to maximize rutabaga production, for example, either it can devise a uniform agricultural policy, or it can assign the task of developing agricultural policy to regional administrators, on the theory that these administrators are better able to account for particular conditions in their area or that the local farmers trust them more. Whatever the reason, however, and whatever the level of decentralization, the goal remains the one that the central government has established: to produce more rutabaga. In a truly federal regime, the subunits are able not only to select their own strategies in the matters allocated to them, but to define their own goals; they possess the policymaking, rutabaga-choosing power of an independent government.

The distinction between federalism and decentralization is worth maintaining because it is necessary for coherent discussion of governmental organization. With the possible exception of some postage-stamp states such as Monaco, San Marino, and Nauru, every nation is decentralized to some extent; they all have territorial subunits exercising some degree of governmental authority. It is virtually impossible to run a government without some reliance on this mechanism. Thus, if we use the term "federalism" to refer to decentralization, every nation is federal, and we will need some other term to distinguish nations such as Belgium or Canada, where the subunits exercise claims of right against the central government (Fitzmaurice 1983; Mackey 1999), from nations such as Japan or France, where they do not.

Why would a nation opt for federalism as a mode of internal organization? Clearly, it would not do so to implement any substantive policy, such as maximizing the production of rutabaga or providing people with greater input into government decisions. For example, if national authorities felt that a regional or local government would be more effective than the central government in implementing a policy of increasing public participation, they would opt for extensive decentralization of governmental functions. They would not opt for federalism because federalism represents a relinquishment of control over the subunits and thus risks the frustration of the policy that the nation, as a whole, wants to achieve. Under federalism, some of the subunits might use their newly acquired autonomy to allow the greater popular involvement that their smaller size, by hypothesis, facilitates, but other subunits might establish autocratic regimes or delegate their authority to the Catholic Church or generate their policy decisions with a computer program. The central government, having relinquished its right to control these subunits, would not be able to reverse such nonparticipatory policies to fulfill its original goal.

The reason nations opt for federalism is that it is an alternative to dissolution, civil war, or other manifestations of a basic unwillingness of the people in some geographic area to live under the central government (Buchanan 1991; Sunstein 1991). Conversely, the reason groups of nations or other polities that want to combine opt to create a federal system, as opposed to a unified one, is that the people in the separate polities are unwilling to submit to unified, central control (Bartkus 1999). In either case, the motivation is a basic lack of national unity, an unwillingness of some groups to submit themselves to centralized control, to regard themselves as members of a single polity that must, for better or worse, reach collective decisions. They may feel that they will be discriminated against in the larger unit; that resources within the geographic region they inhabit will not be used for their benefit; that policies will be imposed on them that they find intolerable; or simply that they want to retain their own identity (Dikshit 1975; Duchacek 1970; Hannum 1990). Federalism is a solution to this problem, a compromise between unity and independence.

Decentralization is not sufficient in a situation where one or several groups are unwilling to submit to central control. The compromise that these groups want is federalism; they want the autonomy of their subunit's government to be protected as a right, not merely recognized as a desirable policy (Friedrich 1968, 188-227). By virtue of this recognition, the autonomy they have secured is placed outside the realm of ordinary politics. The king cannot eliminate it by an ordinary royal order; the voters, or their representatives, cannot do so by a simple majority. In our system, this means that the courts, acting in response to a claim of right, will invalidate normal legislation that trenches on the agreed-upon autonomy of the subunits (Choper 1980). That autonomy can be altered only by a constitutional amendment.

It is apparent that the issue of federalism is closely related to the question of political identity on two levels. First, the question for each citizen is whether she regards herself primarily as a member of the nation or as a member of the subunit to which she belongs. Second, the question for an observer is whether the subunit or the nation as a whole will be regarded as the actor in a given situation. Most political theories refer to collective entities as actors; for institutional theorists, these entities are emergent institutions, with inherent modes of action; for positive political theory, they are rational beings whose behavior can be modeled; for methodological individualists, like microeconomists, they are convenient heuristics; for general will theorists, they are real beings. But who is the collective actor? In a centralized system, it is clearly the nation; we can say that the government of France, or even France, has decided on a certain policy and wants to implement it by using a strategy of decentralization. In a federal regime, however, the central government and the quasi- autonomous subunit both possess a political identity. When we speak of a policy choice, we must decide in advance whether that anthropomor- phized behavior represents the actions of the central government or the government of a quasi-autonomous subunit. In addition to speaking of the national interest, and the interests of the citizens as individuals, we must factor in the interest of the subunits as political actors on their own.

THE BLESSINGS OF
NATIONAL UNITY

From the national perspective, a sense of unity among its citizens, a willingness to act as part of a single polity, is a political resource of enormous value, more valuable than petroleum, molybdenum, or rutabaga. It means that sectional disagreements or rivalries will be resolved within the context of the nation's political process and that a decision, having been reached, will be obeyed. Other disagreements will, of course, remain; there may be conflicts between social classes, ethnic groups, religious groups, or purely ideological alliances, and these conflicts may lead to violence. But the disagreements between groups of people who live in different geographic regions of the nation will not rise to this intensity; people will value their membership in the nation over their sectionally specific views and will compromise those views, or even abandon them, in conflictual situations.

Not only does a sense of national unity remove one major source of political conflict, but it removes the most dangerous source of such conflict. While it is possible for two contending groups that are geographically intermixed to rip a nation and themselves apart, as has occurred in Lebanon, Rwanda, and (at a regional level) Northern Ireland, most intense conflicts tend to be sectional, as Kosovo, Chechnya, Nagorno-Karabakh (Armenia-Azerbaijan), Kurdistan, Eritrea, the Ogaden (Ethiopa-Somalia), Western Sahara, Sudan, Kurdistan, Sri Lanka, and East Timor attest in recent history alone (Buchanan 1991; Cassese 1995). In part, this may be because a geographically defined group lacks the cross-cutting ties with others that racially or religiously defined groups often possess (Hannum 1990). In part, it may be that secession is a viable option only for geographically defined groups and that this extreme solution is an inducement to political extremism

(Buchanan 1991; Dikshit 1975). Whatever the reason, a nation is not only fortunate—it is blessed—if it does not have any such groups, if the people in every region feel a greater loyalty to the nation as a whole than they do to their particular region.

In a democracy, national unity, and the resulting lack of sectional divisions, confers a further, if somewhat more abstract advantage. It conceals from the nation's citizens, and perhaps even from its political theorists, the awkward fact that democratic mechanisms cannot be used to constitute the nation. Creating a nation requires some form of autocracy. The reason is that the defining feature of democracy, in either its direct or representative varieties, is that major decisions are reached by the people themselves or by their elected representatives (Birch 1993, 45-68; Held 1996, 70-120). In practical terms, this means that the decisions are reached by having the people vote, either for the policy itself or for the representatives who in turn select the policy. Before a vote is taken, however, someone must decide who is eligible to vote and what the rules for conducting that vote will be. That decision obviously cannot be determined by a vote; it requires an autocrat of some sort, an individual or an elite, who can establish the initial rules. Thus the principle of democracy, although it may be a perfectly good way to run the ordinary business of government, cannot stand on its own. If we start, either in reality or as a thought experiment, with people in a pregovernmental condition, no government can be established by purely democratic means.

Assume, for example, that there are three contiguous administrative units of a colonial power in a given area, a large one and two smaller ones. All of them rebel and win their freedom. For simplicity, assume as well that all the inhabitants of these units agree that the only viable alternatives are that the separate units form independent nations or that they aggregate into a single nation, and that they further agree on the kinds of people who are entitled to cast votes on political matters and that all votes should be decided by a simple majority. The question then arises whether these separate units should form a single centralized nation, compromise by creating a federalist structure where the preexisting units retain autonomy in certain areas, or become independent of one another. In the large unit, there are 1 million eligible voters, and an overwhelming majority—800,000—favor a unified regime. In the two smaller units, there are 150,000 voters each, and 100,000 favor the independence of their unit, a situation that is not at all implausible, given how the votes will go in a unified regime. If the three units vote as a totality, unification will prevail by a vote of 900,000 to 200,000; if they vote separately, the two smaller units will opt for independence by substantial margins. But who is to decide on the voting procedure? Clearly, this cannot be done by democratic vote, since a vote requires a defined electorate, and the definition of the electorate is precisely the point at issue. Some sort of autocratic decision is required. This awkward problem can be ignored, however, if majorities in all three units favor unification, or separation for that matter. In that case, the result will be the same under either voting pattern. One could say that the vote could be taken once by each method, which would satisfy everyone's preference (by hypothesis) or, alternatively, that it does not violate the principle of democracy to choose the voting method by nondemocratic means, since that choice will not make a difference.

This is not an abstract matter; it is a crucial feature of national politics that implicates the precise issues to which federalism is addressed. From a national perspective, a proponent of representative democracy believes that a constitution should be established, and leaders should be chosen, by a majority of the electorate. But those whose primary loyalty is to a geographic region of this nation will object. "We do not want to be governed by strangers," they will say, "and the fact that those strangers are more numerous than we are only makes the situation worse. We, too, believe in democracy, and we want a majority of the people—our people— to decide whether we want to join your nation, and on what terms. If a majority of our people want to have an independent nation, rather than being part of a larger one, that majority should not be overridden by outsiders." A sense of national unity that is shared by every region of a nation conceals this awkward difficulty in

the theory and practice of democracy by making it essentially irrelevant.

FEDERALISM IN AMERICAN HISTORY

For most of its history, the United States was a nation that needed federalism. The sense of national unity that would have led the voting populace to choose a unified, national regime did not prevail among the 13 American states at the time the Constitution was ratified and the United States was formed (Rakove 1979). People's loyalty to their own state was stronger than their loyalty to the nascent national regime, and thus they opted for a federal system, where the constituent states retained large areas of autonomy as a matter of right (Lutz 1988; Rakove 1996, 161-202). Nor was there sufficient unanimity about the federalist solution to mask the authoritarian origins of the government. While a majority of the people, when considered as a totality, probably favored a federal union, a majority of each state's population did not. In at least two states, North Carolina and Rhode Island, the majority was opposed, so that the autocratic manner in which the ratification process was established made a difference (Main 1961, 249; Van Doren 1948). In fact, these two states joined the Union only because they were compelled by further autocratic means. The same autocratic compulsion was applied to those regions within and beyond the established states with a Native American majority. It may also be assumed that, in any state, or section of a state, where the majority of the people were slaves, that majority would have preferred to establish an independent regime where they were free, rather than joining a nation that continued to enslave them.

During the first half of the nineteenth century, the new, federally organized nation was subject to two conflicting trends. On the one hand, the success of the central government, its general respect for white people's rights, its acquisition of vast territories, and the dramatic increase in national wealth that it seemed to engender all contributed to a growing sense of national unity. People began to think of themselves as Americans, rather than Georgians or New Yorkers (Ackerman 1991, 3-33; Beer 1993, 360-77). At the same time, however, the rejection of slavery in the North (Hildreth 1854; Olmstead 1953) and its enthusiastic continuation in the South (Fitzhugh [1854] 1965) created an ever widening division. To the people of the North, slavery was a violation of the nation's true norms, and the people of the southern states were disruptive members of the polity who were violating those norms. But the white people of the southern states, the only people in those states with a political voice, were more committed to the institution of slavery than they were to the Union; despite their growing commitment to the nation in other areas, enough of their identification with their states remained that this identification could be reasserted, and become primary, when they found themselves unwilling to abide by the decisions of the majority regarding slavery. Consequently, they decided to secede (Stampp 1959).

At this point, of course, the democratic process and every other process of ordinary government broke down. The people of the North could no longer use voting, persuasion, or an appeal to national unity to convince the white people of the South to rejoin the Union because the southerners no longer regarded themselves as part of the same polity. The only remaining approach was to start killing them and devastating their lands until they decided that the amount of misery that was being inflicted on them exceeded their commitment to slavery. At that point, they rejoined the Union on the central government's terms.

Despite this unpromising beginning, the nation was restored and a sense of national unity gradually developed. Slavery was the principal thing that had distinguished the South from the North; the other characteristic features of southern culture had been products of that basic difference. With the military defeat of the South, and the subsequent recognition that slavery was beyond restoration, white southerners began to see themselves once more as members of the United States. Within that general framework, however, they still wanted to retain their familiar social hierarchy and so proceeded, through the Ku Klux Klan, the crop lien system, the Jim Crow laws, and a variety of other mechanisms, to deprive the freed slaves of their newly won rights and the opportunity to improve their political, economic, or social status (Gillette 1979; Litwack 1979; Woodward 1951). As the North's centralizing impulse, fueled by moral outrage at the southern treatment of the slaves, gradually waned, the southern states were allowed to maintain the distinctive institutions that continued African American subjugation. In every other major area—language, religion, culture, race, ethnicity, and political ideology—white southerners and northerners were largely identical, and federalism served no function. Its only purpose, in the period that followed the Civil War, was to allow the southern states to maintain their system of apartheid.

This system, and thus the role of federalism in the United States, lasted for about a century. Beginning in the 1950s, white people in the parts of the United States outside the South began to perceive the southern treatment of African Americans as morally unacceptable. The result was a series of actions by national institutions, which were dominated by these white nonsoutherners, to abolish southern apartheid; they included *Brown v. Board of Education*[1] and other Supreme Court decisions, the Civil Rights Act of 1964, and the executive policies of the Kennedy, Johnson, and Nixon administrations (Harvey 1971; Martin 1979). These actions were perceived, quite correctly, as an abrogation of America's remaining federalist commitment to allow distinctly different normative systems to prevail in different states. The success of the effort eliminated the major difference between the South and the rest of the United States. It contributed, moreover, to the elimination of the more subtle, incremental differences such as the South's lower levels of wealth, industrial development, and education. The New South that emerged during the 1970s and 1980s shared the highly uniform, homogenized commercial culture of the United States as a whole. Any further need for federalism was thus eliminated.

PUPPY FEDERALISM
IN MODERN AMERICA

At present, the United States is a socially homogenized and politically centralized nation. Regional differences between different parts of the nation are minimal, and those that exist are based on inevitable economic variations, rather than any historical or cultural distinctions. Thus North Dakota is somewhat different from Pennsylvania, but most of those differences can be explained by the differences in their economic base; in any country, no matter how culturally uniform, agricultural and industrial districts will exhibit minor but predictable variations in political and social attitudes. There are also variations in the concentration of various religious and ethnic groups throughout the country. The low salience of religious differences in the United States, however, makes these differences virtually irrelevant. Ethnic divisions are, of course, more salient, and the concentration of African Americans in the South prior to the 1950s was one of the bases of the South's distinctive culture and the continued relevance of federalism. The massive migration of African Americans to other sections of the nation has largely eliminated this regional distinction; race relations remain a major problem in America, but it is a problem that now exists in virtually every region, where it is played out in similar terms. Hispanic and Asian ethnicity is also salient, but these groups have also become widely diffused during the postwar era.

With the minor exceptions of Utah and Hawaii, there is no American state with a truly distinctive social profile. Those differences that do exist may loom large to us, but that is because of our insularity; once we compare our differences with the linguistic, religious, cultural, and historical differences that exist in large nations such as India, Indonesia, and Nigeria, or even smaller ones such as Spain, Cameroon, and itsy-bitsy Belgium, ours shrink to insignificance.

Our political culture is more uniform still. The overwhelming majority of Americans identify with one of two major political parties, whose differences, while again salient to us, are minuscule by international standards. Our states, supposedly free to establish their own regimes, have opted for highly similar structures with minor variations (Gardner 1992). No state has instituted a parliamentary system, for example, although that is the dominant pattern for democratic regimes in the world today; only one state, Nebraska, dispenses with the peculiarly American feature of a bicameral legislature; no state denies its courts the power of judicial review. Certainly, no American state has even attempted to establish a theocratic or autocratic regime; thus,

under the current reading of the guarantee clause that restricts it to such matters (but see Merritt 1988), there has been no felt need to invoke the clause, or otherwise intervene in the political process of any state, during the entire course of the twentieth century (Bonfield 1962; Chemerinsky 1994; Choper 1994). Most important, the primary political loyalty of the vast majority of Americans is to the nation. Not only are there no separatist movements in this country, but there is hardly any talk of separatist movements. Virtually no group, no matter how disaffected, even imagines that it would implement its goals outside the nation as it currently exists.

Despite this high level of national unity, there remains a certain nostalgia for our bygone federalist system. This nostalgia arises from at least three sources, and probably more. The first is that the Framers are correctly perceived as having established a federalist regime, for reasons described above, and we incorrectly fear that some horrible consequences will ensue if we admit that we no longer abide by their intentions. Second, the yearning of many Americans for the simplicity of the premodern era, and the more sinister yearning of some Americans for the moonlight, magnolia, and mint-julep era of the antebellum South, slides over to the federalism that prevailed at that time. Third, we dislike the centralized administrative state and see federalism as a welcome antidote to the government that we have created and that we need but do not like.

The result of all this yearning is that we continue to insist that we have a federalist system, even though we neither have it nor need it. The dangerous, debilitating problems that federalism is designed to resolve—the lack of national unity, the persistence of separatism, the underlying social and political differences that are cemented in place by centuries of history and hatred—are mercifully absent in the modern United States. Consequently, we no longer recognize federalism as an unfortunate expedient. The death, destruction, and misery that accompanied our Civil War, and that reflected the problems that federalism addresses, have faded from our memories, to be replaced with movies, history books, battlefield sites, and cutesy battle reenactments that capture the romance of the war and ignore its horrors. Thus we can enjoy the idea of federalism because we have forgotten the grave problems associated with its actuality. What we have instead is puppy federalism, a thin patina of rights talk draped across the areas where we have opted for decentralization as an administrative strategy.

The actions of the Republican-dominated Congress of the last six years illustrate the superficiality of American federalism. In general, the Republicans have declared a stronger commitment to federalism than the Democrats, yet recent Republican Congresses have continued the policies of their Democratic predecessors, enacting statutes that federalize areas previously reserved to state law and contradict the federalism decisions of a Supreme Court

with which they supposedly agree. For example, the 104th Congress enacted the Church Arson Prevention Act of 1996, making destructive acts against religious institutions a federal crime. The act's basis of federal jurisdiction is the one that proponents of federalism often dismiss as a pretext and that was used in the statute struck down by *United States v. Lopez*[2]—interstate commerce. That same Republican Congress also enacted Megan's Law, requiring certain offenders to register with state law enforcement officers—apparently a case of the outrageous, Framer-ignoring, states'-rights-crushing commandeering of state officers that was struck down in *United States v. Printz*.[3] The 104th Congress also enacted the Drug-Induced Rape Prevention and Punishment Act of 1996, which makes the use of "date rape" drugs a federal offense. In spirit, this act is an extension of the Violence Against Women Act, which was passed just before the Republicans took control of Congress and was struck down in *United States v. Morrison*[4] on an interpretation of the interstate commerce clause. Technically, the act extends the Controlled Substances Act and will probably be invulnerable to judicial attack, but this only leads one to wonder why the Republican Congress feels comfortable endorsing and extending a statute drafted in 1970 by one of the most Democratic, nationalizing Congresses in history and taking away the states' police power authority to decide which substances they will forbid their own citizens to ingest. This is, incidentally, a live issue, as indicated by the various states that have tried to modify their prohibitions against marijuana, only to run afoul of federal authorities.

The reason a Republican Congress would enact statutes of this sort is that our federalism is puppy federalism. When state policies correspond to national norms in a given area, or when there is no national norm, that area can be left to state authority. As soon as a national norm emerges, and some states diverge from that norm, federal authorities will act, as they did against the southern states once racial equality became a general goal. In the last two decades, crime has become a matter of grave concern, and the result has been a steady federalization of the criminal law that continues regardless of the party in control of Congress. When the crunch comes, the crunch being a political demand for action, federalism counts for nothing.

The 104th Congress's most significant legislative action, the Personal Responsibility and Work Opportunity Reconciliation Act, might appear to reflect a commitment to genuine federalism, but it does not; rather, it only underscores the absence of any such commitment. It is true that this act changes prior law in providing block grants of federal funds to the states, rather than channeling federal grants to individuals through state administrators as had been the case under the prior Aid to Families with Dependent Children (AFDC) program. But the main reason for this, despite the federalist rhetoric that accompanied its enactment, was that the federal purpose and federal methodology had changed. The purpose is now to discourage the creation of out-of-wedlock children, not to provide these children with support; as the very first sentence of the act declares, "Marriage is the foundation of a successful society." The methodology is to compel the states to achieve specified results in accordance with the stated purposes, rather than compelling them to follow specified procedures. Thus the statute gives block grants and does not specify procedures. This undoubtedly gives the states more latitude in the procedural area, but it imposes much greater demands regarding the results. It defines criteria for an "eligible state" (two different sets of criteria, actually), a "qualifying state," a "high performing state," and a "needy state" (42 U.S.C. § 403(a)). In accordance with these various criteria, it demands that each state submit a plan to show how it will achieve the statutory purpose, sets specific guidelines for rates of out-of-wedlock births and work participation, places numerous prohibitions and limitations on the use of the block grants, provides bonuses to high-performing states, imposes penalties on states that fail to abide by the limits on fund use or fail to achieve specified levels of results, and requires frequent and detailed reports (id. §§ 404-11).

Is this really federalism; is it really the way one sovereign treats another sovereign? It seems to bear a closer resemblance to the way a superior treats a subordinate administrator, and not a very trusted subordinate at that. There is a tone in all these provisions, and particularly in the bonuses and penalties, that is much more demeaning to the states than the AFDC idea that they should administer federal funds in a specified manner. The reason for this apparent breach of federalist etiquette by a Republican Congress is not difficult to discern. Because we have only puppy federalism, the national government will give states control over policy only in areas that are not of national concern. It will retain control over any policy that it regards as truly important. When AFDC was enacted, child poverty was the predominant concern, and the political subtext was that southern states could not be relied upon to treat their African American citizens fairly. With the rise of the New South, and the decline in Congress's commitment to racial justice, this concern no longer predominates. Instead, we have the new moralism, with public policy directed to preventing out-of-wedlock births and ensuring that no one but the severely disabled receive welfare payments without working. The new law reflects those concerns. It does not represent a decrease in federal control but a new methodology for control, a new public policy that the methodology is intended to achieve, and a new political subtext that seeks to discipline licentious New York and indulgent California, rather than racist Georgia and Louisiana.

CONCLUSION

There is no major law reform conclusion to be derived from this discussion. The United States possesses the blessing of national unity, and thus its national government will continue to legislate on any issue that it and the nation in general deem important. One possible conclusion is that the Supreme Court's recent federalism decisions are incorrect—which they are—but as long as the ideology of the justices is not overly divergent from that of the nation as a whole, they are not likely to hand down any decisions with significant impact. The real message of this discussion is for scholars. It is time to stop being fooled by political rhetoric and mistaking puppy federalism for the real thing. Real federalism is gone; America is a centralized administrative state. Rather than mourning its demise, we should feel grateful that our nation no longer needs this unfortunate expedient, and we should focus our attention on complex and important issues, such as decentralization. Instead of a theory of federalism, we need a theory about what policies should be centralized, what policies should be decentralized, and, in both cases, the optimal way for a national government to supervise the regional subordinates that we continue to describe as states.

Notes

1. 347 U.S. 483 (1954).
2. 514 U.S. 549 (1995).
3. 521 U.S. 898 (1997).
4. 120 S. Ct. 1740 (2000).

References

Ackerman, Bruce. 1991. *We the People*. Vol. 1, *Foundations*. Cambridge, Mass: Belknap Press.

Bartkus, Viva. 1999. *The Dynamic of Se-cession*. New York: Cambridge University Press.

Beer, Samuel. 1993. *To Make a Nation*. Cambridge, MA: Belknap Press.

Birch, Anthony. 1993. *The Concepts and Theories of Modern Democracy*. London: Routledge.

Bonfield, Arthur. 1962. The Guarantee Clause of Article IV, Section 4: A Study in Constitutional Desuetude. *Minnesota Law Review* 46:513-72.

Buchanan, Allen. 1991. *Secession: The Morality of Political Divorce from Fort Sumpter to Lithuania and Quebec*. Boulder, CO: Westview Press.

Cassese, Antonio. 1995. *Self-Determination of Peoples*. New York: Cambridge University Press.

Chemerinsky, Erwin. 1994. Cases Under the Guarantee Clause Should Be Justiciable. *University of Colorado Law Review* 65:849-80.

Choper, Jesse. 1980. *Judicial Review and the National Political Process*. Chicago: University of Chicago Press.

———. 1994. Observations on the Guarantee Clause. *University of Colorado Law Review* 65:741-47.

Church Arson Prevention Act. Pub. L. No. 104-155. 110 Stat. 1392 (codified at 18 U.S.C. § 247).

Civil Rights Act. Pub. L. No. 88-352. 78 Stat. 241 (codified in scattered sections of 42 U.S.C.).

Controlled Substance Act. Pub. L. No. 91-513. 84 Stat. 1242 (codified in scattered sections of 21 U.S.C.).

Dikshit, Ramesh. 1975. *The Political Geography of Federalism*. Delhi: Macmilllan Co. of India.

Drug-Induced Rape Prevention and Punishment Act. Pub. L. No. 104-305. 110 Stat. 3807 (codified at 21 U.S.C. 841).

Duchacek, Ivo. 1970. *Comparative Federalism: The Territorial Dimension of Politics*. New York: Holt, Rhinehart & Winston.

Elazar, Daniel. 1984. *American Federalism: A View From the States*. 3d ed. New York: Thomas Y. Crowell.

Feeley, Malcolm and Edward Rubin. 1998. *Judicial Policy Making and the Modern State: How the Courts Reformed America's Prisons*. New York: Cambridge University Press.

Fitzhugh, George. [1854] 1965. *Sociology for the South: Or, The Failure of a Free Society*. New York: B. Franklin.

Fitzmaurice, John. 1983. *The Politics of Belgium: Crisis and Compromises in a Plural Society*. London: C. Hurst.

Friedrich, Carl. 1968. *Constitutional Government and Democracy*. 4th ed. Waltham, MA: Blaisdell.

Gardner, James. 1992. The Failed Discourse of State Constitutionalism. *Michigan Law Review* 90:761-837.

Gillette, William. 1979. *Retreat from Reconstruction, 1869-1879*. Baton Rouge: Louisiana State University Press.

Hannum, Hurst. 1990. *Autonomy, Sovereignty, and Self-Determination*. Philadelphia: University of Pennsylvania Press.

Harvey, James. 1971. *Black Civil Rights During the Johnson Administration*. Jackson, MS: University & College Press of Mississippi.

Held, David. 1996. *Models of Democracy* 2d ed. Stanford, CA: Stanford University Press.

Hildreth, Richard. 1854. *Despotism in America*. New York: Negro University Press.

Kochen, Manfred and Karl Deutsch. 1980. *Decentralization: Sketches Toward a Rational Theory*. Cambridge, MA: Oelgeschlanger, Gunn & Hann.

Kreimer, Seth. 1992. The Law of Choice and the Choice of Law: Abortion, the Right to Travel, and Extraterritorial Regulation in American Federalism. *New York University Law Review* 67:451-519.

Leach, Richard. 1970. *American Federalism*. New York: Norton.

Litwack, Leon. 1979. *Been in the Storm So Long: The Aftermath of Slavery*. New York: Knopf.

Lutz, David. 1988. *The Origins of American Constitutionalism*. Baton Rouge: Louisiana State University Press.

Mackey, Eva. 1999. *The House of Difference: Cultural Politics and National Identity in Canada*. New York: Routledge.

Main, Jackson Turner. 1961. *The Antifederalists: Critics of the Constitution 1781-1788*. Chapel Hill: University of North Carolina Press.

Martin, John. 1979. *Civil Rights and the Crisis of Liberalism: The Democratic Party, 1945-76*. Boulder, CO: Westview Press.

Merritt, Deborah. 1988. The Guarantee Clause and State Autonomy: Federalism for a Third Century. *Columbia Law Review* 88:1-78.

Megan's Law. Pub. L. No. 104-145. 110 Stat. 1345 (codified at 42 U.S.C. § 14071).

Morris, William. 1968. *Decentralization in Management Systems*. Columbus: Ohio State University Press.

Olmstead, Frederick Law. 1953. *The Cotton Kingdom*, ed. Arthur Schlesinger. New York: Knopf.

Personal Responsibility and Work Opportunity Reconciliation Act. Pub. L. No. 104-193. 110 Stat. 205 (codified at 42 U.S.C. §§ 601-17).

Rakove, Jack. 1979. *The Beginnings of National Politics: An Interpretive History of the Constitutional Congress*. New York: Knopf.

———. 1996. *Original Meanings: Politics and Ideas in the Making of the Constitution*. New York: Knopf.

Riker, William. 1964. *Federalism: Origin, Operation, Significance*. Boston: Little, Brown.

Rubin, Edward and Malcolm Feeley. 1994. Federalism: Some Notes on a National Neurosis. *UCLA Law Review* 41:903-52.

Scheppele, Kim. 1989. The Ethics of Federalism. In *Power Divided*, ed. Harry Scheiber and Malcolm Feeley. Berkeley, CA: Institute of Governmental Studies.

Stampp, Kenneth. 1959. *The Causes of the Civil War*. Englewood Cliffs, NJ: Prentice-Hall.

Sunstein, Cass. 1991. Constitutionalism and Secession. *University of Chicago Law Review* 58:633-70.

Van Doren, Carl. 1948. *The Great Rehearsal*. New York: Times Reading.

Violence Against Women Act. Pub. L. No. 103-322. 108 Stat. 1902 (codified in scattered sections of 8, 18, and 42 U.S.C.).

Woodward, C. Van. 1951. *The Origins of the New South, 1877-1913*. Baton Rouge: Louisiana State University Press.

ANNALS, *AAPSS*, **574**, March 2001

Judicial Power and the
Restoration of Federalism

By ROBERT F. NAGEL

ABSTRACT: A series of decisions by the United States Supreme Court raises the question of whether the federal judiciary will help to induce a major shift toward decentralization. Despite the ambitious hopes of some observers and the desperate fears of others, there are reasons to doubt that the Court will implement such a program. The justices are unlikely to persist in protecting states' rights in part because of their own ambivalence and in part because the idea itself is too self-contradictory to support a consistent interpretive agenda. Even if the Court were to overcome these problems, it lacks the capacity to control the relevant behaviors and attitudes. The main potential political allies in a states'-rights campaign—state officials and populist dissenters—are unlikely to have interests compatible with judicial norms or to be effective voices for federalism. In fact, general social and cultural conditions seem to favor further centralization.

Robert F. Nagel is the Ira C. Rothgerber, Jr., Professor of Constitutional Law at the University of Colorado, Boulder. He is the author of Constitutional Cultures *(1989);* Judicial Power and American Character *(1994); and* The Collapse of American Federalism *(forthcoming). His articles have appeared in numerous academic journals as well as in the* Wall Street Journal, New Republic, Washington Monthly, Public Interest, *and* First Things.

I N what appears to be an ambitious campaign to enhance the
role of the states in the federal system, the Supreme Court has recently
issued a series of rulings that limit
the power of the national government. Some of these decisions, which
set boundaries to Congress's power to
regulate commerce and to enforce the
provisions of the Fourteenth Amendment, establish areas that are subject (at least in theory) only to state
regulation. Others protect the autonomy of state governments by restricting congressional authority to expose
state governments to suit in either
state or federal courts and to "commandeer" state institutions for national regulatory purposes. Taken together, these decisions seem to
reflect a judgment—held by a slight
majority of the justices—that the
dramatic expansion of the national
government during the twentieth
century has put in jeopardy fundamental principles of constitutional
structure.

So great is the distance between
modern political practices and traditional principles of federalism that
many jurists, legal scholars, and
journalists see a potential for radical
change in the Court's current program. Indeed, if current trends in the
case law were to continue and
expand, it is imaginable that—like
school desegregation, gender equality, privacy, and freedom of speech—
federalism could eventually become an area where the justices
attempt a program of transformative
interpretation.

Accordingly, the possibility of a
systematic revival of what is popu-
larly called states' rights elicits both
profound fears and great hopes
(Nagel forthcoming). On the one
hand, critics contend that the
authority of the national government
might be so eviscerated that the
nation could not meet basic economic
and environmental needs or pursue
important moral aspirations in the
area of civil rights. They fear that loyalty to the Union could be danger-
ously undermined and even that the
country could begin to split apart. On
the other hand, supporters urge that
devolution of power might make
government less remote and more
responsive, that it might help
reverse a disturbing trend toward
political apathy, and that it might
promote healthy competition and
experimentation.

The impressive scale of these fears
and hopes is puzzling inasmuch as
they are being voiced at a time when
the capacity of the judiciary to effect
major social change has been put into
significant question (Rosenberg
1991). Skeptics contend, for example,
that—notwithstanding lawyers' self-
congratulatory mythology to the
contrary—the desegregation of public schools resulted from legislative
and political action, not judicial initiatives. Or, to take another illustration, even some supporters of the
Court's landmark abortion ruling in
Roe v. Wade[1] now recognize the possibility that establishing a constitutional right to abortion aroused so
much political opposition that the
actual availability of the procedure
may have been reduced over what it
would have been in the absence of
Roe. In the midst of an increasingly
realistic and sophisticated analysis
of the Court's ability to produce even

specific changes in institutional and personal behavior, it is odd that the federalism debate so freely invokes images of massive social consequences like wholesale deregulation and even governmental disunification.

A sober assessment of the stakes involved in the Court's emerging federalism jurisprudence must identify the factors that generally determine whether the judiciary's use of power is likely to be effective and then apply those factors to the subject of federalism. Whether the justices are attempting to induce change by directly influencing behavior or more indirectly by shaping beliefs and attitudes, four factors seem likely to increase the chances that the Court's pronouncements will produce significant results: (1) the inclination of the justices to pursue their goals consistently; (2) the judiciary's capacity to control relevant behaviors; (3) the support of nonjudicial institutions for the Court's goals; and (4) the compatibility of the Court's goals with general social and cultural conditions. Let us consider each of these in turn.

THE INCLINATIONS
OF THE JUSTICES

Obviously, to the extent that members of the Court are only weakly committed to an interpretive program, they are unlikely to persist in implementation or explanation. At the extreme, this can lead to abandonment, as occurred with the Court's earlier period of interest in federalism when, beginning in 1937, the Court began reversing and limiting cases that had defined limits to the commerce power. Short of abandonment, weak commitment can lead to unconvincing explanations, narrow holdings, and conflicting signals.

There are many reasons to doubt that the Court is strongly committed to its current campaign to restore states' rights. While it is true that virtually all the justices occasionally write appreciatively about the importance of states in our federal system, it is also true, as I already indicated, that most of the decisions limiting national authority attract only a bare majority of the justices. As a consequence, the Court has already reversed or severely limited some of these decisions. Perhaps even more revealingly, the justices routinely display distrust, and sometimes even contempt, for the moral and political judgments that underlie state statutes. This is true not only when those statutes arguably conflict with the constitutional rights of individuals but also when they undercut national interests in uniform economic regulation.

For many reasons quite independent of the identity or political affiliation of the particular individuals elevated to the Court, a tenuous inclination to protect state authority should be expected. First, of course, the justices are officers of the national government and identify with the needs and objectives of that government. Moreover, the members of the justices' likely reference groups—faculties at elite law schools, prominent Washingtonians, other federal judges—are also likely to identify with the national government.

Even if a specific justice resists the perspective that is natural to those who sit on the federal bench, the content of the idea of federalism is incompatible with consistent commitment to states' rights. Indeed, it is not too much to say that the principle of federalism is so conflicted and ambiguous that it *cannot* be enforced in any sustained and coherent way. Take, for instance, the undoubted fact that the national government was intended to have only limited and enumerated powers. The problem, as was understood from the beginning of the Republic, is that this intention coexisted with the decision to allow the national government power to regulate areas, such as commerce between the states, that as a practical matter cannot be limited. This leaves the judiciary with only highly artificial conceptual distinctions upon which to justify limitations on national regulatory power. Recently, for example, the Court has placed great emphasis on whether Congress is regulating a commercial activity (such as racial discrimination in restaurants) or a noncommercial activity (such as guns in public schools or violence against women). With respect to activities deemed to be noncommercial, evidence that the regulated behavior has indirect consequences for commerce is either ignored or downplayed.

History demonstrates the difficulty of insisting for long on abstract distinctions in the face of strong empirical considerations. This is partly due, of course, to the political forces that can be expected to respond to judicial decisions that create costs in the real world. But it is also due to an underlying intellectual problem of legal justification: how can the Court convincingly explain that a statute is beyond the constitutional power of Congress when the Constitution itself, making no distinction between direct and indirect consequences, expressly allows control over any activity thought to be necessary and proper for the regulation of commerce? In short, to a significant extent, the Constitution was designed to achieve two deeply conflicting objectives. Since the Supreme Court has no authority to ignore either of these objectives, it is predictable that its decisions will tend to oscillate between them rather than build them into a coherent program.

While popular mythology does not tend to focus on inconsistencies in our founding document, the principle of federalism is hardly the only aspect of the Constitution that contains sharply conflicting impulses. In some of these areas, the Court has demonstrated a capacity for a relatively sustained and determined interpretive agenda. For instance, the modern Court has pursued a significant program of limiting religious expression in public places despite the fact that the principle of separation of church and state competes with the principle of free exercise of religion. Federalism, however, is different in that its underlying nature and rationale are in important respects antagonistic to the practice of judicial review. To understand why this is so, it is necessary to review some basics about the role that the states are supposed to serve in the federal system.

The Founders did not think that the limitations on the power of the national government would be enforced primarily by way of conceptualistic distinctions. They thought that power would check power. Specifically, they thought that citizens would have natural loyalties and affinities to their local governments and that, therefore, these local governments would stand as competitors to national power. "The people," organized by state governments and given voice through these governments, would resist excessive centralization of power. They would "sound the alarm" (Rossiter 1961, Federalist 44, 286) and create "plans of resistance" (Federalist 46, 298). The proponents of the proposed Constitution went so far as to envision the possibility of armed encounters between the national army and state militias "amounting to near half a million of citizens with arms in their hands" (Federalist 46, 299). As Madison put it, it is "the existence of subordinate governments to which the people are attached [that] forms a barrier against the enterprises of ambition" (Federalist 46, 299).

The grounding of constitutional limitations on the capacity of the states to engage in political resistance to national power has a number of important implications. It means, first, that the correct meaning of the Constitution is contestable and, in that sense, open-ended. It means that loyalty to the nation (and its Constitution) is dependent on—not inconsistent with—loyalty to the states. It means that disagreement and even defiance are to some indeterminate degree constitutionally appropriate. It means, as Professor Amar has shown, that national sovereignty resides in people organized by state governments, not in the institutions of the central government (Amar 1987).

Federalism, therefore, is a constitutional principle singularly unsuited for judicial appreciation. Judges are paid to resolve disputes. To perform this task, they need binding authority. Legal understandings are authoritative to the extent to which they are definite, unambiguous, and permanent. To the extent that judges can persuasively articulate this kind of authoritative meaning in constitutional cases, their decisions are the embodiment of national sovereignty. To ask federal judges to enforce federalism, then, is to ask them to undermine their own instincts about legal meaning and to disown their own claim to speak as national sovereign.

CAPACITY TO CONTROL BEHAVIOR

Assuming the justices were inclined to pursue a states'-rights agenda vigorously and persistently, the effectiveness of their campaign would depend upon the availability of incentives for influencing political behavior. While judicial invalidation of national statutes can to some degree discourage federal overreaching, the constitutional system of power allocation is so complex that determined national decision makers can evade almost any judicially imposed restriction. For instance, the landmark decision holding that statutes prohibiting gun possession around public schools are beyond the commerce power does not prevent Congress from using the spending power to induce states to enact the same prohibition. Nor does it prevent Congress from prohibiting the interstate shipment of guns or the possession of a gun that was shipped across state lines.

Similarly, the decisions holding that Congress may not achieve its regulatory objectives by "commandeering" the institutions of state governments do not prevent Congress from regulating directly. Thus, while Congress cannot force local police to perform background checks on gun purchasers, Congress is free to authorize federal agencies to perform exactly the same functions. And, again, the national spending power can be used to induce states to perform the checks.

The complex set of cases that protect unconsenting states from being named as defendants in suits brought by private parties does not have much operational significance either. Municipal governments, school districts, and other similar potential governmental units can still be sued, as can state officials who have actual control over state governmental policies. Furthermore, federal policies can still be enforced against the states themselves by using federal agencies, rather than private parties, to bring suit.

Even when federalism decisions are not readily evaded, their impact is limited. Just as decisions that protect against censorship do not by themselves create vigorous political debate, normal judicial tools cannot directly induce state officials to behave with more vigor or independence or competence. Judges sometimes do elicit active behavior, including behavior by people not directly subject to judicial orders, as when they have managed to get state legislators to appropriate funds for prison reform or to get police to read suspects their *Miranda* warnings. But in such instances, the courts have direct control over some strategic incentive—they can, for instance, threaten to release prisoners if prison conditions are not improved, and they can refuse to accept confessions as evidence if police do not provide the required warnings. It is difficult to imagine any analogous set of incentives that could be used to generate energetic political activity at the state level.

SUPPORT OF
NONJUDICIAL INSTITUTIONS

Even judicial opinions that do not directly constrain behavior can, of course, influence behavior indirectly by shaping attitudes and beliefs. Indeed, to the extent that the educative effect of judicial rulings induces other institutions, especially Congress, to respect state sovereignty, the resolution of specific cases can have far-ranging consequences. And the modern Court's federalism decisions do have important educative and symbolic value (Nagel 1981). They insist that states retain a certain degree of dignity and status, and this is an important precondition to the sort of competition between levels of government that the Framers envisioned. It is probably of at least some value, as well, to remind the members of Congress that they are supposed to give serious thought to the nature and limits of their enumerated powers.

However, because of the natural inclination of judges to favor clear authority, it is doubtful that federal judges can be expected to be effective in promoting the kinds of competitive and sometimes defiant attitudes necessary for a vigorous federal system. Indeed, if studied and taken to heart by politicians, many Supreme Court opinions would discourage the very traits that are required. In one notable decision, for instance, the justices repeatedly and emphatically depicted loyalty to state governments as being incompatible with loyalty to the nation as a whole. Other important decisions severely deprecate the constitutional judgments of state legislators as being threats to—rather than supports for—constitutionalism. In short, while the Court can and does remind other leaders that states are important in our system, it is less inclined to teach the more fundamental lesson about why they are important.

Intellectual influence aside, the judicial decisions can also affect congressional action by arousing or encouraging interest groups that then exert political pressure. The most natural constituency for states'-rights positions, of course, is the leaders of state and local governments. A venerable academic tradition argues that these officeholders have built-in opportunities to influence Congress (Wechsler 1954), and no doubt there is considerable truth in this position. Members of Congress, for instance, are dependent on their local political organizations and thus subject to pressure from state-based politicians. Moreover, as the Founders argued from the beginning, when local policies are more effective than national policies, as could well have been true with respect to welfare programs, Congress can be forced by normal competitive pressures to return authority to state governments.

During modern times, however, the political influence of state and local governments does not seem to have been generally effective in reversing the trend toward centralization of power. One well-known set of reasons involves modern institutional changes that have reduced the influence of state politicians. These include the Seventeenth Amendment, which has state legislators no longer electing senators, and the Court's apportionment decisions, which limit state control over electoral districts. Another reason, as the Court itself recognized in *New York v. United States*,[2] is that the political self-interest of state leaders and the constitutional prerogatives of state governments are not necessarily the same thing. Obviously, it can be politically useful to shift responsibility for controversial issues to Washington. In addition, the enormous sums of money available from the federal government can tempt states not only to yield on substantive policies but also to sacrifice the status and autonomy of state institutions.

A second potential constituency for states' rights is a collection of groups Michael Greve (1999) has called the "Leave-Us-Alone coalition." He defines this movement as "a universe of loosely connected, partially overlapping grass-roots constituencies—property rights advocates, the term limits movement, home school and school choice organizations, right-to-life groups, gun owners, tax limitation initiatives, certain religious denominations, . . . small business owners, and others" (87). These disparate groups, according to Greve, are all dissatisfied with the cumbersomeness of federal regulation and favor state power because it might be more flexible and responsive. In any event, they generally think that state regulation is preferable to national control because exit is possible if a particular state does not exercise power wisely.

It is true, of course, that at any time there will be groups whose political self-interest disposes them to favor states' rights, and Greve may be right that the Leave-Us-Alone coalition is emerging as a fairly permanent opponent of national power. However, to imagine common cause between these populist groups and the justices of the Supreme Court requires heroic imagination. As a cultural matter, it is difficult to name a set of groups less likely to appeal to the elite lawyers who sit on the federal bench. In fact, in *U.S. Term Limits Inc. v. Thornton,* the Supreme Court insisted that the idea of term limits is a threat to national unity;[3] and in *Planned Parenthood v. Casey,* it characterized the pro-life movement as subversive of the rule of law.[4] Many of its decisions are openly hostile to fundamentalist religions. It has shown no inclination to protect the right to gun ownership, and, despite a few limited efforts to enforce the eminent domain clause, it allows pervasive regulation of small businesses.

This cultural divide does not mean that the Court's federalism jurisprudence cannot have the effect of strengthening the political influence of anti-centralization constituencies. Pornographers, who presumably are not esteemed by the justices either, are stronger politically because of judicial protections for free speech. But if Greve is right that the Leave-Us-Alone coalition generally opposes national regulation because its members see advantages in regulatory competition, it is unlikely to get much help from the Supreme Court. This is because the justices are less likely to protect state power in circumstances where significant disagreement about appropriate public policy exists. For instance, its two major decisions limiting Congress's power to regulate commerce both involved statutes—one prohibiting guns in schools and the other penalizing violent acts against women—that were essentially unnecessary because states did not favor contrary policies. In areas like racial segregation in restaurants, where at least at one time local populist groups wanted policies contrary to those of the national government, federal power is secure.

The rest of the modern Court's federalism jurisprudence shows the same tendency. Its rule against the national government's "commandeering" state institutions appeared in a case where the federal policy required state control over low-level radioactive material and had been initiated by way of a compact between state governments. The rule was expanded in a case where the federal policy required background checks on gun purchasers, a procedure that is required in many states and is supported by the National Rifle Association. In contrast, the rule was not applied when the national government—against the vociferous opposition of state governments—sought to set minimum wages and maximum hours for state employees.

Indeed, the Court has held as a general matter that state governments *may* be "commandeered" when the federal statute applies to private behavior along with the behavior of state institutions.[5] This means that in circumstances where state immunity from federal rules could stand as an exception to generally applicable national policy—and thus could function as visible competition to that policy—the Court will not make immunity available. In short, because the Court makes its federalism decisions without full appreciation for the importance of disagreement and defiance, its case law is unlikely to provide support for populist causes in precisely those situations where real challenges to national policy or authority are in play.

GENERAL SOCIAL AND CULTURAL CONDITIONS

In areas of sustained judicial activity like sexual freedom, free speech, and gender equality, where there has been deep public support for radical social change, it is difficult to know how much of that change is attributable to the Court's decisions. Despite the consistency and occasional drama of their support for these causes, the justices may simply be reflecting deeper cultural shifts, not inducing them (Rosenberg 1991). If the tides of history are carrying the American political system toward significant decentralization, the Supreme Court's recent federalism decisions may be more important as signals than as causes. Even so, it is safe to say that judicial initiatives are more likely to have wide impact when they reinforce social trends than when they work against them.

There are plenty of reasons to think that we may be entering an era of political decentralization, if not fragmentation. Many intellectuals (Schlesinger 1991; Huntington 1996) as well as popular observers (Horwitz 1999, 386) see in modern multiculturalism the seeds of political disunification. The "culture wars"—chiefly the domestic struggle over abortion—are so intense and disturbing that sober jurists, including Sandra Day O'Connor, Anthony Kennedy, and David Souter, believe that the anti-abortion movement presents a threat to the American people's belief in themselves as people "who aspire to live according to the rule of law."[6]

While such extreme fears may seem overwrought, it is worth remembering that they are being articulated at a time when some other countries, such as the former Soviet Union and Yugoslavia, have actually broken up. Within our own country, there is the spectral presence of militia groups, the continuing potential for urban riots, and the history of violent opposition to school desegregation.

More prosaic conditions and trends also point toward the possibility of radical decentralization. For instance, transnational institutions, arising in response to international markets that have been made possible by modern computer technology, may be displacing some of the functions of nation-states. Moreover, Keith Whittington (1998) argues that conditions are undermining the centralized bureaucracy that is the basis of much of the domestic power of the modern national government. Like Greve, he points to the growth of political groups disenchanted with centralized government. He also urges that technocratic ideals are being tarnished by the pervasive reality of interest group politics and the success of postindustrial management techniques.

Another set of modern developments, however, points in the opposite direction. Americans, involved with their families and fascinated by their computers and televisions, are increasingly withdrawing from social and political associations (Putnam 2000). What local public life continues (and it does continue, of course) is thinner because high mobility rates and nationalized communication systems mean that local ties are attenuated.

It is true that the privatization of modern life promotes the kinds of disenchantment that Greve and Whittington see as potential causes of decentralization. Disaffection, however, does not necessarily translate into increased support for state and local governments. Social and political isolation can lead not only to intellectual doubts about the centralized administrative state but also to cynicism about government at all levels. It can, moreover, lead to passionate commitment to causes, like gun ownership and militia membership, that can reduce the general public's sympathy for decentralization by continuing and accentuating the unsavory historical associations, especially massive opposition to school desegregation, that burden the cause of states' rights. At the extreme, privatization could evolve into the kind of social atomization that leads to immature yearnings for connection and perfection that can produce a servile need for authority, a nervous inability to tolerate disagreement and conflict, and ultimately to hypernationalism (Nagel forthcoming).

No one, of course, knows whether the current trend toward privatization in American life will continue or, if it does continue, whether the result would be fragmentation or radical nationalization. One sign that our society may be headed toward centralization is the American people's reverence for and dependence on judicial review. In many of the

Court's decisions can be seen strong indications of the very mind-set that is associated historically with hypernationalism. In recent cases, the justices are increasingly demanding supreme and unitary authority over foundational issues.[7] They treat political opposition as subversion[8] and depict moral disagreement as inexplicable if not dangerous.[9] For our society to tolerate and even glorify an institution exhibiting these traits suggests a dangerous affinity for and dependence on authoritarian instincts. To look to that same institution for protection for the very constitutional principle that institutionalizes governmental rivalry suggests that the political imagination necessary to sustain a robust federal system may already be lost.

Another reason to think radical centralization more likely than political fragmentation is the interaction between two newly established but unalterable facts: that the federal government has virtually unlimited jurisdiction and that issues of public concern are now subject to instantaneous nationalized communication. From the time the Constitution was drafted through the nineteenth century and well into the twentieth century, the federal government—either as a matter of law or practice—lacked authority over many issues of importance in everyday life. Moreover, even on those issues over which the national government did have jurisdiction, communication was slow and costly. In the modern era, these limitations no longer exist. Any matter that can be discussed within families, clubs, professional associations, religious organizations, and local governments—including, for instance, child rearing, abortion, marriage, dying, sexuality, and religion—can now also be discussed on the national stage in congressional hearings, Supreme Court opinions, and presidential electoral campaigns. Images and content from this national stage are transmitted everywhere quickly and relatively inexpensively.

The nature of the resulting competition between local and national discourse has implications for the possibility of significant decentralization. Because national discourse always has a potential audience that is larger and more varied than more localized discourse, the subject matter of national discourse will tend to seem more complex and significant than the same subject matter discussed in more limited arenas. In addition, since nationalized discourse is by definition more distant, it will tend to seem less familiar and ordinary—that is, more remote, abstract, and (in these ways) more significant. Both the stakes and the returns are greater for speakers in the national debate.

This set of circumstances has created for politics what Robert Frank and Philip Cook (1996) term a "winner-take-all market." Top political performers can now dominate the vast national political market in the same way that top entertainers or athletes can dominate vast economic markets. Whatever the advantages of winner-take-all markets, one disadvantage, according to Frank and Cook, is that prestige and attention (and other rewards) flow disproportionately to the few national winners while able performers just below the top tend to work in obscurity. The result is hypercompetition for positions at the top.

In the political realm, this means skewed discourse. Politics at the national level tend to attract skilled, larger-than-life figures who successfully personalize issues (which otherwise would seem overwhelmingly important and complex) and exaggerate or distort positions (because each competitor knows that all the others will be tempted by the overwhelming rewards available to those who prevail). In contrast, public discourse at the state or local level tends to be dull and derivative.

To take just one example, consider the contrast between the work product of federal and state supreme court justices. The justices of the United States Supreme Court dominate a national stage. Consequently, the issues they face gain the attention of elite law faculties, whose most brilliant students go on to work closely with the justices as clerks. With these and other aids, the justices are able routinely to engage in highly imaginative, far-reaching constitutional debates. Justices on state supreme courts, on the other hand, are generally not well known. Law faculties at even state law schools tend to ignore state constitutional law, and relatively pedestrian students go on to clerk at the state courts. The result, as Judge Hans Linde (1992) recognized years ago, is that state constitutional law generally consists of a stale and tedious repetition of the doctrines that were generated at the national level.

To the extent that what is true for state court justices is true of state officeholders in general, it seems inevitable that Americans' attention and interest will continue—perhaps increasingly—to center on national political discourse. A striking indication is the debate engaged in by the Pennsylvania state legislators whose anti-abortion statutes were a challenge to the nationalized abortion policy established in *Roe v. Wade* and, indeed, were depicted by justices of the United State Supreme Court in *Casey* as a threat to our sense of ourselves as a people governed by a fundamental law. These supposedly dangerous legislators knew that the power and prestige of the Court would dwarf the status of their own legal arguments on abortion. Therefore, during their debates, they argued that their statute was consistent not only with the Court's likely decisions in the future but also with its original decision in *Roe* (Pennsylvania 1989, 1755). Even as they sought to perform, at least according to their lights, the fundamental function of state institutions in a robust federal system—that is to speak as "the people" in limiting abuses of national authority—they claimed their action accorded with the very national action they condemned.

In a "winner-take-all" society, then, even intensely angry critics of national power are under pressure to frame their positions in ways that reinforce the prestige of national institutions. Under such conditions, it is not at all certain that growing atomization and cynicism, if those are what lie ahead, would result in a regenerated and decentralized political system. To the extent that national authority dominates the moral landscape even of dissidents, the stronger possibility would seem to be the growth of the sort of unqualified longing for identification with national symbols and authority that can lead eventually to radical nationalism.

In any event, growing social isolation and political cynicism are hardly inevitable. In fact, optimism and even perfectionism are deeply rooted in the American ethos and might well continue to be a major cultural force. A pragmatic, can-do independence has long undergirded local organizational activity and political participation in decentralized government. The concentration of public attention on the national stage, however, might tend to convert energetic hopefulness into a form of utopianism that cannot abide the variety and imperfection that inevitably characterize a robust federal system.

The hypothesis that nationalized discourse is linked to utopianism is supported by much of the record of the Supreme Court in the second half of the twentieth century. Certainly, the announced goals of the Court's initiatives in areas like school desegregation, sexual freedom, gender equality, and freedom of speech are grand indeed. Moreover, it is arguable that to a considerable degree the Court has pushed its programs without sufficient attention to social cost and without much concern about the need for local variation (Horowitz 1977). More generally, while Americans have always been fascinated with the Constitution as an embodiment of political idealism, contemporary support for using constitutional law as a vehicle for highly detailed, programmatic reforms may indicate a shift toward utopianism.

Under these conditions, the effort to use judicial power to achieve significant limitations on the power of the national government is puzzling. This effort may turn out to be more significant as an indication of anxiety about the great centralizing trends now in place than as a barrier against them.

Notes

1. 410 U.S. 113 (1973).
2. 505 U.S. 144 (1992).
3. 514 U.S. 779 (1995).
4. 505 U.S. 833, 868 (1992).
5. See *Garcia v. San Antonio Metro. Transit Auth.*, 469 U.S. 528 (1985).
6. *Planned Parenthood v. Casey*, 505 U.S. 833, 868 (1992).
7. See *City of Boerne v. Flores*, 521 U.S. 507 (1997); *Planned Parenthood v. Casey*, 505 U.S. 833 (1992).
8. See *Planned Parenthood v. Casey*, 505 U.S. 833 (1992).
9. See *Romer v. Evans*, 517 U.S. 620 (1996).

References

Amar, Akhil Reed. 1987. Of Sovereignty and Federalism. *Yale Law Journal* 96:1425-1520.

Frank, Robert H. and Philip J. Cook. 1996. *The Winner-Take-All Society*. New York: Penguin Books.

Greve, Michael S. 1999. *Real Federalism*. Washington, DC: AEI Press.

Horowitz, Donald L. 1977. *The Courts and Social Policy*. Washington, DC: Brookings Institution.

Horwitz, Tony. 1999. *Confederates in the Attic*. New York: Vintage Books.

Huntington, Samuel P. 1996. *The Clash of Civilizations*. New York: Simon & Schuster.

Linde, Hans A. 1992. Are State Constitutions Common Law? *Arizona Law Review* 34:215-29.

Nagel, Robert F. 1981. Federalism as a Fundamental Value. *Supreme Court Review* 1981:81-109.

———. Forthcoming. *The Collapse of American Federalism*. New York: Oxford University Press.

Pennsylvania. 1989. *Journal of the House* 2:1755. 24 Oct.

Putnam, Robert D. 2000. *Bowling Alone*. New York: Simon & Schuster.

Rosenberg, Gerald N. 1991. *The Hollow Hope*. Chicago: University of Chicago Press.

Rossiter, Clinton, ed. 1961. *The Federalist Papers*. New York: New American Library.

Schlesinger, Arthur M., Jr. 1991. *The Disuniting of America*. Knoxville, TN: Whittle Direct Books.

Wechsler, Herbert. 1954. The Political Safeguards of Federalism. *Columbia Law Review* 54:543-60.

Whittington, Keith E. 1998. Dismantling the Modern State? The Changing Structural Foundations of Federalism. *Hastings Constitutional Law Quarterly* 25:483-527.

Federalism and Freedom

By SETH F. KREIMER

ABSTRACT: The argument for devolution of power to state and local governments in contemporary Supreme Court cases regularly relies on claims about the virtues of federalism as a means of maintaining individual liberty. This article explores the plausibility of the argument that supplanting federal with state authority is likely systematically to protect individual liberty. The article argues that if there is a viable argument for "federalism as freedom," it must go beyond the sense that two governments are more repressive than one or that the federal government is more inclined to curtail liberty than is a state or local authority. The plausible claims rely on the abilities of autonomous state governments to provide a competing source of norms and to allow escape from oppressive laws. The availability of sanctuaries in other states is a function of rights of interstate travel and territorial limitations on state jurisdiction, which themselves require federalized constraints on state and local autonomy.

Seth F. Kreimer is a professor of law at the University of Pennsylvania Law School, where he teaches courses on constitutional law, constitutional litigation, and freedom of expression. He clerked in the chambers of Judge Arlin M. Adams of the United States Court of Appeals for the Third Circuit in 1977-78. After three years in private practice, he joined the faculty of the University of Pennsylvania in 1981. He has written and litigated widely in the areas of federalism and the constitutional rights to bodily autonomy, reproductive freedom, privacy, free expression, and interstate travel.

I T comes as no news to thoughtful observers that the Supreme Court is reviving judicially enforced constitutional limits on national power under the banner of federalism. On a number of fronts, a five-member majority of the current Court is moving systematically to substitute state for federal authority as enthusiastically as at any point in the Court's history. In the past two terms, the Court has invalidated six federal statutes as inconsistent with its vision of federalism,[1] a rate unsurpassed since the judicial reaction against the New Deal during 1935-36. Earlier Courts rooted constraints on national power primarily in claims about historical fidelity to founding principles, the "slogan 'Our Federalism,' born in the early struggling days of our Union,"[2] or the legal status of reserved rights of states. By contrast, the argument for devolution of power to state and local governments in contemporary cases regularly relies on claims about the virtues of federalism as a means of achieving other values. Prominent among these claims has been the proposition that federalism is important as a means of avoiding tyranny and maintaining individual liberty.[3]

When I first encountered such arguments, they seemed to embody a peculiarly morbid variety of humor. States'-rights federalism had, after all, begun as a mechanism that found its most prominent calling in defending the "peculiar institution" of slavery against national intervention (Scheiber 1996). It had underpinned the evisceration of Reconstruction.[4] In my formative years as a lawyer and legal scholar, during the late 1960s and 1970s, it was regularly invoked as a bulwark against federal efforts to prevent racial oppression, political persecution, and police misconduct. The most recent spasm of judicial activism has taken its toll on protections against official discrimination based on age, official appropriation of intellectual property, and misogynist violence. On its face, federalism seemed to me an odd candidate for the role of palladium of liberty.

Yet the end of the twentieth century has seen an emergence of some state legal regimes that provide recognizably more protections to individual liberties than their federal counterparts. From medical marijuana in California to assisted suicide in Oregon, from protections of minors' rights to abortion in Florida and New Jersey, to access to handguns in Montana, to gay partnership in Vermont, states provide protections denied by federal law. This article will explore the plausibility of the arguments that the process of supplanting federal with state authority is likely systematically to protect individual liberty, and the constitutional presuppositions that underpin the most plausible arguments.

ARE TWO GOVERNMENTS MORE DANGEROUS THAN ONE?

Initially, if one defined liberty simply as freedom from government constraint, one might believe that curtailing the reach of federal power would be likely to increase the liberty of citizens by limiting the number of sovereigns who may set constraints. If a particular activity, whether it is abortion, marijuana use, or gun ownership, is subject to potential regulation by both state and federal authorities, the chances of governmental intermeddling might be thought to double. Where two sovereigns may issue commands, before an individual may engage in the practice in question, she must comply with two sets of rules. Interests seeking to limit a practice can succeed by obtaining either state or federal regulation.

But this perception is not necessarily accurate, for under the supremacy clause of Article VI of the federal Constitution, federal regulation can preempt the effect of state rules. If an area lies within the sphere of federal competence, the federal government may reserve regulation of that area for itself, and if federal rules are more permissive than the rules states may wish to impose, federal authority increases, rather than decreases, liberty. In the founding generation, federal preemption liberated interstate steam transportation from local impediments;[5] during the McCarthy era, it prevented enforcement of the most draconian of state sedition laws;[6] in the struggles of the 1990s, federal preemption was invoked to bar enforcement of California's Proposition 187 against undocumented immigrants.[7] Strikingly, in recent terms, even as the Supreme Court has begun to prune the scope of some federal powers, it has aggressively employed preemption doctrine to immunize a variety of business activities from state regulation in areas that remain within federal authority, invalidating four exercises of state

authority in the last year alone.[8] But it is not only business that benefits from federal supremacy. Where the federal government affirmatively seeks to constrain the state's exercise of its monopoly on coercive violence—by, for example, limiting the state's authority to incarcerate mentally ill citizens in secluded institutions[9] or by constraining the authority of local police to abuse the citizenry at large—federal authority unambiguously protects personal liberty.

In most thoughtful definitions, moreover, governments are not the only threats to liberty. Allowing murder, rape, and robbery to go unpunished reduces the amount of government constraint in society, but it is hard to envision the shambles of civil society in contemporary Sierra Leone or Albania as paradigms of individual liberty. A reasonable sense of liberty entails not simply the absence of government constraint, but the absence of unjust private constraints. The addition of federal to state and local authority to prevent unjust private impositions, therefore, may systematically increase liberty either by providing greater sanctions and enforcement agents to enforce common civil norms or by protecting against private violence where state law does not.

In this sense, the extension of federal power has regularly protected liberty. Federal protections against violence directed at citizens who sought to vote or to organize for civil rights or to utilize integrated public facilities clearly increased the liberty of those citizens—though at the cost of decreasing the liberty of their prospective assailants. Conversely, in the aftermath of Reconstruction, the Supreme Court's decision that private racial violence lay outside of the province of federal authority effectively reduced the liberty of African American citizens. More recently, the removal of federal protections against gender-motivated violence in *United States v. Morrison*[10] decreased the liberty of potential victims of those crimes.

If there is a viable argument for federalism as freedom, therefore, it must go beyond the sense that two governments are more repressive than one.

IS THE FEDERAL GOVERNMENT MORE INCLINED TO CURTAIL LIBERTY?

A second support for devolution as a method of protecting liberty would arise if, as compared with state and local authorities, federal authorities are more likely to seek to interfere with individual liberty and less likely to protect it. Strains of such assumptions accompanied the debates on the framing of the Constitution, and there is certainly reason to believe that, for any individual citizen, ceteris paribus, her potential influence on government is likely to be greater at the local than the national level. Yet responsiveness is no guarantee against repression, for citizens may seek to impose constraints upon others as well as to resist constraints against themselves. Ultimately, a presumption of local virtue is more characteristic of the vanquished Anti-Federalists than of the prevailing Framers. Indeed, one of Madison's arguments for an "extended republic" was precisely that the variety of cross-cutting factions within a larger polity makes oppressive triumph of any one less likely (Rossiter 1961, Federalist 10, 78, 80, 83; Federalist 51, 324-25; Federalist 9, 71, 75). And, despite periodic claims that federal agents are more subject to capture by special interests than are states due to the difficulty of national organization by diffuse interest groups (Rapaczynski 1985, 341, 386-88), there is certainly an adequate stock of examples of state-level special interest oppression in American history—not least in the area of race relations—to leave the issue of whether state or federal governments are more disposed to protect individual liberty at best a subject of debate.

The most reasonable resolution of this debate, to my mind, is that both sides are right. For any particular constellation of policy preferences among the electorate, on any given issue, some states will be more oppressive than a unitary national regime, while some will be more vigilant in protection of individual liberties. Remitting a matter to local governments will result in a wider variance of policy outcomes, for unless each state is precisely reflective of the national balance of opinion, it is inevitable on any linear scale that the median voters in particular states will be arrayed around the national median. As a first approximation, it is hardly clear whether such variance is a net gain or net loss for individual freedom, since gains in freedom in the more protective states seem to be balanced by losses in the less protective ones.

DIVERSITY AND FREEDOM: THE DYNAMIC ARGUMENTS FOR FEDERALISM

Assuming that diffusion of authority to the state level will result initially in a variance in the level of individual freedom around the national norm, two mechanisms nonetheless support the claim that a decentralized system still tends to improve individual liberty. First, devolution may change the nature of the national norm itself by providing a mechanism to limit the oppressive enactments of the national government; second, it may allow escape from oppressive state laws that would be unavailable if a nationally uniform scheme were adopted.

"Double security"

Madison claimed, in a frequently cited argument, that the diffusion of power between state and federal governments provides a check against "usurpation" analogous to the security provided by separation-of-power principles at the federal level: "A double security arises to the rights of people. The different governments will control each other at the same time that each will be controlled by itself" (Rossiter 1961, Federalist 51, 323). Hamilton, similarly, argued,

Power being almost always the rival of power, the general government will at all times stand ready to check the usurpations of the state governments and these will have the same disposition toward the general government. The people by throwing themselves into either scale will infallibly make it preponderate. If their rights are invaded by either, they can make use of the other as an instrument of redress. . . . State governments will, in all possible contingencies afford complete security against invasions of the public liberty by the national authority. (Federalist 28, 181)

In the form in which it was articulated in the *Federalist Papers*, this vision seems both simplistic and a bit of an anachronism. It seems simplistic because, as I have noted, the threats to liberty at the federal level are likely to be supported by some states and opposed by others and "the people" will sometimes be predominantly unprotective of liberty. It seems anachronistic because the core of the redress proposed was a confrontation at arms whose plausibility in the twenty-first century should evoke some skepticism.

Still, if even a few states provide greater protection than the federal norm, the existence of alternatives to the authority of the federal government can legitimate political opposition to repression in ways that would be unattainable in the absence of a diffusion of political authority. At a minimum, the existence of alternative political visions makes it more difficult to demonize and extirpate political dissenters or to claim that the repression in question is unassailably valid. Beyond that, local political bases provide the platform for efforts to oust potentially repressive leaders by political means.[11] From Madison and Jefferson challenging the Alien and Sedition Acts in the legislatures of Kentucky and Virginia, to Ronald Reagan critiquing the Great Society in California, to Bill Clinton, in Arkansas, building a successful challenge to a sitting president, the existence of state-level alternatives to the nationally dominant political orthodoxy has made an electoral—if not a military—challenge to that orthodoxy more likely. The threat of electoral competition is a check on the temptation of political abuse, and the availability of a variety of exemplars of political values in action increases the variety of live choices that citizens may consider at the ballot box.

At the political level, to the extent that unjust limitations on liberty are often the result of exaggerations of the danger of the alien or unfamiliar, or a miscalculation of the benefits of regulation, the availability of a variety of venues for policy makes it less likely that unjust infringements on liberty will survive. On the one hand, experimentation with policy alternatives will allow the empirical impeachment of claims that liberty will generate a parade of horrors. The positive experience with allowing patients the right to refuse treatment after the *Quinlan* case[12] laid the basis for a national consensus on patients' rights that was unavailable a decade earlier. The fact that recognition of gay couples in Vermont does not wreak havoc with the state's family structure will provide a basis for allowing similar rights in other states. Conversely, if a deprivation of liberty in one state fails to provide the hoped-for benefits, one may join Chief Justice Taft's "hope that the tendency to error in the weakening of constitutional guaranties that is going on in some states may be halted by the . . . actual experience

[that] . . . will ultimately bring back the nation to sounder views" (Post 1992, 68).

It is worth remembering, however, that the challenged national orthodoxy may itself preserve liberty. The history of local resistance to national civil rights initiatives is a sobering reminder that local autonomy may come at a cost to individual freedom. A priori, there is no reason to maintain that repressive movements launched from protected enclaves of local authority will be less prevalent than crusades of liberation. Nonetheless, in the last two generations, while it is easy enough to come up with recent examples of state-level innovations that have spread liberty to the national scene—abortion, gay rights, and the right to refuse medical treatment come immediately to mind—it is more difficult to call to mind contemporary examples of local repression that have successfully infected the national polity.

Exit and sanctuary

While the "double security" argument for the linkage between federalism and individual liberty is plausible, it rests on a series of debatable political predictions. A final basis for the claimed linkage between federalism and freedom, however, relies on an analytically unimpeachable claim: state-by-state variation leaves open the possibility to each individual of choosing to avoid repression by leaving the repressive jurisdiction. A nationally applicable norm is unavoidable short of exile; a state law can be avoided with a moving van.

At a minimum, where states adopt different positions on issues of irreducible moral disagreement, the variety of local political regimes gives citizens a choice of the rules they live under that would be unavailable in a centralized system. In its strong form, the argument would hold that as long as there is at least one state on any issue that adopts a position as libertarian as the most libertarian position that a national regime could adopt, a national regime cannot improve on a local regime—since those who value the liberty can migrate to the libertarian state—while national uniformity risks the adoption of a uniform and inescapable repressive norm.

The value and possibilities of geographical sanctuary run through American history. America was, after all, founded in part by immigrants who sought and found sanctuary from political and religious repression. The closing of the western frontier by Great Britain was adduced as one of the justifications for independence (Chafee 1956, 182); after independence, Article IV of the Articles of Confederation expressly protected the right of migration, providing that "the people of each state shall have free ingress and regress from any other state." We see the reflection of the possibilities of interstate escape in the fugitive slave clause, the extradition clause, the full faith and credit clauses of Article IV of the Constitution, and the free soil arguments and personal liberty laws that preceded the Civil War (Finkelman 1981, 293-338; Smith 1997, 809).

After the Civil War, Mormons moved from Illinois to Utah, while African Americans migrated from the Jim Crow South (Bernstein 1998, 781). Rail travel and, later, automobiles and airplanes enabled residents of conservative states to escape constraints on divorce and remarriage.[13] In the years before *Roe v. Wade*,[14] women from states with restrictive abortion laws sought reproductive autonomy in more sympathetic jurisdictions (Kreimer 1992, 451, 453-56). Today, the lesbian who finds herself in Utah, like the gun lover who lives in Washington, D.C., and the gambler in Pennsylvania, need only cross a state border to be free of constraining rules. These are liberties that come only with the variations in local norms made possible by federalism.

To be sure, this exit option is no panacea; the strong form of the argument cannot be maintained, for "only" crossing a border is often no mean hurdle. To the citizen who is unwilling or unable to abandon her current residence, the availability of a freer life in the next state is cold comfort. For the citizen who lacks access to information, funds, or transportation, the legal possibility of liberty in a neighboring state may provide no succor. Between 2 and 3 percent of Americans change their state of residence every year, and two in five live outside of the state of their birth, but a majority never emigrate (*Statistical Abstract of the United States* 1999, 31; United States Census Website). Still, if a species of oppression is so extravagant as to overwhelm ties to job and home and hearth—or if it can be avoided by an extraterritorial excursion—an adult citizen may escape it.

PREREQUISITES OF FEDERALISM AS FREEDOM

On its face, the judicial enforcement of federalism is concerned primarily with constraining the federal government, and most of the attention in this volume focuses on the emergence of doctrines of this sort. But the more plausible, dynamic theories connecting federalism and freedom presuppose a series of features of the federal system that limit the states themselves. In particular, the argument that federalism is linked with freedom by virtue of the availability of exit and sanctuary requires not only that states be self-governing but also (1) that citizens have the right to move between states (for if state A may prevent its citizens from moving to state B, the possible sanctuary in state B is worthless); (2) that citizens who migrate be entitled to the same rights as those who are native born (for if new emigrants from state A cannot obtain the same rights as the native born, they will be unable to take advantage of the sanctuary that state B offers); and (3) that states' jurisdiction be territorially limited (for if state A may enforce its norm within state B, state B can offer no sanctuary).

In fact, amid the fanfare accompanying the recent enthusiasm for the Tenth and Eleventh Amendments, we also observe the Supreme Court enforcing these libertarian presuppositions against both state and federal governments.

Right to travel and interstate migration

The constitutional protection for the first two prerequisites, travel and migration, has been a matter of derivation rather than explicit statement. Although Article IV of the Articles of Confederation included an explicit protection of the rights of "ingress and regress," Article IV of the Constitution of 1787 did not carry forward that language. Rather, the parallel section of the Constitution, Article IV, Section 2, simply stated that the "citizens of each state shall be entitled to all the privileges and immunities of citizens in the several states." Before the Civil War, there was wide agreement in both Congress and the judiciary that the privileges and immunities clause of Article IV prevented states from interfering with the rights of citizens to travel between states of the Union (Kreimer 1992, 501-4), though the Supreme Court found no occasion to enforce those rights.

The triumph of nationalism in the Civil War brought with it an authoritative affirmation by the Supreme Court that the right to interstate travel was constitutionally protected. Striking down a tax imposed by Nevada on local citizens departing from the state, the Court in 1871 proclaimed,

For all the great purposes for which the Federal government was formed we are one people, with one common country. We are all citizens of the United States, and as members of the same community must have the right to pass and repass through every part of it without interruption, as freely as in our own States.[15]

The Court treated the right as one that arose from the nature of the federal structure.

In adopting the citizenship clauses of the Fourteenth Amendment, which bestowed state citizenship by virtue of residency and birthright national citizenship, the framing members of Congress expected the new regime to secure the right of citizens to travel and migrate throughout the country. First, by making clear that African Americans were citizens of the states in which they resided, the Fourteenth Amendment was thought to establish authoritatively that the Article IV privilege of interstate travel and settlement extended to newly freed slaves. Second, by recognizing birthright national citizenship, and guarding the privileges and immunities of that citizenship, the Fourteenth Amendment provided direct protection and authority for Congress to protect national rights of travel and migration.[16] But the Framers failed to embed these expectations in clear constitutional language, and they were not the centerpieces of discussion.

During the next 70 years, the Supreme Court regularly affirmed the right of citizens to interstate travel and migration in dicta but failed to enter decisions enforcing those rights. The Court upheld statutes burdening the efforts of "emigrant agents" to facilitate migration out of the Jim Crow South,[17] and it denied relief to residents of Arizona driven from the state by private violence.[18] In *Edwards v. California*,[19] the Court finally struck down a California statute—adopted in 1901—that punished the act of bringing a nonresident indigent into the state. A minority of four justices relied on a personal right to interstate travel; the majority rested their decision on the proposition that the statute was inconsistent with federal authority over interstate commerce.

It was only the Warren Court that began to enforce a right to interstate travel as a constitutional privilege of national citizenship. *United States v. Guest* relied on the "constitutional right to travel from one State to another, . . . [which] occupies a position fundamental to the concept of our Federal Union" to uphold a federal prosecution of a conspiracy against out-of-state civil rights workers.[20] In subsequent cases invalidating durational residency requirements for state welfare benefits designed to discourage indigents from migrating away from their home states,[21] as well as durational residency requirements for voting[22] and medical benefits,[23] the Warren Court majority reiterated the proposition that the right to travel was a "fundamental" constitutional right that precluded discrimination against newly arrived migrants. But the justices remained opaque as to the source of that right or its precise parameters, relying alternatively on the equal protection clause, the privileges and immunities clause, the due process clause, and inferences from the structure of the federal union.

The right-to-travel analysis splintered during the next two decades. Though the Court struck down durational residency requirements for some tax and social welfare benefits,[24] it upheld durational residency requirements for divorce[25] and stringent residency requirements for access to public education.[26] The justices engaged in increasingly fractious disagreement as to the proper source and scope of the right to interstate travel and migration.

Based as it had been in inferences from constitutional structure and open-ended analysis of equal protection norms, one might have imagined that the right to interstate travel and migration would fall victim to the hostility of the Rehnquist Court to extratextual individual rights. When the Court granted certiorari in 1998 to address the constitutionality of a California statute that limited welfare benefits available to arrivals from out of state during the first year of their sojourn in California to those the migrants would have received in their state of origin, only three justices remained on the bench who had previously addressed the right-to-travel issue. Each of them had dissented from Burger Court cases upholding right-to-travel claims. Moreover, the California statute was specifically authorized by a part of the recently enacted Personal Responsibility and Work Opportunity Reconciliation Act of 1996 through which Congress sought to devolve authority over welfare expenditures to the states, thereby giving color to the claim that the interests of the nation as well as the states supported the challenged limitation.

Yet when the opinion was released in *Saenz v. Roe*,[27] Justice Stevens wrote for all but two justices in striking down California's statute. The opinion reaffirmed the propositions that the Constitution protects

the right of a citizen of one State to enter and to leave another State, the right to be treated as a welcome visitor rather than an unfriendly alien when temporarily present in the second State, and, for those travelers who elect to become permanent residents, the right to be treated like other citizens of that State.[28]

Invoking the citizenship and privileges and immunities clauses of the Fourteenth Amendment in place of the equal protection analysis that underpinned the Warren Court decisions, Justice Stevens announced that "citizens of the United States, whether rich or poor have the right to choose to be citizens of the state wherein they reside" while "the states, however, do not have any right to select their citizens."[29] The Court held that Congress has no more authority to dilute this right than any other guarantee of the Fourteenth Amendment.

The broad support of these forceful declarations makes perfect sense if the purpose of federalism is to preserve individual liberty, for it is the opportunity to choose a new home and take advantage of the benefits it offers that underwrites the claim that state autonomy serves the purpose. For justices who see federalism as a guardian of liberty, neither the states nor the federal government should be able to interfere with that opportunity, either by direct prohibition or by indirect discouragement and denial of the fruits of the citizen's choice of residence.

Territorial limits

The final prerequisite to the availability of exit and sanctuary is so much a matter of common experience that we may fail to notice it: in general, states are territorially defined. When I drive across the border between Pennsylvania and New Jersey, I assume, correctly, that the speed limit with which I must comply becomes New Jersey's rather than Pennsylvania's. I can return to Pennsylvania's law by returning to its territory, and in general, I am subject to only one state's law at any given time.[30]

This limitation of state authority—and its attendant guarantee of exit and sanctuary—is familiar, but it is neither a natural fact nor a political inevitability. Pennsylvania may have reason to seek to control my actions outside of its territory, whether because they have effects within Pennsylvania (as if I were to post a letter bomb to Pennsylvania from a New Jersey address) or because the state believes that its interests are otherwise affected (as if Pennsylvania sought to prevent me from gambling in Atlantic City or prevent New Jersey doctors from providing abortions to young Pennsylvania women without parental consent). Unless otherwise constrained, it can punish me directly for my extraterritorial actions if and when I return to Pennsylvania, and, under the extradition powers and the full faith and credit clause of Article IV, it can invoke federal authority to impose its sanctions even if I choose to remain away.

Often states limit the reach of their laws to their own borders as a matter of comity, but in an increasingly mobile and interconnected society, the occasions to abandon this rule of self-restraint increase. During the first hundred years of the Republic, state courts treated the territorial limitation of state power as a presupposition of the federal structure, underwritten by the privileges and immunities clause of Article IV; after the adoption of the Fourteenth Amendment, the Supreme Court found a basis to enforce territorial limitations on state authority in the due process clause (Kreimer 1992, 464-72).[31] The New Deal constitutional revolution worked a change in this area as in others; the Supreme Court's due process jurisprudence has come to recognize a wider array of state interests and local effects to constitute reasonable bases for the exercise of prescriptive jurisdiction (Kreimer 1992, 473- 78).[32] The Court has continued, however, to discern in the commerce clause and the federal structure limits on the authority of states to seek to regulate extraterritorially.[33]

Even as the Court in recent years has reinforced state authority against federal intervention under the banner of federalism, it has reaffirmed the existence of limits on the authority of any state to seek to control actions within the territory of one of its fellows. The Court has reiterated that "a State does not acquire power or supervision over the internal affairs of another State merely because the welfare and health of its own citizens may be affected when they travel to that State";[34] it has held that "it follows from [the] principles of state sovereignty and comity that a State may not impose economic sanctions on violators of its laws with the intent of changing the tortfeasors' lawful conduct in other States";[35] it has determined that "Michigan has no authority to shield a witness from another jurisdiction's subpoena power in a case involving persons and causes outside of Michigan's governance."[36] These limits not only preserve the possibility of exit and sanctuary, but they respond to the underlying argument for devolution that "the Constitution ... contemplates that a State's government will represent and remain accountable to its own citizens."[37] To the extent that states seek to control citizens of other jurisdictions, they lose the political accountability that the analysis of the Courts' opinions holds as a crucial safeguard against overreaching.

CODA: THE INTERNET AND THE FUTURE OF FEDERALISM

Many of the recent federalism cases have sought to preserve liberty by contracting federal authority. I have highlighted the fact that other cases—less celebrated—have preserved the underlying libertarian presuppositions of the federal system by constraining state authority. As the Internet emerges as a primary mode of interaction, the next generation will confront the Court with increasingly insistent calls for broader limits on state authority based on the same logic that now underpins devolution.

Given current technology, any posting to a Web page ineluctably makes that posting available to viewers in every state. Every state, therefore, has an incentive and a colorable claim to regulate that posting in the service of its preferred policies, even if the posting is entirely lawful both at its point of origin and under the laws of most states where the Web page is accessed. Conversely, because current technology provides no method for a Web-page poster or a chat-room participant to accurately determine the physical locations to which their information may be directed, prospective posters can find no sanctuary short of leaving the Internet entirely. Every state, if it can exercise jurisdiction over Web-page content, can effectively ban the material from all other states. Far from allowing citizens to achieve the most libertarian result offered by any state, therefore, the devolution of regulatory authority to the states would impose the least permissive state regime on the citizens of all other states. On the Internet as currently constituted, state-protective federalism will be unambiguously tipped from an arguable bastion of liberty to an engine of repression.

In light of these concerns, several lower courts have held that state efforts to regulate the content of Web sites are unconstitutionally extraterritorial.[38] To the extent that this proposition survives, regulation of the Internet will be remitted to federal jurisdiction. And federal regulation is likely to be uniform; in a case that the Supreme Court will almost inevitably review, the Court of Appeals for the Third Circuit has held that by incorporating local community standards of decency into the Child Online Protection Act, Congress violated the First Amendment, since the standards of the community most likely to be offended by any message are effectively imposed on residents of more broad-minded communities.[39]

Any functional justification for a legal regime is hostage to the facts that inform predictions about the regime's effects. To the extent that the newly assertive federalism of the Court is based in a linkage between freedom and federalism, the values that underlie the Court's recent forays against federal power are likely to move the regulation of cyberspace—and with it an increasingly pervasive aspect of the nation's life—away from the states and toward the federal government.

Notes

1. See United States v. Morrison, 120 S. Ct. 1740 (2000); Kimel v. Florida Bd. of Regents, 528 U.S. 62 (2000); Alden v. Maine, 527 U.S. 706 (1999); College Sav. Bank v. Florida Prepaid Postsecondary Educ. Expense Bd., 527 U.S. 666 (1999); Florida Prepaid Postsecondary Educ. Expense Bd. v. College Sav. Bank, 527 U.S. 627 (1999); Saenz v. Roe, 526 U.S. 489 (1999).

2. Younger v. Harris, 401 U.S. 37, 44 (1971).

3. See Alden, 527 U.S. at 758 (1999) (Kennedy, J.); College Sav. Bank, 527 U.S. at 689 (1999) (Scalia, J.); Printz, 521 U.S. at 921 (1997) (Scalia, J.); United States v. Lopez, 514 U.S. 549 (1995) (Kennedy, J., concurring); New York v.

United States, 505 U.S. 144, 181 (1992) (O'Connor, J.); Gregory v. Ashcroft, 501 U.S. 452, 458-59 (1991) (O'Connor, J.); Coleman v. Thompson, 501 U.S. 722, 759 (1991) (Blackmun, J., dissenting).

4. See Civil Rights Cases, 109 U.S. 3 (1883); United States v. Harris, 106 U.S. 629 (1883); Slaughter-House Cases, 83 U.S. (1 Wall.) 36 (1873).

5. See Gibbons v. Ogden, 22 U.S. (1 Wheat.) 1 (1824).

6. See Pennsylvania v. Nelson, 350 U.S. 497 (1956).

7. See League of United Latin Amer. Citizens v. Wilson, 908 F. Supp. 755 (C.D. Cal. 1995).

8. Norfolk Southern Ry Co. v. Shanklin, 120 S. Ct. 1467 (2000) (preempting state tort liability); Crosby v. National Foreign Trade Council, 120 S. Ct. 2288 (2000) (preempting municipal effort to require contractors to boycott Burma); United States v. Locke, 120 S. Ct 1135 (2000) (preempting state regulation of oil tankers); Geier v. American Honda, 120 S. Ct. 1913 (2000) (preempting state tort liability for failure to install airbags).

9. See Olmstead v. L. C., 527 U.S. 581 (1999).

10. 120 S. Ct. 1740 (2000).

11. See Federalist 28 ("Projects of usurpation cannot be masked under pretenses so likely to escape penetration.... The [state] legislatures will have better means of information. They can discover danger at a distance, and possessing all the organs of civil power and the confidence of the people, they can at once adopt a regular plan of opposition.") (Rossiter 1961, 181).

12. In re Quinlan, 355 A.2d 647, 664 (N.J. 1976).

13. Hendrik Hartog gives an account of the effects of mobility and the successive roles of Indiana, Illinois, Rhode Island, Iowa, South Dakota, Arizona, Utah, and Nevada as "divorce havens" between the Civil War and the 1950s (Hartog 2000, 19-23, 247, 282).

14. 410 U.S. 959 (1973).

15. Crandall v. Nevada, 73 U.S. (1 Wall.) 35, 48-49 (1867) quoting Passenger Cases, 48 U.S. (7 How.) 283, 492 (1849) (Taney, J., dissenting).

16. See generally Kreimer 1992, 504-6.

17. See Williams v. Fears, 79 U.S. 270 (1900); see also Bernstein 1998.

18. See *United States v. Wheeler*, 254 U.S. 281 (1920).

19. 314 U.S. 160 (1941).

20. 383 U.S.745, 757 (1966). See also *Griffin v. Breckenridge*, 403 U.S. 88, 106 (1971) (relying on right of interstate travel to uphold congressional power to grant civil rights action).

21. See *Shapiro v. Thompson*, 394 U.S. 618 (1969). The Court rejected efforts by states to reimpose durational residency requirements. See, for example, *Lopez v. Wyman*, 329 F. Supp. 483 (W.D.N.Y. 1971), aff'd, 404 U.S. 1055 (1972); *Rivera v. Dunn*, 329 F. Supp. 554 (D. Conn. 1971), aff'd, 404 U.S. 1054 (1972).

22. See *Dunn v. Blumstein*, 405 U.S. 330 (1972).

23. See *Memorial Hosp. v. Maricopa County*, 415 U.S. 250 (1974).

24. See *Attorney General of New York v. Soto-Lopez*, 476 U.S. 898 (1986). See also *Hooper v. Bernalillo County Assessor*, 472 U.S. 612 (1985); *Zobel v. Williams*, 457 U.S. 55 (1982).

25. See *Sosna v. Iowa*, 419 U.S. 393 (1975).

26. See *Martinez v. Bynum*, 461 U.S. 321 (1983).

27. 526 U.S. 489 (1999).

28. Id. at 500.

29. Id. at 510-11.

30. Since states have no authority comparable to the supremacy clause to immunize conduct from each other's sanctions, horizontal limitations on state authority (unlike limitations on federal authority) unambiguously function to protect against imposition of a double set of governmental constraints.

31. For antebellum thinking, see *Lemmon v. People*, 20 N.Y. 562 (1860). For analysis after the Fourteenth Amendment, see *Huntington v. Attrill*, 146 U.S. 657 (1892); see also *Allgeyer v. Louisiana*, 165 U.S. 578 (1897).

32. See *Phillips Petroleum v. Shutts*, 472 U.S. 797 (1985); see also *Sun Oil Co. v. Wortman* 486 U.S. 717 (1988).

33. See *Bigelow v. Virginia*, 421 U.S. 809 (1975). See also *Healy v. Beer Institute*, 491 U.S. 324 (1989); *Edgar v. MITE Corp.*, 457 U.S. 624 (1982).

34. *BMW of North America, Inc. v. Gore*, 517 U.S. 559, 571 n. 16 (1996), quoting *Bigelow*, 421 U.S. at 824.

35. *BMW of North America, Inc.*, 517 U.S. at 572.

36. *Baker v. General Motors Corp.*, 522 U.S. 222, 240 (1998). See also *Quill Corp. v. North Dakota*, 504 U.S. 298 (1992) (holding physical presence necessary for state taxation of income).

37. *Printz v. United States*, 521 U.S. 898, 920 (1997).

38. See *ACLU v. Johnson*, 194 F.3d 1149 (10th Cir. 1999). See also *Psinet Inc. v. Chapman*, 2000 U.S. Dist. LEXIS 11621 (E.D. Va. 2000); *American Library Assn. v. Pataki*, 969 F. Supp. 160 (S.D.N.Y. 1997); *Cyberspace Communications, Inc. v. Engler*, 55 F. Supp. 3d 737 (E.D. Mich 1999). Cf. *Consoidated Cigar Corp. v. Reilly*, 218 F.3d 30 (1st Cir. 2000). For an earlier discussion, see Burk 1996, 1095.

39. See *ACLU v. Reno*, 2000 U.S. App. LEXIS 14419 (3d Cir. 2000).

References

Bernstein, David. 1998. The Law and Economics of Post Civil War Restrictions on Interstate Migration by African Americans. *Texas Law Review* 76: 781-847.

Burk, Dan L. 1996. Federalism in Cyberspace. *Connecticut Law Review* 28:1095-1136.

Chafee, Zechariah, Jr. 1956. *Three Human Rights in the Constitution of 1787.* Lawrence: University Press of Kansas.

Finkelman, Paul. 1981. *An Imperfect Union: Slavery, Federalism and Comity.* Chapel Hill: University of North Carolina Press.

Hartog, Hendrik. 2000. *Man and Wife in America: A History.* Cambridge, MA: Harvard University Press.

Kreimer, Seth F. 1992. The Law of Choice and Choice of Law: Abortion, the Right to Travel, and Extraterritorial Regulation in American Federalism. *New York University Law Review* 67: 451-519.

Post, Robert C. 1992. Chief Justice William Howard Taft and the Concept of Federalism. In *Federalism and the Judicial Mind*, ed. Harry N. Scheiber.

Berkeley: Institute of Governmental Studies Press.

Rapaczynski, Andrzej. 1985. From Sovereignty to Process: The Jurisprudence of Federalism After Garcia. *Supreme Court Review* 1985:341-419.

Rossiter, Clinton, ed. 1961. *The Federalist Papers*. New York: New American Library.

Scheiber, Harry N. 1996. Redesigning the Architecture of Federalism—An American Tradition: Modern Devolu-tion Policies in Perspective. *Yale Journal on Regulation* 14:227-95.

Smith, Douglas G. 1997. The Privileges and Immunities Clause of Article IV Section 2, Precursor of Section 1 of the Fourteenth Amendment. *San Diego Law Review* 24:809-920.

Statistical Abstract of the United States. 1999. Washington, DC: Government Printing Office.

United States Census Website. www.census.gov/population/socdemo/migration/pob-rank.txt. Visited 25 Aug. 2000.

ANNALS, *AAPSS*, **574**, March 2001

Judicial Solicitude
for State Dignity

By EVAN H. CAMINKER

ABSTRACT: The Supreme Court's recent decisions holding that Congress cannot authorize individuals to sue states proclaim that such sovereign immunity serves the states' "dignitary interests" by emphasizing "the respect owed them as members of the federation." What is the interpretive significance of the Court's apparent references to the social meaning of suits against states? This article explores whether the Court's professed concern with maintaining state dignity might be justificatory rather than rhetorical, with the Court invalidating statutes subjecting unconsenting states to private suit because those statutes entailed social meanings that contravene federalism values. Specifically, various expressivist rationales for the Court's sovereign immunity jurisprudence are sketched, and it is suggested that each rationale confronts significant difficulties that undermine the propriety of expressivist reasoning in this context.

Evan Caminker is a professor at the University of Michigan Law School. He clerked for Justice Brennan and taught at UCLA School of Law before joining the Michigan faculty. He wrote this article while on leave as deputy assistant attorney general at the Office of Legal Counsel, United States Department of Justice.

PERHAPS the most aggressive of the Supreme Court's recent federalism decisions are those pronouncing a sweeping principle of state sovereign immunity. Overruling prior precedent, the Court held that Congress cannot authorize private individuals to sue unconsenting states seeking damages for violations of federal statutory rights in federal or state court.[1] The Supreme Court repeatedly proclaimed in these cases that immunity from private suits serves the states' "dignitary interests." As a general matter, the Court explained, the Constitution reserves to states "a substantial portion of the Nation's primary sovereignty, together with the dignity and essential attributes inhering in that status."[2] More specifically, immunity from private suit " 'accords the States the respect owed them as members of the federation,' "[3] whereas congressional authorization of private suits against unconsenting states "present[s] the indignity of subjecting a State to the coercive process of judicial tribunals at the instance of private parties"[4] and "denigrates the separate sovereignty of the States."[5]

What should we make of these and numerous other references to the inherent "dignity" of states and the wrongfulness of Congress's "denigration" thereof? It is tempting to dismiss these articulations as mere rhetorical flourishes, window dressing on federalism walls constructed from other methodological building blocks. Indeed, the Court supported its conclusions with more traditional originalist and functionalist arguments as well, appealing both to the

original understanding and contemporary notions of effective governance.

But it is quite possible that the Court's focus on state dignity reflects an alternative approach to constitutional interpretation, one focusing on "expressive harms" wrought by governmental conduct. As Richard Pildes (1998) explains, "an expressive harm is one that results from the ideas or attitudes expressed through a governmental action rather than from the more tangible or material consequences the action brings about" (755). Either because of the means through which governmental action seeks to achieve its objectives or because of the reasons for this action, such action might "express" a meaning that contravenes constitutional values. Indeed, various scholars claim that the Supreme Court has recently employed such an "expressivist" approach in defining the contours of both the equal protection and establishment clauses, invalidating governmental actions in large or whole part because those actions entail social meanings that contravene constitutional values by visiting expressive harms on individuals (Pildes and Niemi 1993 [voting rights jurisprudence]; Marshall 1996 [establishment clause jurisprudence]; Anderson and Pildes 2000, 1533-51 [voting rights and establishment clause jurisprudence]).

Until now, however, scholars have paid little attention to the possibility that a concern for expressive harms might have application to intergovernmental relations.[6] Might the Court's persistent focus on protecting the states' "dignity" from "denigration" by Congress plausibly reflect the assertion of an expressive constitutional norm, with explanatory rather than merely rhetorical force? If so, what is the nature of the claim, and can it be persuasively defended?

DIGNITY CLAIMS IN STATE SOVEREIGN IMMUNITY JURISPRUDENCE

It is certainly possible that the Supreme Court's repeated invocation of the states' sovereign status and dignity is intended merely as rhetorical window dressing for a conclusion reached on independent grounds. Certainly, the Court has proffered more conventional methodological justifications for its state sovereign immunity doctrine, relying primarily on an originalist account (arguing that the Framers understood unconsenting states to be immune from private suits for damages) supplemented by various functional arguments (including that this immunity preserves political accountability). Perhaps these more conventional arguments provide the analytical justification for the Court's state sovereign immunity jurisprudence, with the references to states' dignitary interests merely providing rhetorical flourish or perhaps purporting to characterize the Framers' own presuppositions.

There are compelling reasons, however, to take seriously the possibility that the Court's phraseology has independent justificatory significance. One reason that should speak to immunity doctrine's many critics is that the Court's articulated originalist and functionalist justifications are simply inadequate to the task. Numerous scholars have bolstered the dissenting justices' claims that neither the originalist account of the Framers' vision of state sovereign immunity nor the functional claims that modern doctrine preserves either state or federal political accountability can withstand close scrutiny. If this is so, one must wonder whether the Court majority might view the preservation of state dignity as bearing some, perhaps even significant, weight in the mix of doctrinal justifications.

Second, the Court's references to dignitary interests and injuries do not appear in casual and isolated snippets but, rather, are characterized as an affirmative rationale for state sovereign immunity. As early as 1887, the Court proposed that state sovereign immunity purports to avert "the indignity of subjecting a State to the coercive process of judicial tribunals at the instance of private parties."[7] More recently, the Court explained that state immunity from suit "accords the States the respect owed them as members of the federation,"[8] invoked "the dignity and respect afforded a State, which the immunity is designed to protect,"[9] and stated that concerns for "the States' solvency and dignity . . . underpin the Eleventh Amendment."[10] And most recently, in *Alden v. Maine*, the Court gave dignitary interests center stage in explicating the role state sovereign immunity plays in our constitutional structure. In addition to quoting each of these previous references to state dignity, the Court added that states "retain the dignity, though not the full authority, of sovereignty";[11] admonished that "Congress must accord States the esteem due them as joint participants in a federal system, one beginning with the premise of sovereignty in both the central Government and the separate States";[12] warned that "Congress has ample means to ensure compliance with valid federal laws, but it must respect the sovereignty of the States";[13] and concluded that "a congressional power to authorize private suits against nonconsenting States in their own courts would be even more offensive to state sovereignty than a power to authorize the suits in a federal forum."[14] Moreover, similar phrases adorn the Court's recent anti-commandeering jurisprudence as well. The Court recently emphasized that "the Constitution established a system of 'dual sovereignty'"[15] and decried commandeering as "reduc[ing] [the states] to puppets of a ventriloquist Congress" by "dragoon[ing]" state officials.[16]

Finally, a concern with the expressive significance of certain types of congressional action fits well with the patchwork of judicially recognized exceptions to and waivers of state sovereign immunity. Current doctrine permits private suits against state officials for prospective relief, congressionally authorized private suits against states to enforce constitutional restrictions imposed by the Reconstruction Amendments, private suits against states litigated in the Supreme Court of the United States after initial prosecution in state court, and suits brought by the United States or

sister states (Chemerinsky 1994, 383-419). While others have shown that these exceptions and waivers cannot easily be explained on historical or functional grounds, dignitary concerns provide a plausible basis for the Court's line drawing. Suits brought against state officials are less of an affront than those brought against the state itself; suits brought by federal or state officials representing a superior or at least coequal sovereign pose less of an affront to states than suits by private persons; suits brought to enforce constitutional rather than statutory rights at least render states subject to the commands of the Constitution rather than to Congress; and the waiver for suits appealed to the Supreme Court at least limits states' involuntary exposure to the highest court in the land.

In the end, it is difficult to know for sure whether the Court's professed concern about congressional denigration of state dignity is justificatory or rhetorical. For purposes of this exploratory essay, I want to take this concern at face value, as at least a partial justification for the doctrine of state sovereign immunity.

STATE DIGNITY AS AN
INTRINSIC EXPRESSIVE NORM

Both a statute and a judicial decision can have expressive significance by articulating and reinforcing norms that are constitutive of a society's very identity and self-understanding. The Court's state sovereign immunity jurisprudence thus might be viewed as framing and enunciating the "political identity" of this nation, to wit: ours is a federalist system in which states enjoy the status of dual sovereigns, exercise significant governing authority as such, and deserve recognition and treatment befitting entities with this status and role. Understood this way, the Court's jurisprudence is nonconsequentialist: it protects the dignity of states because this affirmance of the fundamental structural commitments embedded in our constitutional system of governance matters for its own sake, not as a means to achieving some other end.

Taken at face value, the Court's discussions of state dignity suggest that the states themselves suffer a cognizable expressive harm when their rightful dignitary status is impugned by private suits. This view seems to mirror the Court's apparent recognition of disrespect as a cognizable expressive harm in various individual rights contexts. The Court's equal protection and establishment clause jurisprudence suggests a sensitivity to the ways in which laws can send a message of exclusion and denigration—laws that segregate people along racial lines or distinctly burden racial minorities send a message that minorities are unworthy of equal concern and respect; laws that endorse particular religious viewpoints similarly send a message that adherents to other religions or nonreligion are outsiders. In the sovereign immunity cases, the Court similarly talks as though it views the prospect of private suit as subjecting states to an analogous psychic injury by violating their own sense of dignity and self-esteem.

But this characterization of the Court's concern is surely silly. Unlike persons, states have no feelings of dignity to be protected; the Court's apparent anthropomorphization of states simply reflects a category mistake. Perhaps there are reasons to preserve the dignity of state governments, but they cannot be to make the states themselves "feel" included and valued within the national polity.

A far more plausible characterization of the Court's language does not similarly depend on pretending that states have human qualities; rather, it holds that disrespectful treatment of states should not be tolerated because it contravenes the proper understanding of our governmental regime. The claim here is that constitutional rules governing issues of federalism should conform with and reflect the nation's political identity.[17] Such an expressivist approach might well have informed recent decisions invalidating particular exercises of *state* power. In *Saenz v. Roe*,[18] for example, the Court held that state welfare laws limiting new state immigrants' benefits to the level they would have enjoyed in their prior home state violated the Fourteenth Amendment's citizenship and privileges or immunities clauses. One might view this decision as driven, at least in part, by the recognition that state creation of "degrees of citizenship" for the purpose of distributing state benefits contravenes our political identity by denying the constitutional mandate that U.S. citizens are also full citizens of their chosen state of domicile.[19] The Court's language in *Alden* and other decisions similarly suggests a concern for the expressive significance of governmental action with respect to federalism themes, but here the focus is on the proper role of the states. Arguably, as dissenting then-Justice Rehnquist once complained, a state is not "just another individual or business enterprise,"[20] and when Congress treats the state as such rather than as a constitutive sovereign, this disrespectful treatment intrinsically undermines our sense of political identity by devaluing half of our dual-sovereign heritage.

On reflection, however, this application of intrinsic expressivist reasoning is unpersuasive. It fails to take account of *countervailing* expressive norms that the protection of state sovereign immunity itself violates, and it reflects an anachronistic view of states' role in our federalist system.

To begin with, this intrinsic expressivist claim reflects an impoverished sense of the relationship between state sovereign immunity and our political identity. On its face, the particular language with which the Court proclaims the states' entitlement to dignified treatment appears to exalt states as having a status superior to individuals. To this extent, the Court's language expresses a view at odds with our foundational notion of popular sovereignty, according to which the instruments of government, both federal and state, were created "of the people, for the people, and by the people." As James Madison proclaimed, "The federal and State Governments are

in fact but different agents and trustees of the people, instituted with different powers, and designated for different purposes. . . . the ultimate authority, wherever the derivative may be found, resides in the people alone" (Cooke 1961, Federalist 46, 315). In this sense, both governments have a "common superior," the people, who can control the governments' efforts to usurp their proper powers (315). In short, states are subservient to the people who created them and continually define their delegated powers. But the Court's language sends a contrary message. The view that states have self-esteem concerns suggests that states, once created, acquire a life and interests independent of those conferred upon them by the people. Put differently, the notion that states are organically bestowed with a dignity incident to all sovereigns rests in tension with the notion that states are mere creatures of and subservient to the truly sovereign people.

Moreover, in the specific context of sovereign immunity, the prioritization of states' dignitary interest over individuals' competing interest in compensation for injuries caused by state wrongdoing arguably expresses a message that individuals are subordinate to states rather than the other way around. I do not mean here to be making the general point that sovereign immunity frustrates the rule of law, another cornerstone of our nation's constitutional identity; while there is surely something to this expressive concern, it goes only so far because the rule of law is arguably satisfied by alternative remedies, such as suits for injunctive relief against state officials. But the specific exclusion of private suits against a state from the panoply of available suits to control state misconduct sends a more narrow, but still salient, disturbing message. The Court's decision to single out private rights of action against states as uniquely demeaning, while simultaneously allowing states to be sued by the United States or sister states, suggests that individuals are at the bottom of the pecking order when it comes to determining the relative status of constituent parts of the American polity. Indeed, according to the Court's phraseology, it is precisely *because* private persons are deemed beneath the states in station that suits by the former constitute an "indignity" to the latter. Dignity assumes hierarchy, and the hierarchical relationship between persons and states embedded within the doctrine of sovereign immunity runs precisely counter to the hierarchy entailed by the distinctively American principle of popular sovereignty.

The Court might respond to this line of expressive argument that its recent sovereign immunity cases focused more on the relationship between the states and Congress rather than between the states and individuals. If the state and federal governments are viewed as coequal sovereigns, then permitting Congress to override the states' erstwhile immunity improperly suggests that Congress is hierarchically superior to the states. Of course, one can persuasively argue that this suggestion is entirely proper, under principles captured in the Constitution's supremacy clause. But in any event, the Court's hypothetical rejoinder misses the mark. The Court is quite willing to allow Congress to govern state behavior and even seek compensation for state misconduct to individuals so long as Congress authorizes recovery through suits by the executive branch; it is only when Congress authorizes the same recovery through suits by private parties that the Court's concern for dignity materializes. One therefore cannot easily confine the sovereign immunity doctrine to making a statement about the proper relationship between Congress and the states; it necessarily makes a statement about the relationship between people and the states as well, and here the expression seems squarely antithetical to that presupposed by popular sovereignty.[21]

I do not mean to suggest that the Supreme Court *intends* in its sovereign immunity jurisprudence to express the view that states' interests are superior to those of the individuals they purportedly serve (nor that by abrogating states' immunity Congress intends to express the contrary view). Nor do I mean peremptorily to dismiss the possibility that one might construct a sophisticated analytical defense of sovereign dignity as an interest bestowed on states by the people and hence more consonant with popular sovereignty. I merely mean that the Court's doctrine and explanatory language can quite plausibly be understood by a reasonable observer as expressing the view that states are organically superior to individuals, whether intended or not—just as governmental actions might be understood by a reasonable observer to "endorse" a religious tenet whether or not the government intended to do so. And this is precisely why expressive interpretive methodologies can be quite messy. Because social meaning does not turn solely or even primarily on the actor's subjective intent, actions often have multiple social meanings, perhaps even operating at different levels of perception. And, as here, some meanings might be disturbing even as others are laudable. This recognition does not argue against the use of expressive reasoning in all contexts, but surely it calls for caution and nuance.

The second fundamental difficulty with intrinsic expressive reasoning in this context is this: to the extent that the Court's sovereign immunity jurisprudence reflects its conviction that treating states disrespectfully contravenes a central tenet of our current political identity, the Court's understanding of that identity is strikingly anachronistic. Perhaps the Framers viewed the states as "first among equals" with respect to the status-related attributes of sovereignty. James Madison posited that

the State Governments will have the advantage of the Federal Government, whether we compare them in respect to the immediate dependence of the one or the other; to the weight of personal influence which each side will possess; to the powers respectively vested in them; to the predilection and probable support of the people; to the disposition and faculty

of resisting and frustrating the measures of each other. (Cooke 1961, Federalist 45, 311)

In the Framers' world, it was "beyond doubt, that the first and foremost natural attachment of the people will be to the governments of their respective States" (Federalist 46, 316). If this were ever to change, mused Madison, if "the people should in future become more partial to the federal than to the State governments, the change can only result, from such manifest and irresistible proofs of a better administration, as will overcome all their antecedent propensities" (Federalist 46, 317).

Madison was right; over the course of two centuries, we have become a unified nation with primarily national rather than state affiliations and loyalties. The prevailing early sentiment that states were better guardians of individual liberty was substantially repudiated in the Civil War era, with the opposite sentiment being reflected in the Reconstruction Amendments' broad grants of congressional power to enforce individual rights against states.[22] The prevailing early sentiment that states were primary and better repositories of the general police power was substantially repudiated in the New Deal era, when Congress acquired concurrent authority to exercise a good deal of the modern police powers. Indeed, the domestic issues most prominently addressed by national politicians today include education, crime, medical care, and welfare—the staples of the states' traditional police powers. Finally, modern developments in transportation and communication technologies have enabled a physical mobility and communicative connectedness that, by and large, lead us to perceive ourselves as national citizens first and state citizens second (if much at all).

While it might well be methodologically appropriate at times for the Supreme Court to articulate constitutional rules that reflect expressive norms constitutive of our political identity, doing so is justifiable only if the Court's perception of prevailing norms is accurate. But to the extent the justices exalting the states' dignitary status as coequal sovereigns purport to be describing and reifying a central aspect of our current national identity, they are sadly behind the times.

STATE DIGNITY AS AN INSTRUMENTAL EXPRESSIVE NORM

The preceding observation may suggest, however, that rather than purporting to reify a core tenet of *current* political identity, the Court is engaged in a *revisionary* project to recapture the Framers' political identity. More specifically, one might view sovereign immunity jurisprudence as employing expressive reasoning instrumentally to inculcate values to induce attitudinal or behavioral change.[23] Might the Court's protection of state dignity be justified as an effort to reinvigorate a long-dormant cultural attitude—affinity and respect for state government—that would promote the structural values of federalism in today's world?

The allocation of significant regulatory authority to the states within a federal system is frequently defended as serving the following structural values: enhancing the responsiveness of government to the specific interests of members of a heterogeneous society, both by decentralizing decision making and by generating competition for a mobile citizenry; enabling states to act as laboratories experimenting with diverse solutions to economic and social problems; and stimulating the development of democratic skills and attitudes by increasing citizen participation in self-governance. Moreover, the mere existence of states as independent institutions serves as a structural check against the risk that Congress will either assert power that does not lawfully belong to it or wield the power it does lawfully enjoy too frequently or indiscriminately. As observed by Alexander Hamilton,

The State legislatures . . . will constantly have their attention awake to the conduct of the national rulers, and will be ready enough if anything improper appears, to sound the alarm to the people, and not only to be the VOICE, but, if necessary, the ARM of their discontent. (Cooke 1961, Federalist 26, 169)

Consider this possible application of instrumental expressivist reasoning. Judicial protection and exaltation of state dignity will encourage people to internalize, as a political norm, the importance of having strong and vibrant states exercising significant governmental authority. This norm-internalization will help lead to an actual revival of such state power, thus securing the above-mentioned advantages of decentralization within the federal structure. One could ask whether this causal chain might work through influencing the attitude or behavior of governmental officials (Adler and Kreimer 1998, 134-40), but the more interesting question is whether this causal chain might work through influencing the attitude or behavior of the people themselves.

Adam Cox (2000) has sketched an elaborate argument with respect to the Court's recent jurisprudence forbidding Congress from "commandeering" state officials to implement federal policies, one that focuses exclusively on the anti-tyranny value of strong state institutions. Cox argues that commandeering expresses a message that undermines public perceptions of states as autonomous political actors; if internalized, this message will make state citizens less likely to view their state government as capable of credibly representing their interests; and this in turn undermines the capacity of states to act as political counterweights to federal government overreaching. By invalidating congressional commandeering, the Court sends the opposite message that state autonomy matters, which, if internalized, will in fact make state autonomy matter in precisely this desired manner.

In the sovereign immunity context, the argument might be cast in even simpler and broader terms. If people internalize the attitude that states have the dignified status of coequal sovereigns, they might once again come to view themselves meaningfully as state citizens as well as national citizens. This reinvigorated sense of affinity for and affiliation with states would make the people more comfortable leaving regulatory tasks to states rather than Congress, which could cultivate a political mood leading to such a state of affairs, which would secure all of the aforementioned structural values of decentralized governance. Just as the Supreme Court once suggested that the presidency "needs to maintain prestige" in order to preserve the "element of Presidential influence,"[24] so the Court might claim that states similarly need to maintain prestige in order to preserve their influence within the federal regime.

While superficially plausible, this instrumental justification for modern immunity jurisprudence raises a host of empirical questions. Can the Court correctly predict how the people, even assuming they are aware of the issue at all, will perceive and internalize judicial protection of states from private damages claims? Is the Court's message sufficiently clear, given the numerous exceptions to sovereign immunity allowing suits against states in various circumstances? With respect to the states' anti-tyranny function, are strong states still needed to check federal overreaching given the emergence of judicial review that serves this function to an appreciable degree?

Even assuming favorable answers to such empirical questions, the instrumental justification also raises a host of normative concerns. In general, one might worry about the practical—and even expressive!— implications of having courts intentionally engage in social engineering, even engineering designed to influence political rather than personal relations. For those already worried about judicial accountability, one might argue that Court efforts to manipulate public attitudes have the effect, at least theoretically, of enabling it to circumvent the only real check on its power, namely, long-term popular resistance.

Moreover, this instrumental effort to induce attitudinal transformations comes with an immediate and appreciable cost: individuals are denied compensation for injuries caused by state misconduct. By what constitutional rubric does the Court weigh the speculative long-term advantages of an improved federal-state balance of power against both the tangible and expressive costs of denying individuals the most direct remedy for violation of their federal rights? Perhaps in other contexts, no such trade-off is presented. The costs of outlawing segregation to counteract the expressive message of white supremacy and of prohibiting governmental actions that endorse religion, for example, might be viewed as largely illegitimate and hence properly discounted. But here the costs are real, and the trade-off deserves open acknowledgment and frank consideration by the Court. In my judgment, immunity doctrine cannot be persuasively justified on this instrumentalist ground.

CONCLUSION

Legal scholars are just beginning to explore the intriguing possibilities and pitfalls of expressive reasoning in general and its relevance for structural constitutional principles in particular. Both intrinsic and instrumental expressive theories are promising interpretive tools, and each has its proper place. But doctrines designed to forestall expressive harms (whether individual or structural) can themselves have expressive as well as tangible drawbacks. To the extent it is designed to serve expressive purposes, a blanket rule of state sovereign immunity rests on a flimsy foundation.

Notes

1. See *Seminole Tribe of Florida v. Florida*, 517 U.S. 44 (1996); *Alden v. Maine*, 527 U.S. 706 (1999).

2. *Alden v. Maine*, 527 U.S. at 714.

3. Id. at 748, 749, quoting *Puerto Rico Aqueduct and Sewer Auth. v. Metcalf & Eddy, Inc.*, 506 U.S. 139, 146 (1993).

4. Id. at 749, quoting *In re Ayers*, 123 U.S. 443, 505 (1887).

5. Id.

6. Adam Cox (2000) has recently explored one aspect of an expressivist defense of the Court's anti-commandeering decisions. For brief treatments of expressivism and federalism doctrine, see Anderson and Pildes 2000, 1551-64 (dormant commerce clause and anti-commandeering doctrine); Adler and Kreimer 1998, 140-42 (anti-commandeering doctrine).

7. *In re Ayers*, 123 U.S. 443, 505.

8. *Puerto Rico Aqueduct and Sewer Auth. v. Metcalf & Eddy, Inc.*, 506 U.S. 139, 146 (1993).

9. *Idaho v. Couer d'Alene Tribe of Idaho*, 521 U.S. 261, 268 (1997).

10. *Hess v. Port Authority Trans-Hudson Corp.*, 513 U.S. 30, 52 (1994).

11. *Alden v. Maine*, 527 U.S. at 715.

12. Id. at 759.

13. Id.

14. Id. at 749.

15. *Printz v. United States*, 521 U.S. 898, 918 (1997).

16. Id. at 928.

17. See Hampton 1998, 23 ("the expressive nature of certain laws can be essential in the creation, maintenance or revision of a unifying identity for that society"); Adler and Kreimer 1998, 140-41 (laws' social meaning can play the "intrinsic role of constituting 'the political identity of a state' ").

18. 519 U.S. 489 (1999).

19. Id. at 506.

20. *Fry v. United States*, 421 U.S. 542, 557 (1975).

21. By contrast, one might plausibly argue that the Court's anti-commandeering doctrine speaks only to the Congress-state relationship and not the people-state relationship, and thus the conclusion that being made a federal "puppet" constitutes a cognizable affront to state dignity does not express any view at odds with popular sovereignty.

22. This more modern perspective on national protection of liberty against state interference is reflected in *Fitzpatrick v. Bitzer*, 426 U.S. 445 (1976), where the Court held that states waived their erstwhile sovereign immunity from private suits authorized by Congress to police the boundaries of the Fourteenth Amendment.

23. For discussion of the influence of legal norms on social norms and hence behavior, see various articles included in Social Norms 1998.

24. *Nixon v. Fitzgerald*, 457 U.S. 731, 757 (1982).

References

Adler, Matthew D. and Seth F. Kreimer. 1998. The New Etiquette of Federalism: New York, Printz, and Yeskey. *Supreme Court Review* 1998:71-143.

Anderson, Elizabeth S. and Richard H. Pildes. 2000. Expressive Theories of Law: A General Restatement. *University of Pennsylvania Law Review* 148:1503-75.

Chemerinsky, Erwin. 1994. *Federal Jurisdiction*. 2d ed. Boston: Little, Brown.

Cooke, Jacob E., ed. 1961. *The Federalist*. Middletown, CT: Wesleyan University Press.

Cox, Adam B. 2000. Expressivism in Federalism: A New Defense of the Anti-Commandeering Rule? *Loyola of Los Angeles Law Review* 33:1309-49.

Hampton, Jean. 1998. Punishment, Feminism, and Political Identity. *Canadian Journal of Law & Jurisprudence* 11:23-45.

Marshall, William P. 1996. We Know It When We See It: The Supreme Court and Establishment. *Southern California Law Review* 59:495-550.

Pildes, Richard H. 1998. Why Rights Are Not Trumps: Social Meanings, Expressive Harms, and Constitutionalism. *Journal of Legal Studies* 27:725-63.

Pildes, Richard H. and Richard G. Niemi. 1993. Expressive Harms, "Bizarre Districts," and Voting Rights: Evaluating Election-District Appearances After Shaw v. Reno. *Michigan Law Review* 92:483-587.

Social Norms, Social Meaning, and the Economic Analysis of Law. 1998. *Journal of Legal Studies* 27:537-823.

ANNALS, *AAPSS*, **574**, March 2001

The Elusive Safeguards
of Federalism

By MARCI A. HAMILTON

ABSTRACT: The Supreme Court has issued a series of opinions that turn on the Constitution's inherent principles of federalism, decisions that have alarmed many a legal scholar. The Court has been attacked for overstepping its bounds and, by some, on the grounds that the federalism-state balance should be maintained through the political process rather than judicial review. This criticism of the judicial enforcement of federalism fails as a matter of constitutional history and on empirical grounds. The Supreme Court in this era deserves praise, not criticism, for its recent federalism jurisprudence.

Marci Hamilton is a visiting professor of law at New York University School of Law and the Thomas H. Lee Chair in Public Law of the Benjamin N. Cardozo School of Law, Yeshiva University. An internationally recognized scholar on constitutional issues who often writes on federalism, Professor Hamilton successfully challenged the Religious Freedom Restoration Act before the U.S. Supreme Court in Boerne v. Flores, 521 U.S. 507 (1997). *She is frequently asked to advise Congress on issues pertaining to federalism and the First Amendment.*

WITH his opinion for the Court in *Garcia v. San Antonio Metropolitan Transit Authority, Inc.*[1] reversing *National League of Cities v. Usery*,[2] Justice Harry Blackmun's rejection of a judicial role in policing the boundaries of federalism set the stage for the Supreme Court's current federalism jurisprudence. *Garcia* is the strongest statement to date of the theory that judicial review over federalism is contrary to the constitutional design. The opinion charged that the Court's federalism doctrine was "unworkable," "inconsistent," and, most important for purposes of this article, unnecessary. Justice Blackmun declared that the structure of the Constitution was sufficient to prevent the federal government from impinging on the states, reasoning that the

composition of the Federal Government was designed in large part to protect the States from overreaching by Congress. The Framers thus gave the States a role in the selection both of the Executive and the Legislative Branches of the Federal Government. . . . the Framers chose to rely on a federal system in which special restraints on federal power over the States inhered principally in the workings of the National Government itself, rather than in discrete limitations on the objects of federal authority. State sovereign interests, then, are more properly protected by procedural safeguards inherent in the structure of the federal system than by judicially created limitations on federal power.[3]

Justice Blackmun relied on the work of professors Herbert Wechsler and Jesse Choper to reach his conclusion.[4] Wechsler (1954) articulated

this theory of the "political safeguards of federalism" with a brief essay in 1954, Choper (1980) further explained it, and in a recent article, Professor Larry Kramer (2000) has supported Wechsler's conclusion, even if he takes issue with some of Wechsler's theses. They argue that the courts should not police the boundary between the federal and state governments because politics are adequate to protect state interests (Wechsler 1954, 558; Choper 1980, 175-84; Kramer 2000, 215, 219). Their trust in the invisible hand of politics is misplaced.

Two errors sit at the base of the procedural safeguards thesis. First, it is wrong as a matter of constitutional history. Second, it is untrue as an empirical matter.

THE CASE FOR JUDICIAL REVIEW OF FEDERALISM IN THE HISTORY OF THE CONSTITUTION

The political safeguards theorists would deprive the judiciary of its only means—judicial review—of checking congressional self-aggrandizement vis-à-vis the states. The burden of persuasion rests on the procedural theorists to show that judicial review, while appropriate in separation of powers and church-state disputes, is inappropriate in the federalism context. While there is no debate that the courts appropriately draw the boundary lines of power between the federal branches and between church and state, professors Wechsler, Choper, and now Kramer argue that the federal-state balance should be nonjusticiable. Yet the federal-state balance is as crucial to liberty as the other two means of separating power. In Justice Kennedy's words, "It was the insight of the Framers that freedom was enhanced by the creation of two governments, not one."[5]

The Framers treated power as a single, dangerous phenomenon, and their task as the division, dispersion, and assignment of power to various entities. From the Framers' perspective, the nature of the constitutional division of power between the federal government and the states is not different from the divisions between the federal branches or between church and state. All three arenas include players that will be tempted to exercise power for self-aggrandizement in unanticipated ways and, therefore, demand a neutral body, shielded from political influence, to read the Constitution and to impose its divisions on such entities.[6] If there is a cardinal failure among the procedural safeguards theorists, it is this failure to explain the difference in the division of power between the federal and state governments and that between the federal branches and between church and state—a difference the Framers did not identify or embrace.

By the time the Philadelphia Convention was called, the colonies and then the states had witnessed abuses of power by the King, by the Parliament, by the state legislatures, and by the people. They placed no great faith in any entity, including the people (Hamilton 1997). This sentiment of distrust that suffused the society also permeated the Convention, where Madison succinctly remarked that "the truth was that all men having power ought to be distrusted to a certain degree" (Farrand 1911, 1:584, 1:421, 1:578, 2:3, 2:32; Hamilton 2000). In particular, centralized power, including congressional power, should be distrusted, because, in Justice Harlan's words, our ancestors "were suspicious of every form of all-powerful central authority" (Harlan 1963, 944).

The crux of the procedural safeguards theory—that the framing generation did not "fear that the Congress might pose a serious threat"—is simply wrong (Kramer 2000, 246). The Philadelphia delegates, and both sides in the ratification debates, deeply feared the abuses of power that would flow from a federal legislature. The Framers believed that Congress would be the most dangerous branch and consciously crafted Congress against the backdrop of the degradation of state legislatures under the Articles of Confederation, analyzing governmental structures qua structures and seeing in the federal legislature the potential for cabal, corruption, and intrigue exhibited by the state legislatures (Farrand 1911, 2:35). In Madison's words,

Experience has provided a tendency in our governments to throw all power into the legislative vortex. The Executives of the States are in general little more than Cyphers; the legislatures are omnipotent. If no effectual check be devised for restraining the instability & encroachments of the latter, a revolution of some kind or other will be inevitable. (Farrand 1911, 2:35)

And in Morris's words, "The legislature will continually seek to aggrandize & perpetuate themselves; and will seize those critical moments produced by war, invasion or convulsion for that purpose" (Farrand 1911, 2:52).

Although Federalist leaders like Alexander Hamilton, James Madison, and James Wilson argued, both at the Convention and in the ratification debates, that a bill of rights was unnecessary in that only limited and enumerated powers were delegated to Congress, this judgment did not reflect a confidence in the self-restraint of Congress but a belief that the structure they had crafted—a structure that included judicial review—would hold Congress in check. Hamilton, who famously maintained that a bill of rights was not needed (Rossiter 1961, Federalist 84, 510-15), likewise famously emphasized the importance of judicial review (Federalist 78, 466). Similarly, Wilson ([1787] 1986) explained during the Pennsylvania ratification convention:

The legislature may be restrained, and kept within its prescribed bounds, by the interposition of the judicial department. . . . I had occasion, on a former day, to state that the power of the Constitution was paramount to the power of the legislature, acting under that Constitution. For it is possible that the legislature, when acting in that capacity, may transgress the bounds assigned to it, and an act may pass, in the usual mode, notwithstanding that transgression; but when it comes to be discussed before the judges—when they consider its principles and find it to be incompatible with the superior power of the Constitution, it is their duty to pronounce it void. (550-51)

The opponents of the Constitution were, of course, even more distrustful of the proposed national government than its supporters were. They, too (or at least some of them), recognized that the Supreme Court would review the constitutionality of congressional enactments, but they feared that this power would be used to legitimate rather than prevent encroachments. Thus the pseudonymous Brutus ([1788] 1986), perhaps the most influential of the Anti-Federal publicists, wrote that Congress "might pass one law after another, extending the general and abridging the state jurisdictions, and to sanction their proceedings would have a course of decisions of the judicial to whom the constitution has committed the power of explaining the constitution" (434-35).

The rationale for judicial review was classically stated by Chief Justice Marshall in *Marbury v. Madison*:

The powers of the legislature are defined and limited; and that those limits may not be mistaken, or forgotten, the constitution is written. To what purpose are powers limited, and to what purpose is that limitation committed to writing, if these limits may, at any time, be passed by those intended to be restrained? . . .

It is emphatically the province and duty of the judicial department to say what the law is. Those who apply the rule to particular cases, must of necessity expound and interpret the rule. If two laws conflict with each other, the courts must decide the operation of each. . . . [The Constitution] is superior to any ordinary act of the legislature.[7]

In his other great foundational decision, *McCulloch v. Maryland*, Marshall made it clear that this rationale applies to issues of federalism no less than issues of individual rights. Under the procedural safeguards thesis, the Court would not have addressed the question presented in *McCulloch*, namely, whether federal bank legislation chartering the Second Bank of the United States displaced Maryland's legislation taxing the branches within its boundaries. The opinion extensively discusses the relevant sovereignty of the state and federal governments, saying "that the powers of the [federal] government are limited, and that its limits are not to be transcended," while the "sovereignty of a State extends to everything which exists by its own authority, or is introduced by its permission."[8] To determine whether Congress has exceeded its power, the *McCulloch* Court established the test that continues to be operative in today's federalism decisions:[9] "Let the end be legitimate, *let it be within the scope of the constitution*, and all means which are appropriate, which are plainly adapted to that end, which are not prohibited, but consist with the letter and spirit of the constitution, are constitutional."[10]

Neither of these early landmark cases contains any indication that the division of power between state and federal government was or was intended to be a question beyond the courts' purview. Quite the contrary (Rakove 1997). Rather, they anticipate Justice Kennedy's concurrence in *Lopez*: "The federal balance is too essential a part of our constitutional structure and plays too vital a role in securing freedom for us to admit inability to intervene when one or the other level of Government has tipped the scales too far."[11]

THE FAILURE OF
POLITICAL SAFEGUARDS
AS AN EMPIRICAL MATTER

The political safeguards theory rests on a faulty empirical base. Kramer rests his defense of the theory on the broad factual assertion that states continue to make a great deal of law and therefore must be winning the war against federal takeover; hence the constitutional balance has been maintained (Kramer 2000, 220, 227).

Yet the fact that the states make law, even a great deal of law, misses the point. There is no question that Congress frequently legislates, despite or in willful ignorance of state interests. It is incontrovertible that Congress has never been more activist than in recent decades, spinning out laws that touch on every conceivable topic including school safety,[12] violence against women,[13] gun registration,[14] and even local land use by churches (U.S. House 2000b; U.S. Senate 2000). In addition, it has vehemently criticized the Supreme Court when the Court has held that Congress does have limits (U.S. House 1997, 1998, 2000a; U.S. Senate 1995a, 1995b).

With each federal law, Congress holds the trump card of preemption (U.S. Constitution, Art. VI, Cl. 2), a larger purse (20 times larger than the largest state budget), and ready access to the national media. These tools have been exploited by Congress to the detriment of state autonomy.

Kramer argues that America's decentralized political party system ensures respect for state sovereignty by linking "the fortunes of federal officeholders to state politicians and parties and in this way assure[s] respect for state sovereignty" (Kramer 2000, 276). This contention, however, mistakenly conflates the interests of state politicians with the interests of the states. While one man may be a politician and a representative, each role places distinct (and often conflicting) demands on him. The political parties may serve the ambitions of the politicians, but not necessarily the interests of their constituents.

The argument that states' rights are protected through the political party structure reduces the role of the representative to the day of election, erroneously treating legislators as ciphers for those they represent. This is an oversimplified understanding of the actual part that the representative plays in the constitutional scheme. The Constitution extends the representative's role well beyond election day, into those days between elections when he is delegated authority to exercise independent judgment as a trustee on behalf of his constituents (Hamilton 1994). The Constitution institutes a republican form of government to direct representatives' views away from mere preference aggregation, away

from the raw will of the people, and toward the common good (Hamilton forthcoming).

Justice Breyer has defended the procedural safeguards thesis, declaring that "Congress is institutionally motivated to [defend state interests]. Its members represent state and local district interests. They consider the views of state and local officials when they legislate, and they have even developed formal procedures to ensure that such consideration takes place."[15] In a similar vein, Kramer (2000) argues that national politicians are beholden to state political structures and therefore make laws with the interests of the states in mind. Neither Breyer's nor Kramer's empirical assumptions are borne out by recent legislative practice at the federal level.

While there are undeniable connections between state and federal officials, those connections do not accrue to the benefit of states' rights, for three reasons. First, state politicians kowtow to federal politicians, because they want to be their colleagues. The most powerful political players in the states, the ones who would be most capable of standing up to federal officials—the governors— have become the crop from which the United States harvests likely presidential and senatorial candidates. If a governor aspires to national politics, it is not in his political interest to alienate national politicians or interest groups on behalf of his state, even if there is much at stake for his state. Every time a state politician publicly opposes a federal politician's treasured agenda, he risks being labeled a traitor to the man or the party. A state official is not nearly as invested in making a success of his state institutions, which Madison, in Federalist 51 (Rossiter 1961), thought would motivate him, as he is in currying favor in the national spotlight. State officials in this era may rail against Washington or national politicians, but that railing is calculated to appeal to a broad (translate "national") audience, not to further state interest. As the following examples show, state officials in this era have sacrificed state interest for personal political gain.

Second, the same lobbies that hound the federal government hound the states. State legislators and officials are as fearful of offending national lobbies as are federal legislators and officials. There has been a virtual avalanche of feel-good, look-good legislation that is irrational for the states to support but that has been politically impossible for state politicians to criticize. State attorneys general and governors have disappointed the aspirations of the Constitution in this era by letting their political ambitions take precedence over their representative roles.

Third, political parties are national organizations that demand allegiance to their national agenda's stars. Local politicians receive nationally raised money and the support of national politicians who come to their districts to campaign for them. With the current cost of campaigning, they are driven to subservience to the national party.

For example, the Religious Freedom Restoration Act of 1993 (RFRA) required strict scrutiny of *every* generally applicable state law that substantially burdens any religious entity or individual, an obvious and expensive imposition. If Kramer's theory were correct, the federal politicians dependent on the state politicians would not have enacted RFRA. Congress, however, not only failed to defer to state interests; it did not even give them an airing. Despite the fact that RFRA made it harder to enforce every state law, no state, official, or organization was asked to testify about its many burdens. Nor were states or state organizations brought into the drafting process. In the end, the interests of politicians in looking strong and positive on religion prevailed over the fiscal and autonomy interests of their states. After it was enacted, many jurisdictions forbade their lawyers to challenge RFRA's constitutionality because it would look politically unattractive to be attacking a benefit for religion; others, like California, challenged RFRA but then toned down their criticisms in the face of questions concerning their devotion to religion and ultimately failed to take a position when the issue reached a national forum, the Supreme Court.

When RFRA arrived at the Supreme Court, the states should have been the most likely amici in support of the petitioners, the City of Boerne, Texas (which I represented). While some states did support the petitioners and argued against RFRA,[16] a number of others filed briefs praising RFRA and arguing irrationally that its provisions should be applied to every state law.[17] The Supreme Court's decision invalidating RFRA[18] owed little to the inputs of the states.

When Congress moved to enact the Religious Liberty Protection Act (RLPA) to replace RFRA after its invalidation, members of Congress were loath to appear against it, even if they thought it foolhardy. Indeed, the common wisdom was that most members of Congress were praying that RLPA would just fade away.

RLPA did not simply fade away; instead, it was sliced. A portion of it—applying strict scrutiny to local land use laws and to state and local institutions, like prisons—recently became law (Religious Land Use and Institutionalized Persons Act [RLUIPA]). Kramer's thesis that federal politicians are so reliant on the states that they defer to their requests or needs was disproved in this instance. Ten years after RFRA was first introduced, the National League of Cities, the National Conference of State Legislators, and the National Association of Mayors (and especially Mayor Rudolph Giuliani of New York City) publicly opposed RLUIPA, or parts of it, in strong terms (Otero 2000; Dunlap 2000; Religion 2000). Entities with strong ties to local government and politicians, especially the landmark and historical preservation organizations, also heavily criticized the bill to every member of Congress who would listen. It made no difference. Nor did the Unfunded Mandates Reform Act, on which Justice Breyer relied in his *Morrison* dissent to defend the procedural safeguards hypothesis, because it does not place any meaningful limitations on congressional action but, rather, only on

executive action. When members were told that RLUIPA would, for the first time, bring local land use disputes into the federal courts, a federalism problem if there ever was one, their response was that they simply could not vote against the bill, regardless of the states' needs or interests. The bill was passed by unanimous consent in the Senate and by voice vote in the House within half an hour of each other (U.S. House 2000b; U.S. Senate 2000), to the shock of municipalities, cities, and states coast to coast. It took the Supreme Court to invalidate RFRA on federalism grounds, and it will take the Court to strike RLUIPA's usurpation of state and local power as well.

The same story can be told about the Americans with Disabilities Act of 1990 (ADA). At least as interpreted by the Department of Justice, the ADA is an unreasonable mandatory accommodation statute that places extreme burdens on state and local government. The states, especially their departments of corrections, have borne its expensive and intrusive burdens with a great deal of unhappiness. Yet they have had great difficulty finding means of removing its yoke, because of the political ambitions of state officials. In the course of recent constitutional challenges to the ADA before the Supreme Court, 22 states originally agreed to sign an amicus brief in opposition to the ADA. Once the disabilities lobby was through, that number was down to 7.[19] The first two cases the Court took to address the ADA's constitutionality following the Court's recent spate of federalism decisions worried the American Civil Liberties Union so much that it settled them, and the states' amicus brief became irrelevant. The Court then took another ADA challenge, *University of Alabama at Birmingham Board of Trustees v. Garrett.*[20] By the time the briefs were filed in *Garrett*, 7 states still opposed the law on federalism grounds, but 14 now sang its praises (O'Connor 2000). The threat of making the politicians in those states appear as though they were opposed to the disabled was sufficient to move those politicians from a position of principle on behalf of their states to a moment of silence.

These examples are typical. Environmental laws regularly follow the same pattern (Sandler and Schoenbrod forthcoming). It is common knowledge on Capitol Hill that federalism or states' rights are nonstarters as objections to legislation. Members spout federalism rhetoric to block legislation they oppose for other reasons, but it is never a dispositive consideration.

As a matter of politics, these stories make perfect sense. But they also prove that political parties and structure have not held the line on federal overreaching into the states' business. No less than the politicians they foster, the political parties are captives of powerful national interests. Their attention is trained on reelection, polls, money, and, as the Framers would have expected, increasing their power. That is not necessarily a criticism of them as politicians, but it should make clear that they are not operating as the Constitution intended the people's representatives to operate, and that is with the common good as the highest priority.

CONCLUSION

Congress has taken a mile from the inch they seized during the New Deal, and it needs to be brought back to constitutional proportion. The Court, seeing a congressional aggrandizement of power that is fundamentally at odds with the constitutional design, has employed its only tool to check Congress—judicial review—and set the balance right by instituting effective mechanisms of limitation at a time when other safeguards for federalism are elusive. It is the hero, not the cabal, of this era.

Could the Court transform its current federalism jurisprudence into a means of its own self-aggrandizement, as the procedural safeguards theorists fear? The Framers rightly would have assumed as much. When that time comes, it will be time to unearth the means of bringing the Court back into line. For the time being, however, it is the Court that is most true to the Constitution's ambitions.

Notes

1. 469 U.S. 528 (1985).

2. 426 U.S. 833 (1976).

3. *Garcia*, 469 U.S. at 550-52.

4. See *Garcia*, 469 U.S. at 551 n. 11.

5. See *United States v. Lopez*, 514 U.S. 549 (1995) (Kennedy, J., concurring).

6. See *United States v. Morrison*, 120 S. Ct. 1740, 1754 (2000); *Alden v. Maine*, 527 U.S. 706, 714 (1999).

7. 5 U.S. (1 Cranch.) 137, 176-78.

8. *McCulloch v. Maryland*, 17 U.S. (4 Wheat.) 316, 421.

9. See *Boerne v. Flores*, 521 U.S. 507 (1997).

10. See *McCulloch*, 17 U.S. at 421 (emphasis added).

11. *Lopez*, 514 U.S. at 578 (Kennedy, J., concurring).

12. See *United States v. Lopez*, 514 U.S. 549 (1995).

13. See *United States v. Morrison*, 120 S. Ct. 1740 (2000).

14. See *Printz v. United States*, 521 U.S. 898 (1997).

15. See *Morrison*, 120 S. Ct. at 1777 (Breyer, J., dissenting); Unfunded Mandates Reform Act.

16. See *Brief for Amici States of Ohio, Arizona, Colorado, Delaware, Florida, Hawaii, Idaho, Mississippi, Nevada, New Hampshire, North Carolina, Oklahoma, Pennsylvania, and the Territories of American Samoa, Guam, and the Virgin Islands in Support of Petitioners, Boerne v. Flores*, 521 U.S. 507 (1997) (No. 95-2074).

17. See *Brief of the States of Maryland, Connecticut, Massachusetts, and New York as Amici Curiae in Support of Respondent, Boerne v. Flores*, 521 U.S. 507 (1997) (No. 95-2074); *Brief Amici Curiae of Members of the Virginia House of Delegates and the Virginia Senate in Support of Respondents, Boerne v. Flores*, 521 U.S. 507 (1997) (No. 95-2074).

18. See *Boerne v. Flores*, 521 U.S. 507 (1997).

19. See *Brief for Amici States of Hawaii, Arkansas, Idaho, Nebraska, Nevada, Ohio, and Tennessee in Support of Petitioners, Univ. of Alabama Bd. of Trustees v. Garrett*, 120 S. Ct. 1669 (No. 99-1240).

20. 120 S. Ct. 1669 (2000).

References

Americans with Disabilities Act. Pub. L. No. 101-336.

Brutus. [1788] 1986. XV, 20 Mar. In *The Documentary History of the Ratification of the Constitution*. Vol. 16, ed. John P. Kaminski and Gaspare J. Saladino. Madison: State Historical Society of Wisconsin.

Choper, Jesse H. 1980. *Judicial Review and the National Political Process*. Chicago: University of Chicago Press.

Dunlap, David W. 2000. God, Caesar, and Zoning. *New York Times*, 27 Aug.

Farrand, Max, ed. 1911. *The Records of the Federal Convention of 1787*. Vols. 1-3. New Haven, CT: Yale University Press.

Hamilton, Marci A. 1994. Discussions and Decisions: A Proposal to Replace the Myth of Self-Rule with an Attorneyship Model of Representation. *New York University Law Review* 69:477-562.

———. 1997. The People: The Least Accountable Branch. *University of Chicago Law School Roundtable* 4:1-16.

———. 2000. The Calvinist Paradox of Distrust and Hope at the Constitutional Convention. In *Christian Perspectives on Legal Thought*, ed. Michael McConnell, Angela Carmella, and Robert Cochran. New Haven, CT: Yale University Press.

———. Forthcoming. *The Reformed Constitution: Calvinism, Representation, and Congressional Responsibility*.

Harlan, John M. 1963. Thoughts at a Dedication: Keeping the Judicial Function in Balance. *American Bar Association Journal* 49:943-45.

Kramer, Larry D. 2000. Putting the Politics Back into the Political Safeguards of Federalism. *Columbia Law Review* 100:215-93.

O'Connor, Phillip. 2000. People with Disabilities March Here, Target High Court Case in Alabama. *St. Louis Post-Dispatch*, 10 Oct.

Otero, Juan. 2000. Congress Moves to Federalize Local Land Use Control. *Nation's Cities Weekly*, 7 Aug.

Rakove, Jack. 1997. The Origins of Judicial Review: A Plea for New Contexts. *Stanford Law Review* 49:1031-64.

Religion and Its Landmarks. 2000. *New York Times*. 27 July.

Religious Freedom Restoration Act. Pub. L. No. 103-141.

Religious Land Use and Institutionalized Persons Act. Pub. L. No. 106-274.

Religious Liberty Protection Act. 106 H.R. 1691 (passed in House on 15 July 1999).

Rossiter, Clinton, ed. 1961. *The Federalist Papers*. New York: Penguin Books USA.

Sandler, Ross and David Schoenbrod. Forthcoming. *Government by Decree*.

Unfunded Mandates Reform Act. Pub. L. No. 104-4.

U.S. House. 1997. Committee on the Judiciary. *Hearing Regarding Protecting Religious Freedom After Boerne v. Flores*. 105th Cong., 1st sess. 14 July.

——. 1998. Committee on the Judiciary. *Oversight Hearing Regarding the Need for Federal Protection of Religious Freedom After Boerne v. Flores*. 105th Cong., 2d sess. 26 Feb.; 26 Mar.

——. 2000a. Committee on the Judiciary. *State Sovereign Immunity and Protection of Intellectual Property*. 106th Cong., 2d sess. 27 July.

——. 2000b. Religious Land Use and Institutionalized Persons Act. 106th Cong., 2d sess., H.R. 4862.

U.S. Senate. 1995a. Committee on the Judiciary. *Constitution, State Sovereignty, and Role of Federal Government*. 104th Cong., 1st sess. 11 July.

——. 1995b. Committee on the Judiciary. *Regarding S. 890—The Gun-Free School Zones Act of 1995*. 104th Cong., 1st sess. 18 July.

——. 2000. Religious Land Use and Institutionalized Persons Act. 106th Cong., 2d sess., S. 2869.

Wechsler, Herbert. 1954. The Political Safeguards of Federalism: The Role of the States in the Composition and Selection of the National Government. *Columbia Law Review* 54:543-60.

Wilson, James. [1787] 1986. Speech to the Pennsylvania Ratifying Convention (Dec. 1, 1787). In *The Documentary History of the Ratification of the Constitution*, ed. John P. Kaminski and Saladino J. Gaspare. Madison: State Historical Society of Wisconsin.

Conditional Federal Spending and States' Rights

By LYNN A. BAKER

ABSTRACT: With its 1995 decision in *United States v. Lopez*, the Rehnquist Court made clear that the commerce clause does not grant Congress a plenary police power. Prevailing spending clause doctrine, however, permits Congress to use conditional offers of federal funds in order to circumvent seemingly any restrictions the Constitution might be found to impose on its authority to regulate the states directly. This article first explores three normative arguments in favor of the Court's abandoning the existing test, set forth in *South Dakota v. Dole*, in favor of one that would better safeguard state autonomy while simultaneously preserving for Congress a power to spend that is greater than its power directly to regulate the states. It then proposes a new test under which the courts would presume invalid that subset of conditional offers of federal funds to the states that, if accepted, would regulate them in ways that Congress could not directly mandate. The presumption would be rebutted, and the offer of funds permitted, by a determination that the offer of funds constitutes "reimbursement" spending rather than "regulatory" spending.

Lynn Baker is the Thomas Watt Gregory Professor at the University of Texas School of Law.

A MIDST all the attention afforded the Supreme Court's recent federalism decisions, one important fact has gone largely unnoticed: the greatest threat to state autonomy is, and has long been, Congress's spending power. No matter how narrowly the Court might read Congress's powers under the commerce clause and Section 5 of the Fourteenth Amendment, and no matter how absolute a prohibition the Court might impose on Congress's "commandeering" of state and local officials, the states will be at the mercy of Congress so long as Congress is free to make conditional offers of funds to the states that, if accepted, regulate the states in ways that Congress could not directly mandate.[1]

THE CASE LAW

On several occasions beginning in 1923, the Court has explicitly stated that a conditional offer of federal funds to the states is constitutionally unproblematic because it "imposes no obligation but simply extends an option which the State is free to accept or reject."[2] Because a state has "the 'simple expedient' of not yielding to what she urges is federal coercion,"[3] the Court has concluded that "the powers of the State are not invaded"[4] and there is no Tenth Amendment violation.

In its 1987 decision in *South Dakota v. Dole*, the Court made clear that conditional federal spending affords Congress a seemingly easy end run around any restrictions the Constitution might be held to impose on Congress's ability to regulate the states. The *Dole* Court reaffirmed both that "objectives not thought to be within Article I's 'enumerated legislative fields' . . . may nevertheless be attained through the use of the spending power and the conditional grant of federal funds"[5] and that the "Tenth Amendment limitation on congressional regulation of state affairs [does] not concomitantly limit the range of conditions legitimately placed on federal grants."[6] The Court cautioned that "the spending power is of course not unlimited . . . but is instead subject to several general restrictions articulated in our cases."[7] Unfortunately, none of the stated restrictions was portrayed as having much bite.

The most promising constraints on conditional federal spending noted by the *Dole* Court were a "germaneness" requirement and a "coercion" threshold. With regard to "germaneness," the Court observed that "conditions on federal grants *might be* illegitimate if they are unrelated 'to the federal interest in particular national projects or programs,'" but added that this restriction was merely "suggested (without significant elaboration)" by prior cases.[8] With regard to "coercion," the Court opined that "in some circumstances the financial inducement offered by Congress *might be* so coercive as to pass the point at which 'pressure turns into compulsion.'"[9] The Court concluded that a threatened loss to states of 5 percent of their otherwise

obtainable allotment of federal highway funds, for example, did not pass
this critical point, but the Court did
not suggest what percentage of these
(or any other) funds might.[10]

For those who lament the fact that
any constitutional limits on Congress's regulatory powers can apparently be circumvented through combined use of the taxing and spending
powers, *Dole* leaves three important
issues unresolved. First, although
the *Dole* Court suggested that the
spending clause did not authorize
Congress either to coerce the states
unduly[11] or to impose conditions
"unrelated 'to the federal interest in
particular national projects or programs,' "[12] it provided neither a workable definition of these critical "coercion" and "germaneness" standards
nor any actual or hypothetical example of their violation.

Second, the *Dole* Court attempted
no answer to the central normative
question raised by its suggestion that
there *are* limits on Congress's power
to offer the states conditional funds:
why should Congress *not* be able to
attach any conditions it chooses to
the federal funds it offers the states?
As the Court itself has repeatedly
observed, a state is always free to
decline an offer of federal funds that
it finds unattractive.[13] Why, then, is
additional, judicial protection
needed to ensure the states' autonomy? Third, to the extent that *Dole*
would relegate control over conditional federal spending to the federal
political process, one might question
the ability of the states to protect
themselves from Congress within
that process.

TOWARD A NORMATIVE THEORY OF CONDITIONAL FEDERAL SPENDING

There are at least three good reasons for the Court to abandon the
Dole test in favor of one that would
better safeguard state autonomy by,
for example, presuming invalid those
offers of federal funds to the states
that, if accepted, would regulate
them in ways that Congress could not
directly mandate. First, the federal
government has a monopoly power
over the various sources of state revenue, which renders any offer of federal funds to the states presump-
tively coercive. Second, many conditional offers of federal funds will
actually pose a choice only to a small
subset of states, and this minority
cannot effectively protect themselves
against the majority of states
through the political process. Third,
federal regulatory spending is especially likely to reduce aggregate
social welfare by reducing the diversity among the states in the package
of taxes and services, including state
constitutional rights and other laws,
that each offers to its residents and
potential residents.

Sources of state revenue

A conditional offer of federal funds
to the states implicitly divides them
into two groups: (1) states that
already comply, or without financial
inducement would happily comply,
with the funding condition(s) and for
which the offer of federal money
therefore poses no real choice; and (2)
states that find the funding condi-
tion(s) unattractive and therefore

face the choice of forgoing the federal funds in order to avoid complying with the condition(s) or submitting to undesirable federal regulation in order to receive the offered funds.

When the federal government makes a conditional offer of funds, states in the second group are severely constrained in their decision making by the lack of equivalent, alternative sources of revenue. There is no competitor to the federal government to which these states might turn for substitute financial assistance. And, although each state has the power to raise funds by taxing income, purchases, and property within its borders, this power, too, is subject to federal control, albeit indirectly. Since the adoption in 1913 of the Sixteenth Amendment, which granted Congress the power to tax income "from whatever source derived, [and] without apportionment among the several States," the states implicitly have been able to tax only the income and property remaining to their residents and property owners after the federal government has taken its yearly share.

This means, in addition, that when the federal government offers a state money subject to unattractive conditions, it is often offering funds that the state readily could have obtained *without those conditions* through direct taxation—if the federal government did not also have the power to tax income directly. Moreover, should a state decline proffered federal funds because it finds a condition intolerable, it receives no rebate of any tax dollars that its residents have paid into the federal fisc. In these cases, the state (through its residents) contributes a proportional share of federal revenue only to receive less than a proportional share of federal spending. Thus, when the federal government offers the states money, it can be understood simply as offering to return the states' money to them, often with unattractive conditions attached.

Protections of the political process

One might be less concerned about the level of judicial scrutiny accorded conditional offers of federal funds to the states if one were confident that the states could protect themselves through the political process. Professor Herbert Wechsler has observed in this context that the Senate, in which all states are equally represented, "cannot fail to function as the guardian of state interests as such" and that "federalist considerations . . . play an important part even in the selection of the President" (Wechsler 1954, 548, 557). He has therefore concluded that

the Court is on weakest ground when it opposes its interpretation of the Constitution to that of Congress in the interest of the states, whose representatives control the legislative process and, by hypothesis, have broadly acquiesced in sanctioning the challenged Act of Congress. (559)

While the state-based apportionment of representation within the federal government may well ensure that "*state interests as such*" are protected against federal oppression, *federal* oppression is not the problem. The problem, rather, lies in the ability of *some states* to harness the federal lawmaking power to oppress *other states*. Not only can the state-based allocation of congressional representation not protect states against this use of the federal lawmaking power, it facilitates it.

Recall that a conditional offer of federal funds to the states implicitly divides them into two groups. One would therefore expect such conditional funding legislation to be enacted only if a (substantial) majority of states fell within the group of states that already willingly complied with, or favored, the stated condition, and the conditional offer of funds would therefore be no less attractive to them than a similar unconditional offer. Few congressional representatives, after all, should be eager to support legislation that gives the states money only if they comply with a condition that a majority of their own constituents would independently find unattractive.

Congressional representatives from the states that happily will or already do comply with a particular funding condition might prefer a conditional to an unconditional offer of funds for any of several reasons: (1) to "entice" outlier states into amending or adopting some provision(s) of state constitutional or statutory law whose adoption, at least after *New York*[14] and *Lopez*,[15] Congress could not directly mandate; (2) in the hope that some state(s) might decline the offer of federal funds, leaving more money in the federal fisc for other purposes that might (dispropor-

tionately) benefit their own state; or (3) in order to secure majority support for legislation that would be much less politically palatable without the attached conditions (for example, excluding abortions from coverage might facilitate passage of a bill offering states funds for providing certain medical services to their low-income residents).

In summary, the state-based apportionment of representation in Congress facilitates the ability of some states to harness the federal lawmaking power in order to burden other states to their own advantage. Whatever a particular legislator's motivation might be, supporting a conditional grant of federal funds to the states is likely to make her state (and therefore herself) better off, and should only rarely make it (and herself) worse off, if her state already voluntarily complies, or without federal financial inducement would happily comply, with the funding condition. For these states and their congressional representatives, a vote in favor of the conditional grant is nearly always a vote to impose a burden solely on other states. Whether a state that is not already in compliance chooses to decline the offer of federal funds or to acquiesce in the stated condition, those states already in compliance may well improve, and will only rarely worsen, their competitive position relative to that state.

Interstate competition and aggregate social welfare

In the usual course of affairs, each of the 50 states chooses the package of taxes and services, including state constitutional rights and other laws, that it will offer its residents and potential residents. In this way, the states compete both for individual and corporate residents and for their tax dollars (Tiebout 1956). As part of its unique package, a state might choose, for example, to permit same-sex civil unions.[16] In the absence of a federal government, a state that does not permit same-sex civil unions would have only two ways to compete with a state that does. The former state could continue to offer its current package of taxes and services, including a prohibition against same-sex civil unions, and seek to attract (and retain) those individuals and corporations who prefer this package. Alternately, the state could make some adjustment(s) to its package, which may include adopting a statutory or constitutional provision making same-sex civil unions available.

But if Congress is permitted to offer the states federal funds on the condition that the states prohibit same-sex civil unions, notwithstanding the fact that Congress likely could not directly mandate the states to do so,[17] a simple majority of states will be able to harness the federal lawmaking power to restrict the competition for residents and tax dollars that would otherwise exist among them. Thus, whenever a state might choose to permit same-sex civil unions, the majority of states, which prohibit such unions, would have a third, competition-impeding option: their congressional representatives could enact an appropriately conditioned offer of federal funds in order to divest the outlier state of any competitive gains from its action.

By supporting legislation that offers the states federal funds on the condition that they prohibit civil unions for same-sex couples, a coalition of the states opposed to intimate same-sex relationships can put any state that does not share that policy preference to an unattractive choice: either abandon the competitive advantage that its more inclusive availability of civil unions presumably afforded or forgo the offered federal funds and accept an obvious financial disadvantage relative to each state that accepts the federal money. In this way, conditional offers of federal funds necessarily make the states that without financial inducement would not willingly comply with the funding condition relatively worse off than they would have been in the absence of the offer, while making all other states, by implication, relatively better off.

Permitting Congress to offer the states funds conditional on the constitutional rights and other laws that they offer their residents and potential residents enables a simple majority of states to harness the federal lawmaking power to force some states to pay more than others (including themselves) for their preferred package of laws. This is especially problematic when the funding condition seeks to reduce—to the minimum mandated by the U.S. Constitution and federal statutes—the heightened statutory or constitutional protection that a small number of outlier states currently provide certain minorities. In these cases, one might expect the increased cost of the protection, measured in terms of forgone federal funds, to cause an outlier state readily to relinquish it. After all, the greatest and most direct benefits of such heightened protection will typically accrue to a relatively small and powerless segment of the state's voters, while the proffered federal funds may well be of direct benefit to a substantial majority.

To permit Congress to offer the states funds on the condition that they not make civil unions available to same-sex couples, notwithstanding the fact that Congress likely could not directly mandate the states to do so, is to authorize an end run around the federal amendment procedure. It is to provide a simple majority of Congress the option of denying states a power reserved to them under the Tenth Amendment—the power to choose what sorts of intimate relationships a state will recognize under state law—without the burden of securing a federal constitutional amendment to that effect. For outlier states, the disadvantage of this option is clear: they are likely to find it more difficult to garner the simple majority in either chamber necessary to block a congressional enactment than to assemble the coalition of 13 states necessary to block an amendment to the U.S. Constitution.

By providing a competition-impeding alternative to interstate competition, conditional offers of federal funds reduce the diversity among the states in the package of

taxes and services, including state constitutional rights and other laws, that each offers. Thus some individuals and corporations may no longer find any state that provides a package (including the availability of same-sex civil unions) that suits their preferences, while other individuals and corporations may confront a surfeit of states offering a package (including a prohibition against same-sex civil unions) that they find attractive. The net result is likely to be a decrease in aggregate social welfare, since the loss in welfare to proponents of same-sex civil unions is unlikely under these circumstances to yield a comparable gain in welfare for those who oppose their availability.

Of course, increased diversity among the states is not always a good thing. Some states, for example, might have laws expressing a moral preference that a majority of Americans consider unacceptable and that a conditional offer of federal funds might persuade these states to repeal. In addition, some conditional offers of federal funds may increase aggregate welfare by impeding welfare-reducing interstate "races to the bottom" or by reducing the costs that disuniformities may impose on corporations and individuals seeking to act in more than one state. These observations, however, do not lead inexorably to the conclusion that Congress should be permitted to offer the states federal funds subject to any conditions that it chooses.

To begin, conditional offers of federal funds are not needed to rid states of their most pernicious laws:

our federal and state constitutions prohibit their enactment and enforcement. State laws that violate no federal constitutional provision but that nonetheless express a moral preference that some find reprehensible—for example, laws making the death penalty available for first-degree murder convictions, providing free abortions to indigent women, or providing legal recognition to same-sex marriages or domestic partnerships—denote areas of significant moral disagreement within our society. These are precisely the areas in which interstate diversity is most valuable and federal homogenization through conditional federal spending will therefore most greatly reduce aggregate social welfare.

Should our society reach a substantial consensus that interstate diversity in some area is no longer acceptable, we can always amend the Constitution to prohibit the practice(s) agreed to be immoral. History offers many examples of our willingness and ability to amend the Constitution to reflect such shifts in our moral sensibilities.

In the end, it is important to keep in mind that permitting Congress to offer the states federal funds subject to any conditions that it chooses is likely often to yield reductions in aggregate social welfare. Thus any benefits that may result from always affording Congress this *additional* legislative means of preventing interstate races to the bottom, and of reducing the costs that disuniformities impose on multistate actors, must be weighed against those substantial costs.

A SUBSTITUTE FOR THE *DOLE* TEST

We have seen that there are good reasons for the Court to abandon the *Dole* test in favor of one that would better safeguard state autonomy while simultaneously preserving for Congress a power to spend that is greater than its power directly to regulate the states. The substitute I propose is for the courts to presume invalid those offers of federal funds to the states that, if accepted, would regulate the states in ways that Congress could not directly mandate. This presumption would be rebutted upon a determination that the offer of funds constitutes "reimbursement" spending rather than "regulatory" spending. "Reimbursement" spending legislation specifies the *purpose* for which the states are to spend the offered federal funds and simply reimburses the states, in whole or in part, for their expenditures for that purpose. Most "regulatory" spending legislation thus includes a simple spending component that, if enacted in isolation, would be unproblematic under the proposed test.

An earlier part of the present article, on a normative theory of conditional federal spending, discussed the rationale underlying the proposed test's presumption of invalidity for the subset of conditional offers of federal funds that, if accepted, would regulate the states in ways that Congress could not directly mandate. The present part, therefore, will focus on the distinction the proposed test would make between reimbursement and regulatory spending legislation. In order to understand this critical distinction, it may be useful to consider two hypothetical statutes (A and B) offering federal funds; each statute seeks to regulate those states that accept the conditional offer of funds in ways that Congress could not directly mandate.

(A) Any state receiving federal Death Penalty Funds ("Funds") must have the death penalty available for first-degree murder convictions; participating states shall receive Funds in the amount of their demonstrated costs of executing those sentenced to death for first-degree murder.

(B) Any state receiving federal Law Enforcement Funds ("Funds") must use the Funds to provide beat cops who will daily patrol the state's urban neighborhoods on foot, and must demonstrate its depth of commitment to the national fight against crime by having the death penalty available for first-degree murder convictions; participating states shall receive Funds in the amount of $1.00 per resident according to the most recent federal census.

Congress has no power under the Constitution to make the death penalty available for certain violations of *state* law or to mandate that the states themselves do so. Thus both Statute A and Statute B would regulate those states that accept the conditional offer of funds in ways that Congress could not directly mandate. Both statutes would therefore be presumed invalid under the proposed test. In each case, however, this pre-

sumption of invalidity can be rebutted, and the conditional offer of federal funds ultimately sustained, if the statute is determined to be reimbursement spending legislation.

Statute A, in fact, is an example of reimbursement spending legislation. It simply specifies the purpose for which the states are to spend the proffered federal funds (here, executing those sentenced to death for first-degree murder) and, critically, offers states an amount of money no greater than that necessary to reimburse them for their expenditures for the specified purpose. Statute B, in contrast, is regulatory spending legislation and has both reimbursement and regulatory spending components. The reimbursement spending component is the offer of Law Enforcement Funds, whose purpose and authorized use are limited to reimbursing the states for some portion of their (or their localities') cost of employing police to patrol the state's urban neighborhoods daily on foot. The regulatory spending component, which renders the entire statute impermissible under the proposed test, is the statute's *additional* requirement that states receiving these Law Enforcement Funds also have the death penalty available for first-degree murder convictions.

In seeking to distinguish between reimbursement spending and regulatory spending legislation, the proposed test, like the *Dole* test, imposes a type of "germaneness" requirement on conditional offers of federal funds to the states. In contrast to that in *Dole*, however, the germaneness inquiry under the proposed test has two separate parts, and a challenged condition will be found germane and subsequently sustained if it meets the requirements of either part.[18]

The germaneness requirement of the *Dole* test focuses solely on the relationship between the funding condition and "the federal interest in particular national projects or programs" and is met if the condition is not "unrelated" to some "federal interest."[19] As applied by the Court, this requirement entails only the weakest form of "rational basis" scrutiny of the relationship between the condition and the federal interest. Moreover, the Court's notion of a permissible "federal interest" is seemingly boundless, expressly including even those regulatory objectives that Congress cannot achieve directly.[20] Under the first part of the proposed test's germaneness inquiry, in contrast, the notion of a "federal interest" is strictly and unambiguously limited by Congress's Article I regulatory powers other than the spending power, and a funding condition will be found to be germane under this part whenever its regulatory effects are ones that Congress *could* otherwise achieve directly.

The second part of the germaneness inquiry under the proposed test is embodied in the distinction between reimbursement spending and regulatory spending, and it applies only to those conditional offers of federal funds that, if accepted, would regulate the states in ways that Congress could *not* directly mandate. It focuses on the relationship of the funding condition to both the purpose for which the funds are offered and the amount of money at issue. A condition will be found to be germane under this portion of the proposed test's inquiry only (1) if it specifies nothing more than how—that is, the purpose for which—the offered funds are to be spent, *and* (2) if the amount of money offered does not exceed the amount necessary to reimburse the state for its expenditures for the specified purpose. The germaneness requirement set out in *Dole*, in contrast, permits conditions that do much more than specify the purpose for which the states are to spend the offered funds, and it permits seemingly any amount of money to be made contingent on a state's compliance with a given condition.[21]

It is important to keep in mind that a germaneness inquiry is merely the means to some normative end. Let us now therefore examine the normative justification for the second part of the proposed test's germaneness inquiry, which centers on the distinction between reimbursement spending and regulatory spending legislation.

Consider Statutes A and B again. Both statutes provide states an incentive to make the death penalty available for first-degree murder convictions. From the perspective of a state that, prior to these federal enactments, preferred not to have the death penalty, however, Statute A is surely preferable. Under Statute A, the cost to a state of not complying with the condition attached to the offered funds is much lower than it is under Statute B. Although a noncomplying state forgoes federal reimbursement for the costs of executing individuals it convicts of first-degree murder and sentences to death, it incurs no such costs. Thus the major cost of Statute A to such a state is an opportunity cost: a portion of the federal fisc is being used to subsidize a project—executing individuals that *other states* have convicted of first-degree murder and sentenced to death—from which the state will not directly benefit (and by which it will in fact be burdened) instead of a project that the state would prefer. The cost of Statute B to a noncomplying state, in contrast, is (1) the opportunity cost represented by that portion of the federal fisc—including its own contributions—that is being used to provide a benefit solely to other states, *as well as* (2) forgone desired Law Enforcement Funds for which the state would have been eligible had it been willing to waive its Tenth Amendment right not to administer the death penalty.

It is important to recognize that a noncomplying state bears a similar opportunity cost under both statutes. Thus the significant difference, both descriptively and normatively, between Statutes A and B is the additional cost of forgone, desired Law Enforcement Funds that a noncomplying state bears only under Statute B. Regulatory spending legislation such as Statute B is normatively problematic precisely because the additional cost that it threatens to impose on noncomplying states makes this legislation especially likely to induce otherwise reluctant states to comply. After the enactment of Statute B, for example, it is quite possible that each of the 12 states in which the death penalty is not currently available[22] would choose to make it available for first-degree murder convictions rather than forgo the offered funds. This means that some individuals, who would prefer to live in a state in which the death penalty is not available and who, in any case, do not want their federal tax dollars used to subsidize the execution of individuals convicted in other states of first-degree murder, will no longer find any state that offers a package of taxes and services, including state constitutional rights and other laws, that they find attractive. Meanwhile, other individuals may now confront a surfeit of states offering a package of taxes and services—including the availability of the death penalty for first-degree murder convictions—that suits their preferences.

The net result is likely to be a decrease in overall social welfare, since the aggregate loss in welfare to death penalty opponents from the decrease from 12 to zero in the number of non-death penalty states seems likely to be greater than the aggregate gain in welfare to death penalty proponents from the increase from 38 to 50 in the number of death penalty states.

Of course, reimbursement spending legislation such as Statute A will also impose costs on noncomplying states. These opportunity costs, which all conditional offers of federal funds impose, may give states some (likely small) incentive to conform with the conditions imposed by reimbursement spending legislation. But regulatory spending enactments such as Statute B impose costs *in addition to* these opportunity costs and thus typically provide states a greater incentive to conform. This in turn means that regulatory spending legislation is more likely than reimbursement spending legislation to yield interstate homogeneity and a concomitant reduction in aggregate social welfare. In the end, then, the normative distinction to be made between reimbursement and regulatory spending is one of degree rather than of kind.

Thus the problem is to decide where on the continuum of incentives to conform that conditional offers of federal funds always provide the states, mere "encouragement" ends and "coercion" begins. In *Dole*, the Court simply stated that it would draw the line at the point where the "pressure" exerted by the financial inducement "turns into compulsion."[23] The Court did not acknowledge that since all conditional offers of federal funds to the states provide them some incentive to conform, any determination of the point at which "compulsion" begins is inevitably arbitrary or subjective. The *Dole* Court never defined "compulsion" or "pressure," never explained how one should or could consistently distinguish between the two, nor provided any example of an impermissibly "coercive" offer of federal funds to the states.

The "coercion" inquiry of the proposed test, in contrast, is embodied in its distinction between reimbursement and regulatory spending legislation. The proposed test would draw a line between conditional offers of federal funds that impose opportunity costs on noncomplying states (permissible reimbursement spending legislation) and offers that impose both opportunity costs *and*

additional costs on noncomplying states (impermissible regulatory spending legislation).

In some instances, the line that the proposed test would draw between reimbursement and regulatory spending legislation may not comport with our intuitive or subjective notions of when coercion begins: the additional costs that render a statute impermissible regulatory spending legislation may sometimes seem insignificant in amount. Against this disadvantage, however, one must weigh the substantial advantages of having a line that is bright, straight, readily and consistently drawn, and normatively justifiable.

THE FUTURE OF *DOLE*

Is there any chance that the Court might reconsider *Dole*, whether or not it adopts my proposed standard of review? I am cautiously optimistic. Only three members of the *Dole* majority are still sitting—Chief Justice Rehnquist and Justices Stevens and Scalia—and the possibility of change is, therefore, real.[24] Moreover, there is evidence that several of the sitting justices are aware of the problem posed by *Dole*. Justice O'Connor dissented in *Dole*,[25] and Justice Kennedy has remarked publicly that conditional federal spending, rather than the Court's interpretation of the commerce clause, is the major states'-rights issue facing the country today.[26]

In addition, Justice Scalia observed in *Printz* that many federal statutes that "require the participation of state or local officials in implementing federal regulatory schemes" exist as "conditions upon the grant of federal funding [rather] than as mandates to the States."[27] He went on to observe that the *Printz* Court would "not address these or other currently operative enactments that [were] not before [it]," but he added suggestively that there "will be time enough to do so if and when their validity is challenged in a proper case."[28] Assuming Justice Thomas would vote to overturn *Dole*, Chief Justice Rehnquist remains the key to a "states'-rights" majority on this issue; ironically, he authored both the majority opinion in *Lopez* and the majority opinion in *Dole* that threatens to render *Lopez* and the rest of the Court's states'-rights revival moot.[29]

An even more intriguing possibility is suggested by Justice Breyer's 1999 dissent in *College Savings Bank*,[30] joined by Justices Stevens, Souter, and Ginsburg. Justice Breyer contended that certain conditional offers of federal funds to the states might be more "coercive" than a constructive or implied waiver of sovereign immunity attached to certain federally regulated conduct in which a state voluntarily elects to engage:

Given the amount of money at stake [more than $20 billion in 1998], it may be harder, not easier, for a State to refuse highway funds than to refrain from entering the investment services business.... It is more compelling and oppressive for Congress to threaten to withhold from a State funds needed to educate its children than to threaten to subject it to suit when it competes directly with a private investment company.[31]

Writing for the majority in *College Savings Bank*, Justice Scalia agreed that the "intuitive difference" between a "denial of a gift" and a "sanction," which makes a congressional threat to impose the former seemingly less coercive than the latter, might indeed "disappear[] when the gift that is threatened to be withheld is substantial enough."[32] The majority reaffirmed *Dole*'s holding that some conditional offers of federal funds " 'might be so coercive as to pass the point at which "pressure turns into compulsion," ' " en route to its conclusion that "the point of coercion is automatically passed—and the voluntariness of waiver destroyed—when what is attached to the refusal to waive [sovereign immunity] is the exclusion of the State from otherwise lawful activity."[33]

Because the Court in *College Savings Bank* held constructive waivers of sovereign immunity to be inherently coercive, and because both the majority and dissent agreed that certain conditional offers of federal funds to the states are *even more* coercive, all nine justices might now be more inclined not only to invalidate certain conditional offers of federal funds to the states but also to engage in meaningful judicial review of such offers.[34] If so, they may find the standard of judicial review proposed in this article to be a welcome alternative to *Dole*'s vague and historically toothless "coercion" standard.

Notes

1. For a comprehensive examination of this argument, from which this article is substantially derived, see Baker 1995.

2. *Massachusetts v. Mellon*, 262 U.S. 447, 480 (1923).

3. *Oklahoma v. United States Civil Service Commission*, 330 U.S. 127, 143-44 (1947); *Mellon*, 262 U.S. at 482 ("If Congress enacted [the statute] with the ulterior purpose of tempting [the states] to yield, that purpose may be effectively frustrated by the simple expedient of not yielding.").

4. *Mellon*, 262 U.S. at 480.

5. *Dole*, 483 U.S. 203, 207 (1987) (citing *United States v. Butler*, 297 U.S. 1, 65-66 (1936)).

6. *Dole*, 483 U.S. at 210.

7. Id. at 207.

8. Id. (emphasis added).

9. Id. at 211 (emphasis added) (citing *Steward Machine Co. v. Davis*, 301 U.S. 548, 590 (1937)).

10. See id. Two years later, the Ninth Circuit upheld even those provisions of the Federal Highway Act that required 95 percent of federal highway funds to be withheld from states that did not post a 55-mile-per-hour maximum speed limit, and the Supreme Court denied certiorari. See *Nevada v. Skinner*, 884 F.2d 445, 454 (9th Cir. 1989), cert. denied, 493 U.S. 1070 (1990).

11. See *Dole*, 483 U.S. at 211.

12. Id. at 207 (citing *Massachusetts v. United States*, 435 U.S. 444, 461 (1978) (plurality opinion)).

13. See, for example, *Dole*, 483 U.S. at 210; *Oklahoma*, 330 U.S. at 143-44; *Steward Machine*, 301 U.S. at 595; *Mellon*, 262 U.S. at 482.

14. *New York v. United States*, 505 U.S. 144 (1992).

15. *United States v. Lopez*, 514 U.S. 549 (1995); see also *Printz v. United States*, 521 U.S. 898 (1997); *United States v. Morrison*, 120 S. Ct. 1740 (2000).

16. See Around the Nation 2000, which discusses the Vermont governor's signing of legislation "granting gay couples nearly all of the benefits of marriage" and "allow[ing] gay couples to form civil unions beginning July 1[, 2000]."

17. Both the majority and the dissent in *Lopez* specifically identified family law, albeit in dicta, as an area in which states "historically have been sovereign" and which would therefore likely be beyond the scope of Congress's regulatory power. *Lopez*, 514 U.S. at 564; id. at 624 (Breyer, J., dissenting).

18. It should also be noted that the germaneness inquiry under the *Dole* test is but one of four (albeit quite toothless) prongs that must be met if the legislation is to be sustained. The two-part germaneness inquiry under the proposed test, in contrast, is that test's only prong.

19. *South Dakota v. Dole*, 483 U.S. 203, 207 (1987) (quoting *Massachusetts v. United States*, 435 U.S. 444, 461 (1978)).

20. See *Dole*, 483 U.S. at 207 ("[O]bjectives not thought to be within Article I's 'enumerated legislative fields' may nevertheless be attained through the use of the spending power and the conditional grant of federal funds." (citation omitted)).

21. See *Dole*, 483 U.S. at 208-9.

22. See Claiborne and Duggan 2000, observing that death penalty laws are currently "on the books in 38 states."

23. *Dole*, 483 U.S. at 211 (quoting *Steward Machine Co. v. Davis*, 301 U.S. 548, 590 (1937)).

24. Chief Justice Rehnquist and Justice Scalia were in the majority in both *Dole* and *Lopez*; Justice Stevens joined the majority in *Dole* but dissented in *Lopez*. Cf. *Dole*, 483 U.S. 203 (1987), with *Lopez*, 514 U.S. 549 (1995).

25. See 483 U.S. at 212.

26. Justice Kennedy made this comment to the author on 28 Sept. 1995 at a cocktail party in Tucson, AZ, hosted by the University of Arizona College of Law.

27. *Printz*, 521 U.S. at 917-18.

28. Id. at 918.

29. For one possible explanation for the apparent inconsistency in Chief Justice Rehnquist's concern for "states' rights," see Baker 1995, 1915 n. 13.

30. *College Savs. Bank v. Florida Prepaid Postsecondary Educ. Expense Bd.*, 527 U.S. 666, 692 (1999).

31. Id. at 2236.

32. Id. at 2231.

33. Id.

34. My optimism on this score concerning the *College Savings Bank* dissenters is dampened somewhat by their observation that, notwithstanding the Court's decision, "perhaps Congress will be able to achieve the results it seeks (including decentralization) by embodying the necessary state 'waivers' [of sovereign immunity] in federal funding programs—in which case, the Court's [recent Eleventh

Amendment] decisions simply impose upon Congress the burden of rewriting legislation, for no apparent reason." Id. at 2240. One might have expected justices concerned about the coercive effects of conditional federal spending to indicate some reservations about whether such legislation involving waivers of sovereign immunity would or should be sustained.

References

Around the Nation. 2000. *Washington Post*, 27 Apr.

Baker, Lynn A. 1995. Conditional Federal Spending after *Lopez*. *Columbia Law Review* 95:1911-89.

Claiborne, William and Paul Duggan. 2000. Spotlight on Death Penalty; Illinois Ban Ignites a National Debate. *Washington Post*, 18 July.

Tiebout, Charles M. 1956. A Pure Theory of Local Expenditures. *Journal of Political Economy* 64:416-24.

Wechsler, Herbert. 1954. The Political Safeguards of Federalism: The Role of the States in the Composition and Selection of the National Government. *Columbia Law Review* 54:543-60.

ANNALS, *AAPSS*, **574**, March 2001

The Supreme Court's Federalism: Fig Leaf for Conservatives

By HERMAN SCHWARTZ

ABSTRACT: Throughout American history, states' rights have been used as a cover to hide less respectable interests such as race, class, religion, power, and money. Because reforms in racial justice and social equality have come primarily from the federal government as a result of the Civil War and the New Deal, states' rights have usually been used to promote conservative interests. Today's conservative Supreme Court majority, led by Chief Justice William H. Rehnquist, has imposed limitations on federal power to curtail the rights of women, religious groups, the elderly, racial minorities, and other disadvantaged groups. Asserting a wide range of benefits from strong state sovereignty, few of which do in fact exist, the conservatives have shrunk the scope of the commerce clause, developed implied limitations on federal authority, and narrowly construed the Civil War amendments. Yet, despite their federalist rhetoric, the conservative justices have not hesitated to strike down state and local legislation and other action enhancing individual rights—and this notwithstanding their frequent criticism of judicial activism in other areas.

Herman Schwartz is a professor of law at Washington College of Law, American University. He is the author of The Struggle for Constitutional Justice in Post-Communist Europe *(2000);* Packing the Courts: The Conservative Campaign to Rewrite the Constitution *(1988); editor of* The Burger Years *(1987); and author of numerous articles on American and comparative constitutional law.*

T HE great constitutional divide in the American system of government is between the national government and the states, between nationalists and adherents of states' rights. The great social divide, however, is between races and classes, and regardless of the surface content of the federalism debates, it is the race and class interests that determine the outcome of the federal-state power conflict. Today, the Supreme Court's conservative majority, composed entirely of Reagan-Bush appointees, is using allegiance to states' rights as a fig leaf to disguise its efforts to promote the Reagan-Bush campaign to undermine the civil rights revolution and the New Deal.

During the antebellum period, the states were more powerful than the federal government, which the Southern states used to protect slavery and their other sectional interests. The Civil War and the accompanying amendments and legislation produced a social and constitutional revolution. Unfortunately, interest in the plight of the former slaves soon foundered on Northern indifference and Supreme Court sabotage.

In the decades following the Civil War, America's explosive economic growth created not only massive wealth but also great misery, which was exacerbated by the Great Depression. The states could not cope with this, in part because the Supreme Court had disabled them by annulling their power to enact social legislation but primarily because the problems were too overwhelming for any state to handle. To deal with the crisis, Franklin D. Roosevelt's administration engineered the second great transfer of power to the federal government—the New Deal.

The New Deal was intended to do more than bring recovery to the economy and restore the status quo (Kennedy 1999, 249-87). FDR wanted to go further and reform the American economy so as to provide some basic economic security for the average American. This obviously required a bigger government and higher taxes, which dismayed conservatives and produced a deep political cleavage on economic and welfare issues that persists to this day. Furthermore, though the Roosevelt administration did little directly for racial minorities, its effort to create a social safety net for all Americans produced spillover benefits for blacks. Also, one of the first decisions of the reconstituted Supreme Court was *Missouri ex rel. Gaines v. Canada*,[1] the first of the cases leading to *Brown v. Board of Education*.[2] Over the next six decades, the Supreme Court used both the commerce clause and the Fourteenth Amendment to confirm the New Deal's shift of power to the national government in a consistent series of decisions on both the economy and race.

When Ronald Reagan became president in 1981, he promptly set about trying to tilt the balance back toward the wealthier classes and white privilege. Reagan, his chief legal adviser Edwin Meese, and Reagan's successor, George Bush, targeted New Deal and later social programs, as well as the federal laws and court decisions aimed at achieving racial equality. Their targets were specified in a study by a right-wing think tank, the Center for

Judicial Studies: public assistance claimants, Medicare recipients whose funding was terminated without a hearing, people suing under Civil Rights Acts, union members, refugees, American Indians, handicapped children, claimants under the Age Discrimination in Employment Act, victims of Securities Act violations, public housing tenants, antitrust plaintiffs, and county welfare departments, to mention but a few (Stern 1984, 3).

Reagan and Bush also packed the judiciary at all levels, but particularly the courts of appeals and the Supreme Court, with youthful judges committed to cutting back federal authority who would serve for many years to come (Schwartz 1988, 58-74). In 1991, with the 1986 appointment of William H. Rehnquist as chief justice and the arrival of Anthony Kennedy, aged 52, and Clarence Thomas, 44, the conservative justices had a solid 5-4 majority.

The first assault on the New Deal, however, was led by Rehnquist long before Kennedy and Thomas joined the Court. Raised in a Roosevelt-hating family, Rehnquist has been an arch-conservative since boyhood (Lardner and Saperstein 1986). The last major social legislation of the New Deal was the 1938 Fair Labor Standards Act (FLSA), which set minimum wage and maximum hours requirements. In 1974, Congress extended the FLSA to state and local governments. Two years later, in *National League of Cities v. Usery*, Rehnquist cobbled together a 5-4 majority to strike down the 1974 extension for encroaching on the states' "traditional functions," and

"impair[ing] their sovereignty" and their "ability to function effectively."[3] The result, as Justice John Paul Stevens put it, was to recognize a "sovereign state's rights to pay a substandard wage to the janitor at the state capitol."[4]

After nine years, in *Garcia v. San Antonio Metropolitan Transit Authority*,[5] the Court overruled *National League of Cities* as unworkable. The states did not need judges to protect them, decided the Court, because they could take good care of themselves in the political process in Congress. The Court was right. State and local governments reacted swiftly to the decision, and within months, without a single recorded vote, Congress amended the FLSA to reduce their exposure.[6]

The *Garcia* aftermath was not the first time Congress had responded to state political muscle. Anyone who has spent time on Capitol Hill knows the power of state and local interests. In 1984, Congress freed cities and local officials from any liability for antitrust treble damages after the Court had imposed such liability.[7] Nearly a century earlier, when the Supreme Court denied Iowa the right to bar the sale of liquor imported from another state, Congress immediately passed the Wilson Act to nullify the decision.

In his *Garcia* dissent, an angry Justice Rehnquist had warned that the tide would turn again. He was right. In 1991, a 5-4 majority in *Gregory v. Ashcroft*[8] narrowly interpreted a federal law banning age discrimination as not applying to state judges because it did not contain a "plain statement" that the law covered them, a technique the Court has often used to curtail federal authority.[9] In her opinion for the Court, Justice O'Connor set forth the advantages she saw in strong state sovereignty:

This federalist structure of joint sovereigns preserves to the people numerous advantages. It assures a decentralized government that will be more sensitive to the diverse needs of a heterogeneous society; it increases opportunity for citizen involvement in democratic processes; it allows for more innovation and experimentation in government; and it makes government more responsive by putting the States in competition for a mobile citizenry. . . . Perhaps the principal benefit of the federalist system is a check on abuses of government power.[10]

Unfortunately, these "advantages" are frequently unrealized and offset by very real disadvantages. Few citizens pay much attention to state issues, or even to local issues, unless they are directly involved. Media coverage of state activities is spotty at best and often nonexistent. Voter turnout in state and local elections is even worse than in national elections. Indeed, few voters even know the names of their local representatives other than their mayor and know even less about their state representatives. Whatever the opportunities for citizen involvement at the state and local levels, few seem interested in taking advantage of them. Most voters, however, know who their congressional representatives and senators are and what they are doing.

Moreover, state sovereignty is hardly necessary for either citizen involvement or for much of what states do themselves. As Rubin and Feeley (1994) point out, and as examples throughout the world confirm, decentralization without sovereignty offers many opportunities for meaningful local participation and governmental responsiveness. Indeed, we have two ubiquitous examples in this country—city and county government. Yet both are merely creatures of the state without sovereignty or indeed any constitutional status at all.

As for the "principal benefit" of checking "abuses of power," that kind of check has historically come not from the states on the federal government but the reverse, as Madison predicted in Federalist 10; discrimination against blacks, women, and gays and encroachments on free speech are obvious examples. In fact, most of the time, states' rights has been a weapon of reaction (Hyman 1973, 12 n. 18). Moreover, when the national government has suffered from McCarthyism and similar "abuses of government power," the states have not checked the abuses but have exacerbated them.[11]

There is, however, one area where state sovereignty is necessary— social and other experimentation, especially where the federal government seems unable to act on a problem. State and local action on tobacco, gun control, prescription drug pricing, and campaign finance have required state authority that is truly independent, for decentralization alone would probably have subjected these matters to the same forces that have produced the national impasse. But this does not justify the Court's states'-rights decisions, for these have been in cases where the federal government has indeed acted—in some cases, as will be seen, with the states' approval and encouragement.

Nor is experimentation always a good thing. At least some of it has involved a "race to the bottom," not only in corporate affairs as in Delaware but also in wages, safety conditions, discrimination, and other matters.

There is also the matter of efficiency and corruption. Although most state legislators are now full-time, the sessions are still relatively short: the Texas legislature, for example, meets only once every two years for just four months, and much important legislation is rushed through, unread, in the waning minutes of the session. Conflicts of interest are rife: a recent study found that one in five state legislators "help regulate their own business or professional interests, have financial ties to organizations that lobby state governments, and many receive income from agencies they oversee" (State Legislators Mix 2000).

State and local governments are also often hostile to those down on their luck, particularly if the latter are racial minorities. As Sheryll D. Cashin notes, that is one reason the Republican Party's Contract with America pushed so strongly for more state and local control at the expense of the federal government (Cashin 1999, 553 n. 6). For example, New York City conceded in court in 1999 that workers at "job centers," formerly welfare offices, had illegally denied people food stamps and Medicaid or discouraged people from applying for them. Despite a court order, the city was still doing so a year later (Turning 2000). Some states have made it so onerous to apply for food stamps, which the states administer, that many needy people do not even apply (Bernstein 2000).

With the arrival of Justice Thomas, the assault on social legislation and civil rights by curtailing federal power moved into high gear, drawing on constitutional grounds for decisions that could not be overcome by Congress with a mere "plain statement." These include the Tenth Amendment and assumptions about the structure of the Constitution; limits on Section 5 of the Fourteenth Amendment; limits on the commerce clause power; and the Eleventh Amendment. Space limits preclude discussion of the last, on which there is already a voluminous literature.

The opening shot was fired in *New York v. United States*[12] in 1992. At the behest of the National Governors Association (NGA), in 1980 Congress passed the Low-Level Radioactive Waste Act, based on an NGA proposal. At first, New York fully supported the act but after a while became unhappy with it and challenged some of the compulsory provisions as a violation of the Tenth Amendment. Other states, however, intervened to defend the act.

While recognizing that the text of the Tenth Amendment established no specific powers or even guidelines for drawing the federal-state dividing line, Justice O'Connor ruled that the federal government may not compulsorily "commandeer" the states "to enact or administer a federal regulatory program."[13] When Congress compels the states to adopt or administer federal programs, she wrote, the lines of "accountability" are blurred because the community will wrongly blame state officials if they are unhappy with any burdens imposed by the program.[14] Five years later, the five conservatives used the same accountability reasoning to strike down provisions of the Brady Handgun Violence Prevention Act, which required local law enforcement officers to conduct background checks on prospective gun buyers.[15]

The accountability argument is patent nonsense, especially in the contexts of the specific cases. People involved in the low-level radioactive waste industry know who has set which rules, especially where, as in this case, the legislation is the product of years of experience and negotiation. And is there a gun-buying Rip van Winkle anywhere who does not know that it was the federal government that required the background check? If there is, surely a sign in the gun dealer's shop would make that clear. Moreover, if the lines of accountability in the low-level waste context are blurred, that simply reflects reality because the act was a joint product of the federal and state governments.

Indeed, the *New York* decision does not really promote accountability, for it ignores the consent to this plan of the citizens' duly elected representatives on both the federal and the state levels. This gave Justice O'Connor some pause, but not for long: state sovereignty was not for the benefit of the states or the state officials, she declared, but to pre-

serve the liberties of the citizens of those states. The logic of this is baffling. Political liberty is the freedom to participate in the community's political life and thereby influence public policy. Public officials must therefore be accountable to the voters (Kaden 1979). This accountability, however, is undermined even more when the decision of the duly elected representatives at the state and federal levels is overridden by the federal judiciary than when it is overridden by Congress, since Congress represents the citizenry and is politically accountable to them, whereas the federal courts are not. If there is a danger that New York voters will wrongly blame their local representatives for onerous burdens imposed by Congress, why will the voters of the consenting states not wrongly blame their local representatives for failing to deal with the dangers of radioactive waste when the protections of the act were struck down by the federal court?

The decision also reflects a formalistic approach that has little to do with reality. The lines between federal and state authority are continually blurred, especially since so many federal programs that are indisputably constitutional under, for example, the spending clause, involve a mixture of state discretionary rules and federal requirements.

This disdain for state interests and views on the part of states'-rights supporters on the Court is not unusual. It appeared last year when the five conservatives struck down the Violence Against Women Act (VAWA) despite the support shown for the act by 38 states when it was under consideration in Congress and in an amicus brief by 36 states when the case was heard by the Supreme Court.[16] And it is shown also in civil rights cases where the Court's conservatives have frequently struck down state and local actions that conflicted with their conservative agenda.

The Rehnquist Court's record on civil rights for racial minorities, apart from federalism issues, is a dismal one. Since April 1988, when Justice Anthony Kennedy joined the Court, it has decided some 40 race-related cases, of which 15 have been close—6-3 or 5-4; the others have been fairly clear-cut one way or the other. Of the 15, one 5-4 liberal victory was overturned. Of the remaining 14, the racial minority litigants lost all but 3. Since President George Bush appointed Clarence Thomas to succeed Thurgood Marshall in 1991, racial minorities have fared even worse. Of the 12 6-3 or 5-4 cases from 1992 through January 2000, the conservative bloc held together in all but one case (Schwartz 2000).

Although these decisions have covered school desegregation, employment discrimination, and affirmative action, to mention but a few areas, the voting rights decisions are particularly glaring examples of the conservatives' willingness to override state enactments. Improvement for people of color in this country has come only from their enhanced electoral power. But it is precisely in this area, and especially in the South, where blacks still suffer from voter discrimination, that the Court has been most actively hostile.

Led by Justice O'Connor's decision in *Shaw v. Reno*,[17] the Court has consistently struck down the creation of electoral districts by state legislatures in which minority voters would be a majority and might thereby gain representation approximating their share of the state population. Her opinion piously relied on an ideal of "colorblindness" in a society that is anything but colorblind when it comes to discrimination *against* racial minorities. Also, although ethnically oriented districting has long been a part of American politics, and politically oriented gerrymandering is a permanent and virtually unquestioned fixture of American life, racially oriented districting is, to the conservative majority, very different and so heinous as to be subject to the strictest scrutiny.

The Court has also made it far more difficult for racial and ethnic minorities to improve their economic situation. In 1989, in *Richmond v. J. A. Croson Company*, the Court decided that all state and local affirmative action programs *favoring* racial minorities were to be subjected to the same heavy burden of justification as state action deliberately aimed *against* these minorities.[18] The *Croson* decision doomed some 199 local and 36 state affirmative action plans in the government contract business.[19] Surprisingly enough, Justice O'Connor and Chief Justice Rehnquist interpreted Section 5 of the Fourteenth Amendment as giving the federal government great power to enforce the amendment while disabling the states, an anomalous position for such staunch states' rights advocates. Six years later, however, after Clarence Thomas joined the Court, they abandoned their sudden nationalism and, revealing their real agenda, imposed the same onerous requirements on federal affirmative action programs that they had imposed on the state and local governments.[20] The result was to close off most of the opportunities for blacks and Hispanics to start businesses, to become lawyers, doctors, scientists, or software designers, or just to get a good education.

The Court is not alone in its infidelity toward states' rights when the latter interfere with less respectable but more important interests like race, class, political power, or religion. All branches of government at both the federal and the state levels, and some of our greatest historical figures, have been guilty of the same fickleness. James Madison started out as a fervent supporter of strong central government. To a lesser extent, so did Madison's great collaborator, Thomas Jefferson (Smith 1995, 512-13). But when the Federalist Congress passed the Alien and Sedition Act to punish criticism of the Federalist administration—the target obviously being the rival Republican Party led by Jefferson and Madison—the two became strong opponents of national power and wrote the Kentucky and Virginia Resolutions of 1798 and 1799, in the first of which Jefferson declared that a state could nullify federal laws that it considered unconstitutional, a position later taken up by John C. Calhoun (also an erstwhile nationalist) and the South in defense of slavery and Southern agriculture (Wills 1999, 140-52). Once in office,

however, Jefferson and Madison exercised so much national power that, as Henry Adams put it, they "out federalized the Federalists."

Jefferson and Madison were not the only politicians to switch sides when it suited their political or economic interests. Indeed, their own political rivals, strongly nationalistic Federalists like Timothy Pickering, became ardent states'-righters when their businesses were hurt by Jefferson's embargo and, at the Hartford Convention of 1814, adopted Jefferson's nullification theory (Wills 1999, 153-62).

Defending white privilege is one area where states' rights have always been invoked. From the first year of the first Congress, the South tried to prevent any congressional treatment or even discussion of slavery at the national level, arguing that it was solely a state matter. But that argument was quickly abandoned when it cut against the slave interest. During the antebellum period, the South urged enactment and vigorous enforcement of the federal Fugitive Slave Laws of 1793 and 1850, preemption of state antislavery laws, Post Office interdiction of abolitionist mail banned in the South, and other measures expanding federal power at the expense of the states (Hyman 1973, 13-15).

Today, the Republican Party steadily proclaims the virtues of states' rights. That has not, however, deterred Republicans from promoting bills to cut back tort litigation in product liability cases on behalf of their business supporters and to annul Oregon's legislation allowing assisted suicide, both matters that are inherently local. Perhaps the most prominent recent example of Republican fickleness on this issue was in last year's presidential election when the Republican Party went to the federal court to overturn a Florida state court's ruling; elsewhere in this issue, Rubin provides more examples of Republican deviation from the true faith.

Two years after *New York v. United States*, the Court issued an even more startling decision. For the first time since the later 1930s, a Court majority struck down a federal statute passed under the authority of the commerce clause. In *Lopez v. United States*,[21] the usual 5-4 majority nullified a federal law criminalizing the possession of guns in a school zone because no economic transaction was involved and there was no congressional finding of an effect on interstate commerce. The obvious impact of school violence on the national economy was dismissed, and the fact that most guns move in interstate commerce was ignored. Four years later, the conservative majority used the same argument to strike down the VAWA, denying that it was an "economic" matter even though there was "a mountain of data" that violence against women costs the economy billions each year.[22]

The Constitution does presuppose a line between interstate and local commerce, but in today's world the line is impossible to draw with any precision. Any large-scale phenomenon will have economic effects except in easy cases, and no manageable judicial standards exist for distinguishing interstate from intrastate commerce. Whenever the Court has tried to draw a line limiting federal authority over the economy on behalf of states' rights, reality has soon washed it away.

The implication, of course, is that virtually everything is subject to federal power and that the federal government is not really a government of limited powers. We act on that understanding all the time. For example, it is assumed that what the Court does not allow Congress to do directly under the commerce clause it may do indirectly by imposing conditions on grants under the spending clause.[23] The theory is that the states can refuse the money if they do not like the condition. But the federal government's fiscal power is so great that a state's choice about taking the money is often no choice at all (Meltzer 1996, 53). As *Garcia* recognized, meaningful protections for the states can only be political and they are usually quite sufficient.

There is one area where the courts can impose needed and workable limits on the national government— namely, when federal power encroaches on individual rights. The statutes nullified by the Court's rulings in the matters discussed previously have been based on the commerce clause. But for authority to enact civil rights legislation, Congress has also relied on Section 5 of the Fourteenth Amendment, which authorizes Congress to enact laws to enforce the amendment against state and local governments by appropriate means. In recent years, the Court had allowed Congress a good deal of discretion in deciding how best to enforce the amendment.

That came to a halt in 1997. In 1993, Congress passed the Religious Freedom Restoration Act in order to undo the damage to religious freedom inflicted by a 1990 Supreme Court decision, *Employment Division, Dep't. of Human Resources v. Smith*,[24] that state and local governments do not have to justify forcing religious groups to comply with laws of general applicability even when those laws seriously interfere with religious practice. In his opinion for the Court, Justice Scalia urged religious groups seeking an exemption to use the "political process," and they did so, quite successfully: the act was passed by Congress almost unanimously. That mattered little, however. The Court held in *City of Boerne v. Flores*[25] that Congress had not adopted a merely "remedial" measure to enforce the religious freedom provisions of the First and Fourteenth Amendments but had tried to determine the content of the Constitution, a function held exclusively for the courts. But, as Professor Michael McConnell (1997) has written, it was not originally intended that Congress be denied all power to define the scope of constitutional rights, and on close questions, the congressional judgment should be given much deference (194-95). The Court also said that a remedy under Section 5 had to be found by the Court to be "congruent" and "proportional" to the constitutional violations since otherwise the states would be too heavily burdened. This close scrutiny of the congressional judgment of what constitutes an "appropriate" remedy represents a sharp departure from the Court's traditionally deferential attitude toward similar kinds of congressional judgments in other areas, such as the necessary and proper clause.

In 2000, the Court hit twice again at Congress's use of Section 5 to protect constitutional rights. After rejecting an Age Discrimination in Employment Act suit against Florida for violating the Eleventh Amendment, it refused to find that the suit was justified under Section 5. In the Court's judgment, there was not enough unconstitutional age discrimination by the states to allow Congress to try to remedy it.[26] One would have thought that here, too, such an empirical judgment was for Congress to make. However, despite their criticism of judicial activism when rights are judicially expanded, the Court's conservatives do not hesitate to impose their own judgment when reviewing the federal government's efforts to protect individual rights.

The VAWA case, already discussed, is the most recent example of this tendency. The act was passed because state officials were discriminating against women by failing to enforce the laws against domestic violence. With the encouragement and support of 38 states, the federal government stepped in to remedy that failure and, in the words of Section 5, to "enforce the provisions" of the amendment. To Chief Justice Rehnquist and the conservative majority, all this was irrelevant. Turning to the *Civil Rights Cases* of 1883,[27] they dismissed the suit because it was against private parties and not the state. The 1883 decisions reflected this country's abandonment of the newly freed slaves after Reconstruction; continued reliance on them is unfortunate. Even if still alive, however, the 1883 cases were distinguishable here since there was no state involvement at all in those cases, whereas in the VAWA case, the states admitted being guilty of discrimination against women by not enforcing the law. The act was designed to remedy that *state* discrimination. It is immaterial that the case involved state inaction, rather than state action: nothing in the Fourteenth Amendment restricts its protection to active discrimination by state officials. The failure to enforce the law when women are the victims is, literally, a "den[ial of] the equal protection of the laws" protecting women, in violation of the clear language of the Fourteenth Amendment.

Almost two centuries ago, Professor Nathan Dane wrote that "states rights and state sovereignty are expressions coined for party purposes, often by minorities, who happen to be dissatisfied with measures of the general government" (quoted in Hyman 1973, 12). His observation is as true today as it was then.

EPILOGUE

After the foregoing was written, the Supreme Court overturned decisions of the Florida Supreme Court relating to the Florida law and practice governing the choice of Florida's presidential electors in the 2000 election (*Bush v. Palm Beach County Canvassing Board*; *Bush v. Gore*).[28] The decisions will be analyzed elsewhere in this issue. Here it is enough to point out that nothing could better demonstrate that states' rights is merely a useful tool in the service of more material interests, to be tossed aside when it interferes with those interests, than these two decisions. As shown previously, the five conservative members of the Supreme Court have continually invoked states' rights and lofty rhetoric about our system of dual sovereignty in order to overturn numerous federal laws granting individuals rights against state authority. In the *Bush* cases, the conservative majority ignored all of their prior states'-rights rulings and rhetoric to intervene in the electoral process, and in *Bush v. Gore* found a new equal protection issue to use in order to overturn the Florida Supreme Court's order to recount the contested ballot. The foreseeable and indeed inevitable result of their action was that Governor George W. Bush remained the winner even though numerous contested ballots remained uncounted. So much for states' rights.

Notes

1. 305 U.S. 337 (1938).

2. 347 U.S. 483 (1954).

3. *National League of Cities v. Usery*, 426 U.S. 833 (1976).

4. Id. at 851.

5. 469 U.S. 528 (1985).

6. Fair Labor Standards Amendments of 1985.

7. Pub. L. No. 98-544, 99 Stat. 2750 (codified as amended at 15 U.S.C. §§ 34-36).

8. 501 U.S. 452 (1991).

9. See, for example, *United States v. Jones*, 2000 WL 645885 (2000); *Atascadero State Hosp. v. Scanlon*, 473 U.S. 234 (1985);

Pennhurst State Sch. & Hosp. v. Halderman, 451 U.S. 1, 17 (1981).

10. *Gregory,* 501 U.S. at 456.

11. See, for example, *Slochower v. Board of Education,* 350 U.S. 551 (1956); *Stuyvesant Town Corp. v. United States,* 346 U.S. 864 (1953). See also Johnson 1997; Donner 1990. In 1920, the New York State Legislature expelled five Socialist Party members; see Hentoff 1980.

12. 505 U.S. 144, 188 (1992).

13. Id.

14. Id.

15. See *Printz v. United States,* 521 U.S. 898 (1997).

16. See *United States v. Morrison,* 120 S. Ct. 1740 (2000).

17. 509 U.S. 630, 644 (1993).

18. 488 U.S. 469, 493 (1989) (plurality opinion).

19. Id.

20. See *Adarand Contractors, Inc. v. Pena,* 515 U.S. 200, 227 (1995).

21. 514 U.S. 549 (1995).

22. See *Morrison,* 120 S. Ct. at 1778.

23. Cf. *Printz,* 521 U.S. at 898; *South Dakota v. Dole,* 486 U.S. 203, 205 (1987). See also Meltzer 1996.

24. 494 U.S. 872 (1990).

25. 521 U.S. 507 (1997).

26. *Kimel v. Florida Bd. of Regents,* 120 S. Ct. 361 (2000).

27. 109 U.S. 3 (1883).

28. 531 U.S. ___, No. 00-836 (per curiam) (Dec. 4, 2000); 531 U.S. ___, No. 00-949 (per curiam) (Dec. 12, 2000).

References

Bernstein, Nina. 2000. Bingo, Blood and Burial Plots in the Quest for Food Stamps. *New York Times,* 12 Aug.

Brady Handgun Violence Prevention Act. 18 U.S.C. §§ 921, 922, 924, 924A (1994).

Cashin, Sheryll D. 1999. Federalism, Welfare Reform and the Minority Poor: Accounting for the Tyranny of State Majorities. *Columbia Law Review* 99:552-627.

Donner, Frank. 1990. *Protectors of Privilege: Red Squads and Police Repression in Urban America.* Berkeley: University of California Press.

Fair Labor Standards Amendments of 1985. Pub. L. No. 99-150 (codified as amended at 29 U.S.C.A. § 201).

Hentoff, Nat. 1980. *The First Freedom: The Tumultuous History of Free Speech in America.* New York: Delacorte Press.

Hyman, Harold M. 1973. *A More Perfect Union: The Impact of the Civil War and Reconstruction on the Constitution.* New York: Knopf.

Johnson, Kevin R. 1997. The Antiterrorism Act, the Immigration Act, and Ideological Regulation in the Immigration Laws: Important Lessons for Citizens and Noncitizens. *St. Mary's Law Journal* 28:833-83.

Kaden, Lewis B. 1979. Politics, Money, and State Sovereignty: The Judicial Role. *Columbia Law Review* 79:847, 856-57.

Kennedy, David M. 1999. *Freedom from Fear: The American People in Depression and War, 1929-1945.* New York: Oxford University Press.

Lardner, George, Jr. and Saundra Saperstein. 1986. A Chief Justice with Big Ambitions; Even as a Boy, Rehnquist Hoped to "Change the Government." *Washington Post,* 6 July.

McConnell, Michael W. 1997. Institutions and Interpretation: A Critique of *City of Boerne v. Flores. Harvard Law Review* 111:153, 194-95.

Meltzer, Daniel J. 1996. The Seminole Decision and State Sovereign Immunity. *Supreme Court Review* 1996:1, 50-55.

Religious Freedom Restoration Act. Pub. L. No. 103-141 (codified as 107 Stat. 1488, 42 U.S.C.A. § 2000bb (2000)).

Rubin, Edward L. and Malcolm Feeley. 1994. Federalism: Some Notes on a National Neurosis. *UCLA Law Review* 41:903, 908-26.

Schwartz, Herman. 1988. *Packing the Courts: The Conservative Campaign to*

Rewrite the Constitution. New York: Scribner.

———. 2000. A Force for Civil Rights Now Fights Them. *Los Angeles Times*, 26 Mar.

Smith, James Morton. 1995. *The Republic of Letters*. New York: Norton.

"State Legislators Mix Public and Private Business," Study Says. 2000. *New York Times*, 21 May.

Stern, Craig. 1984. Judging the Judges: The First Two Years of the Reagan Bench. *Benchmark* vol. 1.

Turning the Needy Away. 2000. *New York Times*, 31 July.

Wills, Garry. 1999. *A Necessary Evil*. New York: Simon & Schuster

Wilson Act. 27 U.S.C. § 21.

Violence Against Women Act. 42 U.S.C. § 13981. Pub. L. No. 103-322. 108 Stat. 1941.

ANNALS, *AAPSS*, **574**, March 2001

Inside the Federalism Cases:
Concern About the Federal Courts

By ANN ALTHOUSE

ABSTRACT: This article considers some of the Supreme Court's recent efforts at preserving the role of state and local government despite vigorous congressional attempts at regulating in areas that had traditionally been left to local policymaking. Focusing on the commerce clause cases and cases interpreting Section 5 of the Fourteenth Amendment, this article ties federalism interests to the Supreme Court's concerns about the function of the federal courts: the statutes that prompted the Court's new vigor in limiting congressional power imposed on the workload of the federal courts and on what the Court sees as the judiciary's exclusive role of constitutional interpretation.

Ann Althouse is the Irma M. & Robert W. Arthur-Bascom Professor of Law at the University of Wisconsin Law School. She has written numerous articles on the subject of federalism and the federal courts.

THE efforts of the conservative side of the Supreme Court to enforce federalism as a matter of constitutional law have drawn a good deal of criticism. Many observers had come to feel secure in the belief that it was well settled that Congress alone would decide which matters should be resolved at the national level and which would be left to the states. Thus Court watchers were surprised, even shocked, when, in 1995, *United States v. Lopez* struck down the federal Gun-Free School Zones Act (GFSZA).[1] Further consternation ensued last summer when the Court, in *Morrison v. Unites States*, found part of the Violence Against Women Act (VAWA) unconstitutional.[2] In both of these cases, a bare majority found that an act of Congress exceeded the power granted by the commerce clause.

Since 1937, commerce clause doctrine has allowed Congress to regulate matters that have a "substantial effect" on interstate commerce, and, until 1995, this doctrine had worked to accommodate every single matter Congress saw fit to regulate. For a brief period between 1976 and 1985, the Court had experimented with a doctrine that excepted "traditional state governmental functions" from this broadly expansive congressional power. (Thus Congress could, for example, impose a national minimum wage, but the state as an employer would be able to make some of its own wage decisions free of that federal mandate.)[3] When the Court abandoned even that small excision from federal power in *Garcia v. San Antonio Metropolitan Transit Authority*,[4] the sense that the

Court had permanently retired from the business of enforcing federalism began to take hold. *Garcia* left us with something more than doctrine that seemed to create unlimited national power; it articulated a theory to justify that power. Congress was quite properly the sole decision maker on issues of federalism because the Constitution had structured Congress to embody the interests of the states. With this so-called political safeguard for federalism values,[5] congressional deliberation provided all the protection the states needed against losing legislative control over any given matter and all the protection the constitutional Framers intended to give them.

Garcia, combined with the post-1937 history of expansive commerce power interpretation, seemed to some observers to have permanently sealed the fate of the states. The states' ability to "perform their separate functions in their separate ways,"[6] to tailor legislative solutions to local problems and preferences, and to experiment and innovate would depend on whether or not Congress chose to substitute uniform federal law for the diverse, patchwork approach offered by state and local law.

Garcia depended not merely on a recognition of congressional power but also on a rather abject assessment of judicial capacity. Efforts at defining an area of traditional state governmental functions had not gone very well. There had been far too much burdensome litigation dogging the lower courts; there seemed no end to the questions about where to draw the line between traditional and nontraditional; and there were new questions about whether tradition ought to be the measure of federalism. Different federal courts of appeals had reached different conclusions about whether, say, an urban transit system was a traditional state function. Similarly, the commerce clause cases in the years before 1937 had shown the courts in disarray, obstructing democratic choice without having a confident, predictable method of sorting out what was properly reserved to the states and what could be the subject of federal law. With *Garcia*, there seemed to be a final resting point for federalism-based constitutional law: it was all a horrible mistake, an embarrassment that the Court now quite properly consigned to the doctrinal dustbin.

By contrast, Congress seemed to have won the respect that the case law had given it: its past choices about when to impose uniform national regulation inspired confidence. The economic regulation of the New Deal era had provided the context for the expansion of commerce clause doctrine. The value of this expansion was strongly confirmed when the Court was able to use the commerce clause to uphold the Civil Rights Act of 1964.[7] *Garcia* involved the application of minimum-wage laws to the states as employers. Unlike the bumbling judiciary, Congress stood out as a worthy institution that could reliably perform the task of setting the balance between federal and state power.

Why then did the conservative side of the Court disturb this perceived repose? One might say that the final resting point just described was never really very secure. The conservative members of the *Garcia* Court, who numbered only four at the time, condemned the majority's abdication of the judicial role and wrote of overturning the decision at some future date. But, in fact, the conservatives, though they gained their majority when Justice Thomas replaced Justice Marshall in 1991, have not overruled *Garcia*.

I want to suggest here that the conservative side of the Court, like the *Garcia* majority,[8] looks at the nature of the judicial role and the capacity of the judges to carry out their work to good effect. For this reason, it has not used its majority power to restore the doctrine that *Garcia* overruled. It has not opted to involve the courts once again in the task of defining traditional state functions, which had proven so intractable in the past. The conservative majority has designed its new federalism so that it works not merely to protect the states from intrusions of federal power but also to protect the role of the federal judiciary. This article examines the way federalism-based doctrine connects to concerns about the caseload and the "lawsaying" function of the federal courts.[9]

BURDENING THE
FEDERAL COURTS

Concern about burdens on the federal courts might explain the disinclination to overrule the doctrine established in *Garcia*, despite the fact that a majority of the justices does not subscribe to its foundational belief in the ability of the national political process to protect the interests of the states. More clearly, the concern about burdening the federal courts can help explain the *Lopez* and *Morrison* decisions. In those two cases, the Court found that an act of Congress exceeded the power granted by the commerce clause. Note the practical effect on the federal courts. GFSZA, challenged in *Lopez*, made it a federal crime to possess a gun within 1000 feet of a school zone. VAWA, at issue in *Morrison*, contained a section that created a federal tort claim that one individual could assert against another for "gender-motivated" violence. It should not strain credulity to say that the conservative majority viewed these statutes as cluttering the federal docket with ordinary crime and tort cases—the traditional work of the state courts.

The state courts far outnumber the federal courts, and many of the Court's jurisdictional opinions reflect a concern for the rational allocation of judicial resources. Throughout the Burger-Rehnquist era, the Supreme Court has used jurisdictional doctrine to structure the workload of the federal courts, relegating various matters to the state courts, ostensibly in the name of federalism. Citing deference to state interests, the Court has developed doctrines, in areas like abstention, habeas corpus, and sovereign immunity, that have cleared many cases from the federal courts' dockets.[10] As a matter of simple arithmetic, the great majority of cases must go to the state courts, so the category of cases that belong in federal court must be kept comparatively small, though not everyone will agree about which ones should be excluded.

Federalism-based jurisdiction doctrine is open to the criticism that it undervalues federal constitutional rights by relegating them to state courts. Yet a doctrine that, for example, requires defendants in ongoing state criminal proceedings to present their federal constitutional defenses to the state court rather than initiating new cases in federal court[11] may be justified on the ground that it enlists the much more numerous state courts in the process of enforcing federal law. One might contend that constitutional rights are too important to be entrusted to state courts, yet the routine bypassing of the state courts, with its attendant burden on the federal courts, might undermine the very sympathy toward rights that commentators tend to believe federal judges possess. State judges need to learn to enforce rights as they arise in the context of criminal cases; full protection of rights depends on their becoming deeply ingrained in state court practice. A federal court bypass short-circuits that process. Federal jurisdiction should be shaped to maintain pressure on the state courts to fulfill the obligation to enforce federal law. Thus, for example, habeas corpus access after the state criminal process has concluded should be preferred (as it is) to injunctions of ongoing criminal proceedings.

The jurisdiction cases interpret statutes and design interstitial common law: they do not strike down federal statutes. Since the federal courts remain subject to Congress's strong power over their jurisdiction,[12] judicial notions about federalism and jurisdiction are subject to legislative override. The burdens on the federal courts, however, have come not through expansive jurisdiction statutes[13] but through the congressional creation of new substantive claims. When this occurs, as it did with GFSZA and VAWA, no interpretation of jurisdictional doctrine can reallocate the caseload to the state courts: these cases fall squarely within federal question jurisdiction.[14] The only options are to accept the new caseload or to begin to restrict Congress's legislative powers, by enforcing some restriction on the commerce power. The Court is currently split over these options. Though both sides of the Court have pleaded with Congress to refrain from "the federalization of traditional state crimes and the extension of federal remedies to problems for which the States have historically taken responsibility,"[15] the liberal members of the Court adopt a position of judicial restraint when Congress proceeds to enact these statutes,[16] whereas the conservative justices have taken up activism.

GFSZA and VAWA stirred judicial activism not only because they interfered with the legislative powers of state and local government but because they gave the federal courts a new workload composed of cases that looked too much like the routine work of the state courts. It is one thing for Congress to move into the area previously covered by state law: Congress *chooses* to take on a new task and intrudes only on the state

legislative power. This is an aggrandizement of the federal government at the expense of the states. But consider the jurisdictional effect: this is not necessarily an aggrandizement of federal judicial power at the expense of the state judiciaries. If the new caseload were viewed as genuinely worthy of federal jurisdiction, the loss of state power would translate to a gain in federal power. But to the extent that the new cases are viewed as ordinary torts and crimes, the federal judiciary is diminished by the new burden.

With the federalization of torts and crimes, the interests of the federal judiciary converged with federalism interests. Although no jurisdictional doctrine was available to express judicial resistance to these impositions on the federal courts, principles of federalism did provide an argument to rein in Congress. We cannot know whether the conservative side of the Court would have felt sufficient pressure to enforce limits on the commerce power if only the interests of the states were at stake. But anyone attempting to understand the Court's new federalism should take into account the way it is interwoven with concern about the work of the federal courts.

NATIONAL PROBLEMS,
LOCAL SOLUTIONS?

The problems of guns in schools and violence against women are easily perceived as national problems, and there is some sense to the argument that Congress should be left with the power to decide when the efficiency of a single, national solution is warranted. There is a counterargument that favors judicial intervention to preserve room for the states to address their problems in their own ways. Background beliefs will affect which argument one embraces: are the states likely to come up with good ideas and to respond in helpful ways to local needs, or are they bastions of prejudice and incompetence? Will Congress solve nationwide problems with efficiency and expertise, or will it hastily grasp at the political gains that come from appearing to solve conspicuous problems? The influence of these background beliefs contributes to the conservative-liberal split over the judicial enforcement of federalism. It may be that the liberal justices tolerate the added caseload that comes from letting Congress decide when federal torts and crimes should be created because they are committed to preserving congressional power to overcome the bad choices that they worry the states will make. The conservative justices have no conflict at all: because they favor the diversity and decentralization of state and local law and doubt the ability of Congress to do better, they can rid the federal courts of the new caseload without a sense of sacrifice.

The fact that Congress recognizes the existence of a particular problem does not necessarily mean it should leap to solve it by committing scarce federal court resources. Consider *Lopez*: one boy carrying a gun to school does not amount to the sort of crime that ought to occupy a federal judge's time. Similarly, though violence against women is a serious

matter, an endless stream of tort claims brought by one individual against another should not flow into the federal courts. Just as the Court developed abstention doctrine to prevent one criminal defendant after another from moving constitutional defenses to federal court and to motivate state judges to internalize the requirements of federal constitutional law,[17] the Court has now developed commerce clause doctrine to prevent the use of the federal courts to bypass state judiciaries.

The "substantial effects" doctrine, interpreted broadly, left the federal courts unprotected. Any crime, aggregated with all other crimes of its type, has a "substantial effect" on interstate commerce. Victims of any sort of violence may lose time from their jobs, need to use medical services, and so on, and these effects, taken together, add up to a "substantial effect" on the economy. Quite apart from its impact on the federal courts, the "substantial effects" doctrine, as expansively interpreted by the Court, violated the fundamental constitutional principle of enumerated and reserved power. *Lopez* made the doctrine more restrictive, but only slightly. Although it could have scrapped the "substantial effects" test entirely,[18] it merely limited that test to "activities that arise out of or are connected with a *commercial transaction*, which viewed in the aggregate, substantially affects interstate commerce."[19]

The Congress that passed GFSZA did not address the question of its own power.[20] The *Lopez* majority in the Supreme Court, however, unlike the lower court in *Lopez*, did not rest its decision on that ground—the failure of Congress to make a formal demonstration of the facts establishing the commerce clause basis for its action. The Court wrote that Congress could at most supply additional information that might enable the Court "to evaluate the legislative judgment that the activity in question substantially affected interstate commerce, even though no such substantial effect was visible to the naked eye."[21] Here, as elsewhere, the chief justice asserted a strong conception of judicial control over the definition of constitutional law—in this case, the meaning of substantial effect on commerce. Congress may make a first assessment of whether a particular matter meets that standard, but the Court would have the final word.

Justice Breyer, in his dissent, elaborated the connection between guns in schools and the economy. Indeed, it is easy to make this connection. The "naked eye" needs little help: visualize children as future workers, and everything that affects them affects the economy. This cannot be the test of congressional power, according to the conservative majority, precisely because of how well it works: it would transform Congress's limited powers into unlimited powers. It would enable Congress to act wherever it chose and make it especially easy to reach the very areas that tend to be mentioned first when attempting to identify matters traditionally left to the states: education, family, marriage, and street-level violence.[22]

The Congress that passed VAWA—a year before the Lopez decision—did make an effort to amass evidence of the effect of violence against women on the economy. Yet this evidence relied on the same attenuated causal connection that Justice Breyer would use in his Lopez dissent. Once the majority had repudiated that approach to causation, Congress's attentiveness to constitutional law lost the weight it might have had if GFSZA, with its lack of even a nod to the Constitution, had not come first and provided the final push that led the Court to reinvigorate federalism.

Congress, after winning the respect the Garcia Court gave it, proceeded to lose it by enacting statutes like GFSZA and VAWA. Tempted, perhaps, by the political gains to be won by demonstrating a concern for children, women, and violence, Congress took actions not justified by any real need for national uniformity. Individualized state and local approaches to problems were displaced or overshadowed without much consideration for whether a disuniform approach might be superior. Many problems, such as violence in schools, vary in nature and intensity from place to place. Variation in policy, moreover, can express local preferences and can work as an experiment, yielding a set of tested options that informs the policymaking of other states.[23] To crush this variety and vitality is no small matter.

The congressional decision to displace local decision making about racial discrimination in places of public accommodations, so clearly a worthy decision, encouraged the Warren-era Court to take a generous view of the commerce power.[24] GFSZA represented Congress at the opposite extreme, taking on a problem not because of the poor performance of the states or any demonstrated need for uniformity but out of a self-serving political recognition that voters care deeply about schools and violence. The one-size-fits-all GFSZA visited harsh criminal penalties on children, depriving the local polities of a free space in which to attempt more creative, more benevolent, more effective, or more preferred solutions. Whisking kids away into prison (with the help of federal judges) interfered with experiments like gun-surrender programs and sanctions aimed at parents.[25]

The crude treatment of federalism values in GFSZA roused the Court from the deference it had been willing to give to Congress. Without *Lopez*, VAWA might have looked like a worthy effort in the tradition of the Civil Rights Act of 1964. After *Lopez*, at least to the conservative majority, VAWA seemed to be another unwarranted displacement of state diversity, another voter-pleasing gesture that threatened to crowd the federal courts with cases that really belonged in state court. One would need to accept the Breyer theory of causation to accept VAWA's connection of gender-motivated violence to interstate commerce. Moreover, VAWA was not an attempt to regulate "activities that arise out of or are connected with a *commercial transaction*." Thus what was intended to serve as a dutiful demonstration of the basis for congressional power now appeared to be an attempt to rewrite the Court's constitutional doctrine, a congressional usurpation of the Court's prized constitutional lawsaying role.

THE LAWSAYING ROLE
AND THE
FOURTEENTH AMENDMENT

This struggle over the lawsaying role calls to mind *City of Boerne v. Flores*,[26] the case that struck down the Religious Freedom Restoration Act (RFRA). The Court had recently changed its interpretation of the free exercise clause. No longer would states need to show a "compelling interest" in order to justify statutes of general applicability that may substantially burden but do not target religion.[27] In RFRA, Congress attempted to restore the Court's old doctrine, to rewrite constitutional law with a statute.

As authority for this action, Congress invoked Section 5 of the Fourteenth Amendment, empowering it "to enforce, by appropriate legislation, the provisions of this article." Arguably this provision authorized the statutory expansion of rights. Just as the Civil Rights Act of 1964 had generated broad interpretations of the commerce clause, the Voting Rights Act of 1965 had led to the cases suggesting that Congress could enlarge rights using its enforcement power.[28] Congress won deference because it had attended to a matter that genuinely deserved a uniform, national statement to displace the inadequate efforts of the states. But deference won can also be lost. RFRA proved to be the GFSZA of the Fourteenth Amendment.

Before *Boerne*, one might have thought that Section 5 gave Congress a role in articulating rights: the Court would begin a dialogue about rights, establishing their basic scope, but Congress could then choose to add to those rights. The Court might have given a narrow meaning to a right in order to leave room for democratic decision making, and then that democratic choice could be to enlarge the right. But there is a glaring federalism problem here: the majoritarian processes the Court accommodated by constraining the size of a Fourteenth Amendment right were the legislative processes of the *states*. The statutory expansion of rights embodied in RFRA was a national policy choice that restricted state lawmaking. Congress did not merely define the scope of the free exercise right; it also made a decision about what should be governed by federal law and what should be left to state lawmaking. It was redefining the right and also resetting the federalism balance. Moreover, it had dumped a large number of cases on the federal courts.[29]

In *Boerne*, the Supreme Court responded with a strong statement of its intent to preserve the judicial grip on the lawsaying function. The courts, not Congress, would control the interpretation of constitutional rights. The Court made Section 5 power much more difficult to tap. Henceforth, Section 5 legislation would need to be genuinely remedial of rights as defined by the federal courts. Any purported "enforcement" of those rights would need to be "congruent" with and "proportional" to judicially defined rights.[30] The new

doctrine would unmask "remedies" that reached beyond real-world problems as attempts at redefining rights, impermissibly encroaching on the judicial domain.[31] RFRA openly displayed its intent to supplant judicial interpretation. Since *Boerne*, however, the Court has gone on to restrict the use of Section 5 power in subtler cases in which the Court perceived Congress to be creating remedies beyond the scope of judicially defined rights.[32] Today, the Court closely polices congressional attempts to use the Fourteenth Amendment power. Even when a statute does not target a disfavored Supreme Court opinion the way RFRA did, the Court will not permit the enlargement of rights. Here, as in the commerce clause cases, the conservative majority has designed doctrine that works to protect not only states but the federal courts as well.

THE LAWSAYING
ROLE AND VAWA

We have seen that *Morrison* rejected Congress's attempt to connect violence against women to a substantial effect on the economy. Acts of violence committed by one person against another are not "activities that arise out of or are connected with a commercial transaction." The reason for "federalizing" the violence—gender—makes it less of a "commercial transaction" than a robbery. Yet one might say that gender-motivated violence does have a greater claim to national attention than does robbery, because the states have traditionally taken robbery seriously, whereas there is a history of the states' neglecting the problem of violence against women. A layperson who favored VAWA would probably see it as an easy case for federal authority because it addresses sex discrimination. One doubts that anyone unfamiliar with the case law would think to say that national attention is justified because of the effect on interstate commerce. VAWA would seem to fit neatly into Congress's long-standing concern with individual rights.

The private action provision of VAWA is different from the public accommodations governed by the 1964 Civil Rights Act: the latter statute covered only business establishments. One might wonder why the Fourteenth Amendment would not provide the basis for Congress's power. If the real reason for federalizing violence against women has to do with discrimination, that seems like the right place in the Constitution to look for the needed power.

The problem is the same one that kept the 1964 act from relying on Section 5: the Fourteenth Amendment refers only to state action. The only plausible way to have used Section 5 in *Morrison* would have been to say that the states were indeed violating equal protection and that a properly "congruent and proportional" remedy for those violations by the states would be to permit women to sue their attackers in federal court.

Congress did, in fact, gather evidence showing that some states did not treat gender-motivated violence as seriously as other violence, so it might seem genuinely remedial to permit victims to bypass the inade-quate mechanisms of the states and to employ the federal courts as a friendly forum for suing attackers. Even though the Fourteenth Amendment, without legislative supplementation, permits suits only against state actors, one might argue that to authorize lawsuits against private citizens really is to tailor a remedy for the state's violation of rights. But the majority would not take that theory seriously: it simply saw the lack of state action as a congressional attempt to overrule the Court's precedents imposing that requirement.

Moreover, Congress did not try to identify the states that had done poorly and to tailor a remedy designed to reach them. It had provided an all-purpose bypass of the state judicial system, to be used at the will of an individual plaintiff who, because she would only be suing her attacker and not any state actor, would not be using the federal courts as a way of ending the violation of constitutional rights. Under the VAWA private-action approach, all of the state actors were left alone to continue ignoring the problem of violence against women. The state court resource was left fallow, while the federal courts were enlisted in the ongoing work of providing remedies for victims of violence. There was no targeting of the states that had acted with particular hostility to women, and there was no remedy designed to force the states to change their ways. VAWA's private right of action essentially wrote off the states, rewarding them for their own bad behavior by transferring the work of providing remedies to the federal courts.

Rather than pressuring the states to offer remedies and to take violence against women seriously, the private action provision of VAWA set up a mechanism for bypassing state processes, thus producing the convergence of federalism and federal jurisdiction problems that triggers the activism of the conservative side of the Supreme Court.

CONCLUSION

The Supreme Court's recent development of federalism-based doctrine reflects the interplay between Congress, the states, and the federal courts. The Court initially expanded its interpretation of congressional power in response to statutes that dealt with matters of great national concern and a need for a uniform national response. When Congress took advantage of these interpretations by going too far in the direction of federalizing crimes and torts, imposing not only on the interests of the states but on the resources of the federal courts, Congress lost the deference its earlier work had won.

Despite the clamor over the Court's new federalism doctrine, it has in fact only modestly trimmed congressional power. It has not reverted to its pre-1937 activism but merely alerted Congress to think more carefully about whether federal solutions and federal court access are really needed or whether to rely on state and local laws and state court adjudication. Congress could convince the Court once again that the political process can take full account of federalism concerns. But without key changes in Court personnel,

continued legislation about matters traditionally left to the states, loading federal courts with cases that would otherwise go to state court, will tend to produce new case law expressing the convergent interests of the states and the federal courts.

Notes

1. 514 U.S. 549 (1995) (invalidating 18 U.S.C. § 922(q)(1)(A) (1988 ed. Supp. V)).

2. 120 S. Ct. 1740 (2000) (invalidating 42 U.S.C. § 13981).

3. See *National League of Cities v. Usery*, 426 U.S. 833 (1976).

4. 469 U.S. 528 (1985).

5. 469 U.S. at 551. The *Garcia* Court relied on the analysis in Wechsler 1954. See also Choper 1980.

6. *Younger v. Harris*, 401 U.S. 37 (1971) ("Our Federalism" entails a presumption that things work best "if the States and their institutions are left free to perform their separate functions in their separate ways.").

7. See *Heart of Atlanta Motel, Inc. v. United States*, 379 U.S. 241 (1964); *Katzenbach v. McClung*, 397 U.S. 294 (1964).

8. One member of the *Garcia* majority, Justice Stevens, remains on the Court. The rest of the *Garcia* majority has retired, but each of those justices—with the exception of Justice Marshall, replaced by Justice Thomas—has a successor with similar ideas about federalism and constitutional law.

9. "It is emphatically the province and duty of the judicial department to say what the law is." *Marbury v. Madison*, 5 U.S. (1 Cranch) 137 (1803).

10. This observation is detailed in Althouse 1991, 1994.

11. See *Younger v. Harris*, 401 U.S. 37 (1971).

12. See, for example, *Sheldon v. Sill*, 49 U.S. 441 (1851).

13. Statutes affecting federal court jurisdiction tend to track restrictive judicial policies. See, for example, 28 U.S.C. § 2254 (1994 ed., Supp. III) (part of the Anti-terrorism and Effective Death Penalty Act of 1996) (sharply limiting habeas access).

14. See 28 U.S.C. § 1331.

15. *Morrison*, 120 S. Ct. at 1764, n. 10 (Souter, Stevens, Ginsburg, and Brennan, Js., dissenting) (citations omitted); U.S. Senate 1994, 100-107.

16. *Morrison*, 120 S. Ct. at 1764, n. 10 (Souter, J., dissenting) ("It should go without saying that my view of the limit of the congressional commerce power carries no implication about the wisdom of exercising it to the limit.").

17. See *Younger v. Harris*, 401 U.S. 37 (1971).

18. See *Lopez*, 514 U.S. at 584-602 (Thomas, J., concurring) (noting the more modest position taken in the other opinions and arguing that the "substantial effects" test is in fact an incorrect interpretation of the commerce clause).

19. 514 U.S. at 561 (emphasis added).

20. Congress did amend GFSZA after the Court of Appeals for the Fifth Circuit had stricken down the statute precisely for its lack of constitutional "findings" connecting gun possession to interstate commerce. See *Lopez*, 514 U.S. at 552.

21. *Lopez*, 514 U.S. at 563.

22. See id. at 564-65.

23. See *New State Ice Co. v. Liebmann*, 285 U.S. 262, 311 (1932) (Brandeis, J., dissenting).

24. See *Heart of Atlanta Motel, Inc. v. United States*, 379 U.S. 241 (1964); *Katzenbach v. McClung*, 397 U.S. 294 (1964).

25. See *Lopez*, 514 U.S. at 581-82.

26. 521 U.S. 507 (1997).

27. See *Employment Div., Dept. of Human Resources of Ore. v. Smith*, 494 U.S. 872 (1990), overruling *Sherbert v. Verner*, 374 U.S. 398 (1963).

28. See, for example, *Oregon v. Mitchell*, 400 U.S. 112 (1970) (upholding five-year ban on voter literacy tests, despite Supreme Court opinion that literacy tests do not violate the Constitution); *South Carolina v. Katzenbach*, 383 U.S. 301, 308 (1966) (upholding ban on voter literacy tests related to persons schooled in Puerto Rico).

29. See Herman 1998 (noting large number of prisoner cases using RFRA and the Supreme Court's general hostility to prisoner cases).

30. *Boerne* found the voting rights cases involved genuinely remedial statutory law, because that law responded to evidence that states had violated rights and tailored the provisions by limiting their duration and only to the states that had engaged in the "most flagrant" discrimination. Not only was Congress dealing with a problem that had resisted solution at the state level; Congress also tempered the application and effect of this law on the states. See *Boerne*, 521 U.S. at 525-27. This is the sort of deference to the states that gave rise to the belief in the political safeguards of federalism recognized in *Garcia*.

31. Cf. *Dickerson v. United States*, 120 S. Ct. 2326 (2000) (striking down the federal statute that attempted to replace the well-known *Miranda* warnings, on the ground that it was an attempt to redefine a constitutional right).

32. See *Kimel v. Florida Board of Regents*, 528 U.S. 62 (2000) (Age Discrimination in Employment Act of 1967, 29 U.S.C.S. § 621 et seq., does not fit within the Section 5 power); *Florida Prepaid Postsecondary Educ. Expense Bd. v. College Sav. Bank*, 527 U.S. 627 (1999) (Congress may not use Section 5 to provide for patent enforcement against the states). Note that Congress's powers under Article I easily support employment discrimination and patent law. But Article I powers, unlike the Fourteenth Amendment power, do not authorize Congress to abrogate state sovereign immunity; so much of today's litigation over the scope of the Fourteenth Amendment power really concerns the question of state immunity from retrospective relief.

References

Althouse, Ann. 1991. Tapping the State Court Resource. *Vanderbilt Law Review* 44:953-1005.

————. 1994. Federalism, Untamed. *Vanderbilt Law Review* 47:1207-27.

Anti-Terrorism and Effective Death Penalty Act. 1996. Pub. L. No. 104-132. 110 Stat. 1214 (amending, inter alia, 28 U.S.C. 2254).

Choper, Jesse. 1980. *Judicial Review and the National Political Process*. Chicago: University of Chicago Press.

Gun-Free School Zones Act. 1990. 18 U.S.C. § 922(q)(1)(A).

Herman, Susan N. 1998. Slashing and Burning Prisoners' Rights: Congress and the Supreme Court in Dialogue. *Oregon Law Review* 77:1229-1303.

Religious Freedom Restoration Act. 1993. 42 U.S.C. § 2000bb et seq.

U.S. Senate. 1994. Committee on Appropriations. *Hearings on H.R. 4603*. 103d Cong., 2d sess.

Violence Against Women Act. 1994. 42 U.S.C. § 13981(b).

Wechsler, Herbert. 1954. The Political Safeguards of Federalism. *Columbia Law Review* 54:543-60.

ANNALS, *AAPSS*, **574**, March 2001

Federalism and the Court: Congress as the Audience?

By VICKI C. JACKSON

ABSTRACT: The Supreme Court's revival of federalism as a limit on national power has roots, in part, in the Court's mistrust of the national legislative process and its sense of institutional competition with Congress. To the extent that the Court is concerned about careless legislating, six rules of "care and craft" in drafting legislation are proposed for members of Congress to consider: develop a factual record, reflect the source of constitutional authority, tailor the statute to reach "national" and not "local" matters, consider the implications of decentralized enforcement for surviving constitutional challenges as well as for efficacy, consider whether state governments are treated comparably to the federal government, and be particularly cautious in efforts to overrule the effects of the Court's decisions. To the extent the Court is concerned with its own institutional prerogatives, however, or is committed to a categorical divide between areas constitutionally committed to the states and the federal government, care and craft alone will not be a solution.

Vicki C. Jackson is a professor of law at Georgetown University Law Center. She is the author of many articles on federalism and the Eleventh Amendment and writes and teaches as well in comparative constitutional law. Professor Jackson serves on several academic and professional boards, including the State and Local Legal Center's Advisory Board, the International Association of Constitutional Law Executive Board, and the D.C. Bar Board of Governors.

NOTE: The views expressed herein are those of the author alone.

I N the last decade, the Supreme Court has reinvigorated federalism as a limit on national power in three distinct areas: the anticommandeering rule, the sovereign immunity rules, and the rules of limited enumerated powers. The anticommandeering rule prohibits Congress, at least when acting under its Article I powers, from imposing obligations on state or local governments to enact legislation or to enforce federal laws. Thus, for example, the Brady Law's requirement that local sheriffs perform background checks was held unconstitutional in *Printz v. United States*,[1] and Congress cannot require states to enact legislation to advance federal programs, even when states had informally agreed to such requirements (*New York v. United States*).[2]

Sovereign immunity rules, drawn from the Eleventh Amendment to the Constitution and from broader nontextual principles held to be implicit in the constitutional structure, limit Congress's powers to subject states to private suits for damages, even under valid federal laws that subject others to those suits. *Seminole Tribe v. Florida*[3] held that sovereign immunity of the states was a constitutional principle that limits Congress's powers under Article I and thus invalidated a provision authorizing Indian tribes to sue states under a federal law dealing with gambling on Indian reservations. As a result of *Seminole Tribe* and *Alden v. Maine*,[4] states cannot be sued in either federal or state courts by employees seeking back pay due under the Fair Labor Standards Act, even though other employers (including local governments) can be. Congress may, however, subject states to suits for damages if it acts pursuant to its Fourteenth Amendment powers (*Fitzpatrick v. Bitzer*).[5] It is thus important to know precisely which of its powers Congress can rely on in enacting laws, because the remedies available against states for breach of federal law are more limited where Congress acts only under its Article I powers than where it acts pursuant to the Fourteenth Amendment.

Finally, the Court has insisted that Congress's enumerated powers are limited ones, both under the commerce clause and under Section 5 of the Fourteenth Amendment. In *United States v. Lopez*,[6] the Court held that a statute prohibiting gun possession near schools could not be upheld under the commerce clause because the connection between the asserted effects of such gun possession and the national economy was too remote. In *Boerne v. Flores*,[7] the Court found that Congress had exceeded its powers under the Fourteenth Amendment by extending statutory protections to religious practices that the Court previously had held were unprotected by the Constitution. Congress, the Court said, may invoke its powers to enforce the Fourteenth Amendment only where its legislation is "congruent and proportional" to constitutional violations, a standard that the challenged federal statute in *Boerne* did not meet.

Under its newly invigorated approach to "limited enumerated powers," the Court recently held that Congress lacked power to prohibit and penalize certain forms of gender-motivated assaults. In *United States v. Morrison*,[8] the Court struck down the civil remedy provisions of the Violence Against Women Act (VAWA).[9] Gender-motivated violence was not "in any sense of the phrase, economic activity" as the Court saw it, suggesting that the Court is moving to treat economic activity as some sort of categorical divide between federal and state power under the commerce clause. Moreover, the remedy could not be justified under the Fourteenth Amendment, in part because it was directed at perpetrators of gender-motivated violence rather than at state officials.

Lopez and *Morrison* both insist that the Constitution "requires a distinction between what is truly national and what is truly local." These and other recent decisions can be best understood, however, not as a return to historic first principles, but rather as the cyclical reassertion of judicial authority in a system of separation of powers. There is a close link between the Court's renewed monitoring of asserted federalism-based limits and its reliance on separation-of-powers principles to explain its decision in *Boerne v. Flores*. The Court's new federalism jurisprudence arguably has implications for the legislative process, in both procedural and substantive terms, with an emphasis on "care and craft" in legislative drafting. I conclude, however, by questioning how much such care and craft will matter, in light of the absence of a sound functional theory behind the Court's federalism cases coupled with the Court's institutional competition with Congress.

AN EXPLANATION

This article is too short for a full explanation of the Court's revival of federalism, but I want to suggest that these recent decisions are of a piece in at least one sense. While the decisions are cloaked in claims of originalist commitments to first principles of federalism, the major doctrinal developments cannot convincingly be said to be compelled by original understandings. Evidence of original intent is at best in conflict on these issues and, in some respects, is inconsistent with the Court's decisions. Resort to the rhetoric of originalism fails to capture the degree to which what is being reasserted is as much judicial supremacy as federalism.

In evaluating the accuracy of the historical claims, consider the reach of the anti-commandeering principle. In *New York*, the Court asserted that the 1787 Convention substituted the power to impose obligations directly on the people for the prior power to make requisitions from the states and that federal laws commandeering state legislatures to act were thus unconstitutional. Noting the clear intent of the 1787 Convention to strengthen the national government, some scholars disagree that the federal power to regulate individuals directly was a substitute for, rather than an addition to, the preexisting powers of the nascent national government in 1787.[10] Moreover, Professor Prakash's (1993, pp. 1996-97, 2033-34) sympathetic exploration of the anti-commandeering principle's historical provenance led him to conclude that while the Court was on solid ground with respect to efforts to require state legislatures to enact laws, it was the expectation of the framing generation that state executive and judicial officials would enforce federal law.[11] Yet *Printz* held that the anti-commandeering principle barred federal imposition of duties on state executive officials. The *Printz* Court's strained effort to distinguish the early imposition of federal duties on state "magistracies" as involving only judicial duties is unconvincing, as is its effort to discredit a rather clear assertion in Federalist 27 (relied on by Justice Souter in dissent) that state governments would enforce federal laws.

With respect to the Eleventh Amendment, the Court has chosen to follow the "law office" history of the late nineteenth century rather than either the more contemporary record of how the Eleventh Amendment was interpreted soon after its enactment or the detailed scholarly historical examinations of its adoption. According to the Court in *Hans v. Louisiana*,[12] and again in *Seminole Tribe*, the Court's 1793 decision in *Chisholm v. Georgia*,[13] sustaining jurisdiction over a contract claim against a state by a citizen of another state, created a "shock of surprise" and represented an erroneous reading of the original Constitution; the Eleventh Amendment was intended to clarify the error and assure that the sovereign immunity of the states would be respected. At least one opinion by Chief Justice John Marshall, however, treated the amendment as an inconvenience of pleading, not necessarily intended as a major substan-

tive limit on the federal judicial power over federal law claims.[14] Many scholarly studies, moreover, had concluded that the narrow language of the amendment was best understood as an effort to limit diversity-based heads of jurisdiction over the states, with little or no intended effect on federal question jurisdiction.[15] Although *Seminole Tribe* invoked *Hans* as authority, *Hans* involved a constitutional claim asserted against a state under a general jurisdictional statute and not whether Congress could expressly subject states to suits under otherwise valid federal laws. In 1989 in *Union Gas v. Pennsylvania*,[16] the Court upheld such a congressional power. But *Seminole Tribe* reversed *Union Gas*, purportedly because of *Hans*, while ignoring even older cases that would have supported a narrower scope for state sovereign immunity on federal claims.

The recent decisions focus attention on some aspects of the framing and ratification of the Constitution (largely those relating to the continued role of the states), while ignoring others of at least equal import. Concerns over states' thwarting the national government's effort to maintain and enforce peace agreements with foreign nations, the need for more reliable sources of national revenue than requisitions from the states, the desirability of securing national power to deal with commerce (foreign, domestic, and with Indian tribes), and the benefits of bringing into a more structured union the perceived excesses of some states all formed part of the backdrop for the Convention. The "more Perfect Union" to which the Constitution aspired was one in which the national government had more power, and the states were more constrained, than under the Articles of Confederation. The nation-building, nationalizing impulses behind this Constitution were well expressed in *McCulloch v. Maryland*,[17] where Chief Justice Marshall insisted that it was the people, and not the states, that made the Constitution. Although it is clear that the Constitution is based on the continued existence of the states and guarantees their continued existence and ability to function as governments, there are important strands of originalist thought that are consistent with *McCulloch's* commitment to the national political process of the question of the "degree of necessity" for national legislation. In Federalist 45, Madison wrote,

If . . . the people should in future become more partial to the federal than to the State governments, the change can only result from such manifest and irresistible proofs of a better administration as will overcome all their antecedent propensities. And in that case, the people ought not surely to be precluded from giving most of their confidence where they may discover it to be most due.[18]

First principles, then, are mixed, and invocation of first principles does not fully explain what is going on here. *Boerne v. Flores* suggests that it is at least as much concern for its own role vis-à-vis the political branches as for federalism that may be driving the Court.

The issue in *Boerne* was the constitutionality of the Religious Freedom Restoration Act (RFRA), an act that sought to provide a statutory level of protection for religious liberty rights higher than that which the Court had said the Constitution provided.[19] The Court held that RFRA was unconstitutional because, by exceeding the level of protection the Court had said was necessary to protect against violations of religious liberty, Congress had exceeded the scope of its power under Section 5 of the Fourteenth Amendment, infringing on areas left to the states to regulate. The Court, not Congress, determines what constitutes a violation of Section 1 of the Fourteenth Amendment. While Congress has broad powers under Section 5 to remedy violations of Section 1, its legislation must be aimed at conduct that the Court would agree constitutes a violation of Section 1. The legislative record failed to show that Congress was indeed aiming its legislation at conduct the Court would agree constituted violations of religious liberty, and, the Court found, the legislation was so out of proportion to any such acts that it could not be upheld as an exercise of the remedial enforcement powers of Section 5.

Linked to this federalism holding is the Court's strong sense of offended institutional prerogative.

When the political branches of the Government act against the background of a judicial interpretation of the Constitution already issued, it must be understood that in later cases and controversies the Court will treat its precedents with the respect due them under settled principles, including *stare decisis*, and contrary expectations must be disappointed. RFRA was designed to control cases and controversies, such as the one before us; but as the provisions of the federal statute here invoked are beyond congressional authority, it is this Court's precedent, not RFRA, which must control.[20]

In other words, Congress had threatened the supremacy of the Court's decisions by seeking to overcome the effect of the Court's earlier decision. Both separation of powers and federalism principles, then, the Court found, required invalidation of RFRA.

IMPLICATIONS FOR CONGRESS: CARE AND CRAFT?

What are the implications of these decisions for Congress as the national lawmaker? It is important to note the current Court's lack of respect for the national political process. In 1985, the Court had concluded that the primary protection for the states was in the political safeguards of the national political process[21] and that it was to this process that states must generally look to control the growth and use of national power. This reliance on the political process has been silently, but decisively, disavowed in the last decade, in the Eleventh Amendment cases, in *New York*, and in *Lopez*. *Boerne* represents perhaps the most striking manifestation of the renewed judicial assertiveness about the Court's prerogative to define not only the scope of individual rights under the Bill of Rights but also limitations on national power that, the Court believes, protect the federal system designed by the Framers. In *Reno v. Condon* and

again in *Morrison*, the Court paid lip service to what it called the "presumption of constitutionality," but the reference was pro forma and without weight. This is particularly clear in *Morrison*, where Congress had developed an extensive record before it acted, including a record of support by state attorneys general for the federal legislation.

Indeed, the decisions betray a genuine mistrust of Congress, reflecting the Court's apparent view of Congress as a body that creates laws without real deliberation on the need for federal legislation and without knowledge of or respect for the role of the states, or even as a body that may at times legislate pretextually or on behalf of special interests rather than the longer-term interests of majorities. *Boerne* was read by some as developing the test of proportionality to screen for improper purpose, and *Lopez* as reflecting a concern with poorly deliberated, symbolic legislative gestures. *Florida Prepaid Postsecondary Ed. Expense Bd. v. College Savings Bank*[22] concluded that Congress had failed to identify a pattern of patent infringements and unconstitutional conduct by the states sufficient to warrant the nationwide federal remedy against states for patent infringements that the Court proceeded to hold unconstitutional.

Mistrust of congressional process is further reflected in *Kimel v. Florida Board of Regents*.[23] *Kimel* held unconstitutional a provision in the Age Discrimination in Employment Act (ADEA) authorizing suits against states for violations of that act. The Court did not hold the

ADEA's substantive terms unconstitutional, noting that the ADEA's application to state governments had been upheld by the Court in 1983.[24] Notwithstanding this earlier decision upholding, under the commerce clause, the ADEA's application to states, the *Kimel* Court, in considering whether the ADEA was within Congress's Fourteenth Amendment powers, described the ADEA's extension to the states as "an unwarranted response to a perhaps inconsequential problem." It referred disapprovingly to the quality of the evidence before Congress as falling "well short of the mark," specifically noting a senator's reference to "[l]etters from my own State." In the legislative process in a representative democracy, letters from home states might be considered appropriate evidence on which to rely, so the Court's apparent skepticism may reflect a rather more profound mistrust of the legislative branch. The important implication here is that Congress cannot count on deference (or on a presumption of constitutionality with much bite). Legislation, at least in areas new to federal regulation, will have to earn it.

The relationship between the Court's mistrust of the national legislative process and its interest in reinvigorating federalism-based limits on national power is somewhat uncertain. Even if Congress were perceived as legislating with greater care, craft, and deliberation, to the extent that the Court is determined to assert a categorical division of federal from state responsibilities, careful drafting will help sustain a statute's constitutionality only to the extent that it respects that division. To the extent that the recent federalism cases reflect the Court's skepticism of the adequacy of the national political legislative process, more care in fact-finding, more attention to constitutionally relevant issues, more deliberation, and more careful drafting may help Congress advance its goals by producing legislation that will not be struck down.[25] With these points in mind (and on the assumption that the Court's recent stance toward national legislation is at least partly influenced by its mistrust of the legislative process), I will make six suggestions, based on the recent cases, for what drafters can do to respond to the Court's concerns.

First, legislative hearings should develop a record of the facts supporting the need for the legislation and the claimed basis for the exercise of federal power. The absence of such a factual record may be relied on to condemn legislation, as in *Florida Prepaid*, where the Court noted that there were very few instances of states being accused of violating privately held patents referred to in the record. Similarly, in *Lopez*, the Court noted the absence of any fact-finding by Congress to support the asserted relationship between guns near schools and interstate commerce. Of course, the factual record may come back to "bite" the constitutionality of the legislation, if it suggests that Congress was proceeding on a theory of constitutionality with which the Court disagrees. Thus, in *Boerne*, the Court noted that the legislative record reflected virtually no examples of invidiously motivated religious discrimination, but rather reflected concerns over generally applicable laws not aimed at a religious minority (which the Court had recently held would not violate religious liberty under the First Amendment). Moreover, the presence of an appropriate factual record supporting the need for federal legislation, as well as the constitutional theory of the law, may not be sufficient: a strong legislative record, acknowledged in *Morrison*, did not guarantee success in sustaining the law.

Second, it is important to reflect clearly in the statute the source of constitutional authority for the action. A Court seriously committed to presuming the constitutionality of laws would not necessarily be concerned with congressional recitations of authority but would itself be prepared to consider in litigation plausible sources of authority asserted to support a law's constitutionality. However, the current Court is unprepared to give teeth to any such presumption. Rather, the burden is on the legislation itself to make manifest its authority and justification. Indeed, in *Florida Prepaid* the Court rejected one of the parties' arguments, that the Patent Remedy Act could be sustained on a theory that uncompensated violations of patents amounted to a taking of property without compensation in violation of the Fifth and Fourteenth Amendments, on the ground that Congress had not referred to this theory in the course of adopting the legislation.[26] This suggestion—that if Congress does not rely on a specific theory, the Court need not consider it on a constitutional challenge—might be thought almost to reverse the presumption of constitutionality and suggests that this Court will place on Congress the burden to justify novel legislation.

Third, legislators may try to tailor the statute, where possible, in light of the Court's concern that there be a line between what is national and what is local. For example, when Congress relies on its commerce clause powers to regulate areas heretofore regulated only by the states, it could consider the use of jurisdictional nexus provisions, tailored to the problem it is trying to reach and mindful of the Court's concerns. In light of *Lopez* and *Morrison*, it is especially important to exercise care to establish a connection to interstate commerce in attempts to regulate interpersonal behavior not involving purchase, sale, loan, or exchange of goods or services.[27] For in review of such legislation, the Court's current jurisprudence seems to require that one be able to provide a positive answer to the question, If this is constitutional, then what is it Congress cannot reach?

Fourth, those involved in legislating should think about how issues will be presented to the courts under proposed legislation and specifically about whether enforcement of the law will be centralized (for example, in the federal government) or decentralized (for example, through private lawsuits). In areas of constitutional uncertainty, the sequencing and selection of cases may be able to influence the Court's responses to constitutional questions. If a standard of conduct is enforced by the federal government—for example, through criminal prosecutions—it can exercise control over what cases to bring, on what facts, in what order, with awareness of the Court's concerns.[28] If private civil actions are authorized, such selection and sequencing is much harder to achieve, yet decentralizing enforcement into the hands of those who are the intended beneficiaries of legislation may be the most effective means of enforcement. A careful Congress should consider the implications of centralized and decentralized enforcement mechanisms both for a statute's effective implementation and for its constitutional survivability.

Fifth, note a possibly emerging concern in the Court with how states are treated as compared with the federal government. In *Florida Prepaid*, the majority noted—without explaining the relevance of its comment—that, were it to find that the Patent Remedy Act had validly abrogated states' immunities, states would be subject to a more intrusive and severe range of remedies than was the federal government for comparable infringements.[29] The dissent disputed the magnitude of the asserted differences, again without explaining why this was relevant.[30] I have suggested elsewhere that the Constitution's structure and, in particular, its assumption of the perpetual existence of both the states and the nation as ongoing governments, may form a basis for presuming that exemptions or immunities for one level of government may be required by the other constitutionally guaranteed level of government.[31] In any event, if proposed legislation directly regulates acts by state and local governments, and does or could apply to the federal government as well as the states, a prudent legislator may want to consider and address whether the proposed legislation should apply in the same manner to both levels of government and if not, why.

Sixth and finally, if the goal is to enact legislation that will be upheld, it is important to be particularly cautious in considering legislation to overcome effects of a constitutional decision by the Court. Let me be clear: the proper goal may *not* always be to maximize the chances of a law's being upheld. Congress has its own constitutional responsibilities to exercise its enumerated powers for the benefit of the nation; if it never enacts legislation that in any way challenges the Court's view of contested issues, it will be more difficult for the scope and integrity of controversial rulings to be tested in the courts.[32] On the other hand, one message we can take from *Boerne* is that the Court will be particularly concerned about what it sees as efforts by Congress to seek to overrule, or disagree with, the Court's own constitutional analysis and will, due to separation-of-powers concerns, subject such legislation to sharper scrutiny.

INSTITUTIONAL COMPETITION
AND THE LIMITS OF CARE

The prior section proceeded on the assumption that the Court in part has been responding to what it sees as a lack of deliberation, care, and craft in the drafting of legislation by Congress. But there are other notes in the Court's recent federalism cases that may not be so easily met, to wit, its sense of institutional competition with Congress and its substantive commitment to an ill-defined but categorical division of federal and state powers. Reinforced by commitments to stare decisis in the judicial process,[33] these elements of the Court's federalism jurisprudence may stand as a substantive bar to legislation in some fields regardless of the care and craft with which they are approached.

The Court's recent tightening of limits on Congress's powers to enact legislation under Section 5 of the Fourteenth Amendment was explicitly linked by *Boerne* to the Court's preeminence in defining the rights accorded under Section 1. The result of the Court's decision was a diminution both in Congress's substantive powers to create new rights and in its powers to make those rights fully enforceable through ordinary judicial remedies. It is to the Court, then, and not Congress, that the people must look for the basic articulation of their rights. For a Court whose institutional anxiety is manifest in the most subtle choices of language,[34] its limitation of Congress's ability to enact fully enforceable remedial schemes against the states has the effect of enhancing the Court's own role in providing rights.

Moreover, the Court in *Morrison* has begun to make clear that its concern is not simply with care and deliberation but with sustaining a substantive, categorical line limiting the reach of national power. The Court acknowledged that Congress had compiled an extensive record documenting the pervasiveness of gender-based violence against women having substantial impacts on victims and their families; the legislative record, moreover, had substantial findings connecting such violence to harms to the economy. The Court did not disagree that there was a causal chain connecting those acts to effects on commerce but would not uphold the statute on those grounds because as a logical matter to do so would allow Congress to regulate any subject, since in the interconnected world of today any subject that is of national concern has ultimate effects on the economy. To accept such reasoning, however, the Court said, would be inconsistent with the Constitution's demand that there be a distinction between that which is "truly national" and that which is "truly local."[35]

Given this commitment to developing doctrine that will sustain such a dividing line, we might expect the Court to be prepared to invalidate other laws. On what principle? It is hard to say, other than that the invalidations will probably extend to legislation in areas that Congress has not extensively legislated in before and which are thus seen as traditionally for the states. Congress's powers being thus curtailed (even where there are effects on the national economy), major national problems—including that of gender-based violence against women and states' failures to prevent it—have been put further from the reach of effective national action.

CONCLUSION

The Court's desire to reassert judicial supremacy in defining the boundaries of national and state power may not be affected at all by the care-and-craft approach described in this article. The anxieties may run too deep, or the commitment to a diminished national power too strong, for concern for legislative prudence to have much sway. However, more attention to the Court's articulation of constitutional limits, more careful delineation of what problems need national legislation and why, may improve the deliberative quality of the national legislative process itself even if it does not immunize legislation from invalidation by the present Court.

Notes

1. 521 U.S. 898 (1997).

2. 505 U.S. 144 (1992); see id. at 189-94 (White, J., dissenting). Under *Reno v. Condon* (120 S. Ct. 666 (2000)), however, it is clear that this anti-commandeering principle is a limited one. The Court there upheld the constitutionality of the Driver's Privacy Protection Act, which had been challenged as violating the anti-commandeering rule because it required state motor vehicle bureaus to comply with privacy-protecting provisions for use of driver license information. The Court drew a sharp line between laws requiring states to regulate other persons and laws imposing federal regulation on the state itself.

3. 517 U.S. 44 (1996).

4. 119 S. Ct. 2240 (1999).

5. 427 U.S. 445 (1976).

6. 514 U.S. 549 (1995).

7. 521 U.S. 507 (1997).

8. 120 S. Ct. 1740 (2000).

9. I helped prepare a brief for a group of law professors in support of the constitutionality of VAWA's civil rights remedy in the Supreme Court in *Morrison*.

10. See, for example, Caminker 1995, 1042-59; Jackson 1998, 2199-2200; but cf. Prakash 1993, 1971-72.

11. See also Caminker 1995.

12. 134 U.S. 1 (1890).

13. 2 U.S. 419 (1793).

14. See *Osborn v. Bank of United States*, 22 U.S. 738, 857-58 (1824).

15. See, for example, Fletcher 1983; Gibbons 1983; Jackson 1988. See also Pfander 1998. For a range of other views, see, for example, Young 2000; Marshall, L. C. 1989; Marshall, W. P. 1989; Meltzer 1997; Vazquez 1997.

16. 491 U.S. 1 (1989).

17. 17 U.S. 316 (1819).

18. Admittedly, Federalist 45 goes on to acknowledge that "even in that case the State governments could have little to apprehend, because it is only within a certain sphere that the federal power can, in the nature of things, be advantageously administered." But Federalist 45 does not suggest that the Constitution provides such a limit but, rather, that "the nature of things"—as they then stood—did so. A similar argument concerning the original mix of intentions behind the adoption of the Fourteenth Amendment might be offered in contrast to the Court's current view of its limited and Court-centered impact. Cf. *Boerne v. Flores*, 521 U.S. at 520-24 (suggesting that Section 1 of the Fourteenth Amendment was redrafted to reflect federalism concerns) with Foner 1988, 228-80 (suggesting that Section 1 was redrafted to ensure that the Court would be able to protect rights being secured even if Congress failed to do so).

19. See *Employment Div., Dept. of Human Resources of Oregon v. Smith*, 494 U.S. 872 (1990) (rejecting constitutional challenge to state law's failure to provide exemption for religious uses of peyote). RFRA, which sought to extend protection to claims like those rejected in *Smith*, was similar to other statutes, such as the Pregnancy Discrimination Act or Title VII, which established standards to accord greater protection from discrimination based on race and gender than the Court had held was required by the Constitution.

20. *Boerne v. Flores*, 521 U.S. at 536.

21. *Garcia v. San Antonio Metropolitan Transit Authority*, 469 U.S. 528 (1985).

22. 527 U.S. 627 (1999).

23. 120 S. Ct. 631 (2000).

24. *EEOC v. Wyoming*, 460 U.S. 2326 (1983).

25. See Waxman 2000. Cf. Cushman 1998, 81-84, arguing that the pre-1937 New Deal

Court is misread as being hostile to the whole thrust of New Deal legislation but, rather, for example, in invalidating the Frazier-Lemke Farm Debt Relief Act of 1934, offered specific guidance about what features would require revision in order to be upheld. Although the tenor of the Court's more recent federalism decisions may appear more confrontational than "consultative," its opinions could be read as offering guidance, for example, that prophylactic uses of the Section 5 power to enforce the Fourteenth Amendment are more likely to be upheld if limited to particular periods or geographic areas (see, for example, *Florida Prepaid*, 527 U.S. at 646-47; *Boerne*, 521 U.S. at 532, 535) or that a jurisdictional nexus requirement may permit jurisdiction to be exercised over violent crime that would otherwise be outside the commerce clause power (for example, *Morrison*, 120 S. Ct. at 1750, 1752 and n. 5).

26. See 527 U.S. at 642.

27. Cf. *Reno v. Condon*, 120 S. Ct. at 671 (implying that Congress could presume that any entry of goods into the market for sale would satisfy the commerce clause: "Because drivers' information is, in this context, an article of commerce, its sale or release into the interstate stream of business is sufficient to support congressional regulation. We therefore need not address the Government's alternative argument that the States' individual, intrastate activities in gathering, maintaining, and distributing drivers' personal information has a sufficiently substantial impact on interstate commerce" to support federal constitutional power) with *Morrison*, 120 S. Ct. at 1752-53, 1754 (suggesting by implication that Congress cannot proceed on the assumption that people injured by gender-motivated violence were economic actors, harm to whom would injure the economy, by treating acts with a concededly "serious impact" on victims as not having a "substantial effect" on interstate commerce and asserting that "the regulation and punishment of intrastate violence not directed at the instrumentalities, channels or goods involved in interstate commerce has always been the province of the States").

28. This point is addressed not only to legislators who draft, but also to executive branch officials who enforce, laws.

29. *Florida Prepaid*, 527 U.S. at 648, n. 11.

30. *Florida Prepaid*, 527 U.S. at 662, n. 15 (Stevens, J. dissenting).

31. See Jackson 2000a, 1006-9; Jackson 2000b, 732-38.

32. Even *Boerne v. Flores* implies that Congress could properly enact legislation inconsistent with a Court decision if by conventional stare decisis principles the Court might depart from its prior ruling. On the large subjects of Congress's responsibility and capacity to consider constitutional issues, see, for example, Brest 1975; Mikva 1983; Tushnet 1999.

33. For example, in *Jones v. United States* (120 S. Ct. 1904 (2000)), the Court explained that, in part to avoid a constitutional question under *Lopez*, it was construing the federal arson statute more narrowly than some lower courts had done.

34. See, for example, the Court's insistence in *Alden* (119 S. Ct. at 2246) that its own interpretations are "authoritative."

35. The Court suggested that the reasoning proffered in support of the VAWA would, if accepted, allow Congress to regulate any crime where the nationwide aggregated effects of the conduct being prohibited had a substantial effect on interstate commerce, leading to national power to regulate family law or virtually any other, a result inconsistent with the Court's view that the Constitution requires a dividing line between the national and the local. It accordingly held that Congress could not, under the commerce clause, regulate noneconomic, violent criminal conduct based solely on the conduct's aggregate effects on interstate commerce.

References

Age Discrimination in Employment Act of 1967 (ADEA), Age Discrimination in Employment Act Amendments of 1978. 92 Stat. 189.

Brady Law (Brady Handgun Violence Prevention Act). 107 Stat. 1536.

Brest, Paul. 1975. The Conscientious Legislator's Guide to Constitutional Interpretation. *Stanford Law Review* 27:585-601.

Caminker, Evan. 1995. State Sovereignty and Subordinacy: May Congress Commandeer State Officers to Implement Federal Law? *Columbia Law Review* 95:1001-89.

Cushman, Barry. 1998. The Hughes Court and Constitutional Consultation. *Journal of Supreme Court History* 1998:79-111.

Driver's Privacy Protection Act of 1994. 108 Stat. 2099.

Fletcher, William. 1983. A Historical Interpretation of the Eleventh Amendment: A Narrow Construction of an Affirmative Grant of Jurisdiction Rather Than a Prohibition Against Jurisdiction. *Stanford Law Review* 35:1033-1131.

Foner, Eric. 1988. *Reconstruction: America's Unfinished Revolution 1863-1877*. New York: Harper & Row.

Frazier-Lemke Farm-Debt Relief Act. 48 Stat. 1289.

Gibbons, John J. 1983. The Eleventh Amendment and State Sovereign Immunity: A Reinterpretation. *Columbia Law Review* 83:1889-2005.

Jackson, Vicki C. 1988. The Supreme Court, the Eleventh Amendment and State Sovereign Immunity. *Yale Law Journal* 98:1-126.

———. 1998. Federalism and the Uses and Limits of Law: Printz and Principle? *Harvard Law Review* 111:2180-2259.

———. 2000a. Principle and Compromise in Constitutional Adjudication: The Eleventh Amendment and State Sovereign Immunity. *Notre Dame Law Review* 75:953-1010.

———. 2000b. Seductions of Coherence, State Sovereign Immunity and the Denationalization of Federal Law. *Rutgers Law Journal* 31:691-739.

Marshall, Lawrence C. 1989. Fighting the Words of the Eleventh Amendment. *Harvard Law Review* 102:1342-71.

Marshall, William P. 1989. The Diversity Theory of the Eleventh Amendment: A Critical Evaluation. *Harvard Law Review* 102:1372-96.

Meltzer, Daniel J. 1997. The Seminole Decision and State Sovereign Immunity. *Supreme Court Review* 1996:1-65.

Mikva, Abner. 1983. How Well Does Congress Support and Defend the Constitution? *North Carolina Law Review* 61:587-611.

Patent Remedy Act (Patent and Plant Variety Protection Remedy Clarification Act). 106 Stat. 4230.

Pfander, James E. 1998. History and State Suability: An "Explanatory" Account of the Eleventh Amendment. *Cornell Law Review* 83:1269-1382.

Prakash, Saikrishna Bangalore. 1993. Field Office Federalism. *Virginia Law Review* 79:1957-2037.

Pregnancy Discrimination Act (PDA). 92 Stat. 2076.

Religious Freedom Restoration Act of 1993 (RFRA). 107 Stat. 1488.

Tushnet, Mark. 1999. *Taking the Constitution Away from the Courts*. Princeton, NJ: Princeton University Press.

Vazquez, Carlos M. 1997. What Is Eleventh Amendment Immunity? *Yale Law Journal* 106:1683-1806.

Violence Against Women Act of 1994. 108 Stat. 1902.

Waxman, Seth. 2000. The Physics of Persuasion: Arguing the New Deal. *Georgetown Law Journal* 88:2399-2419.

Young, Ernest A. 2000. State Sovereign Immunity and the Future of Federalism. *Supreme Court Review* 1999:1-79.

ANNALS, *AAPSS*, **574**, March 2001

State Sovereignty and the Anti-Commandeering Cases

By MATTHEW D. ADLER

ABSTRACT: The anti-commandeering doctrine, recently announced by the Supreme Court in *New York v. United States* and *Printz v. United States*, prohibits the federal government from commandeering state governments: more specifically, from imposing targeted, affirmative, coercive duties upon state legislators or executive officials. This doctrine is best understood as an external constraint upon congressional power—analogous to the constraints set forth in the Bill of Rights—but one that lacks an explicit textual basis. Should the Constitution indeed be interpreted to include a judicially enforceable constraint upon national power—and, if so, should that constraint take the form of an anti-commandeering rule?

Matthew Adler is a professor of law at the University of Pennsylvania Law School. He is a former Marshall Scholar and clerked for Judge Harry Edwards and Justice Sandra Day O'Connor. His scholarship generally involves the application of analytic philosophy to problems of public law. He has recently written about constitutional federalism, expressive theories of law, cost-benefit analysis, and the peculiar way in which constitutional doctrine focuses on impermissible rule-types rather than protected act-types.

I N *New York v. United States*,[1] the Supreme Court announced a new and highly significant constitutional doctrine: the anti-commandeering doctrine (Adler and Kreimer 1998; Caminker 1995, 1997; Hills 1998; Jackson 1998). The Court stated that "Congress may not simply . . . commandee[r] the legislative processes of the States by directly compelling them to enact and enforce a federal regulatory program,"[2] and it proceeded to invalidate a federal statute, the Low-Level Radioactive Waste Policy Amendments Act. Five years later, in *Printz v. United States*,[3] the Court confirmed and extended the anti-commandeering doctrine and relied upon it to strike down a second federal statute, the Brady Handgun Violence Prevention Act. The doctrine was at issue yet again in *Reno v. Condon*,[4] which, unlike *New York* and *Printz*, was a unanimous decision. The Court in *Condon* rejected an anti-commandeering challenge to the Drivers' Privacy Protection Act but, also unanimously, reaffirmed "the constitutional principles enunciated in *New York* and *Printz*."[5] In this article, I will explain the importance of the case law just described within our regime of constitutional federalism, and I will explore the grounds for applauding or deploring this new limitation on federal power.

OUR FEDERAL SYSTEM
AND ITS SOVEREIGN STATES

It is a shibboleth of the Court's recent federalism cases—not only the anti-commandeering cases but also commerce clause decisions such as *United States v. Lopez*[6] and *United States v. Morrison*[7] and sovereign immunity decisions such as *Seminole Tribe of Florida v. Florida*[8] and *Alden v. Maine*[9]—that in our constitutional system the state governments, and not merely the national government, are sovereigns. State sovereignty means more, I suggest, than the sheer existence of states. One can imagine a constitutional system in which geographically defined subdivisions, called "states," exist; in which the residents of each such subdivision are declared to be "citizens" of that state; in which citizens of each state are protected from discrimination by other states; in which the states have some important constitutional role, for example, in electing key officials in the national government; but in which (1) the national government is a government of unlimited, rather than limited and enumerated, powers, and further (2) the national government, in the exercise of these powers, is free to define the structure of state government and the rights and responsibilities of state officials, just as it is free to define the structure of national administrative agencies and the rights and responsibilities of the persons who staff those agencies (Rubin and Feeley 1994, 910-15). It would be counterintuitive to describe the states of this imaginary federal system as sovereign; and, in any event, these imaginary states do not have the features that the Supreme Court in *Printz, New York, Lopez, Seminole*

Tribe, and other such cases means to identify when it invokes the concept of state sovereignty.

Just as state sovereignty means more than the sheer existence of states, so it means less than sovereignty in the international-law sense (Rapaczynski 1985, 346-59). International sovereigns (nation-states) are coequal; no such sovereign is either legally subordinate, or legally supreme, to any other. Where the laws of two international sovereigns come into conflict, this clash is resolved by neutral choice-of-law rules that refer to the territorial locus of the relevant events, or the citizenry of the persons involved—not by a rule that gives automatic priority to the laws of one nation-state over those of another. If, for example, it were a principle of international choice-of-law that the laws of France always trumped the laws of Italy, then Italy would not be properly described as a full-fledged, international sovereign. But the U.S. Constitution contains, quite explicitly, a choice-of-law rule that gives automatic priority to the laws of the national government over state law (Gardbaum 1994, 770-73). Thus the supremacy clause of Article VI:

This Constitution, and the Laws of the United States which shall be made in Pursuance thereof . . . shall be the supreme Law of the Land; and the Judges in every State shall be bound thereby, any Thing in the Constitution or Laws of any State to the Contrary notwithstanding.

What might state sovereignty involve, if not full coequality with the national government, at one extreme, and the mere existence of the states, at the other? I have already hinted at the answer. First, states could be seen as sovereign in possessing governmental powers that are not held by the national government (Rapaczynski 1985, 350-51). For example, if a unitary national government would have the power to regulate all activities within the territorial confines of the nation that affect the welfare of its citizenry or some part thereof, the national government might be empowered to regulate only those activities with multistate welfare impacts—activities that affect the well-being of citizens from multiple states—while the power to regulate activities whose welfare effects are wholly intrastate would be reserved to the states. Second, states could be sovereign in holding certain rights or entitlements against duly empowered national action (Merritt 1988). The Constitution could grant the national government various powers (perhaps a wide set, perhaps a narrower subset) but then constrain the national government from exercising these powers in a way that infringed certain, constitutionally protected interests of the states, just as the First Amendment constrains the national government from exercising its powers in a way that infringes constitutionally protected interest of individuals in free speech.

A particularly robust scheme of state sovereignty would employ both these strategies, while a yet stronger scheme would employ both and then add the feature of judicial enforcement (Sager 1978); constitutional courts would be authorized to invalidate a federal statute that was unsupported by any power constitutionally granted to the national government or that was supported by some such power but nonetheless violated a state sovereignty constraint (Yoo 1997).

So much for hypothetical constitutions. What about our actual Constitution? First, does our Constitution limit the powers of the national government and reserve regulatory powers to the states? The answer—and it is hard to see how there could even be reasonable disagreement on this score—is yes. Article I, Section 8, enumerates the powers of Congress—most significantly the power set forth in the so-called commerce clause of Section 8, the power to "regulate Commerce with foreign Nations, and among the several States, and with the Indian Tribes." Implicit in the fact of enumeration, and explicit in the Tenth Amendment, is the proposition (1) that Congress cannot legitimately enact a statute unless the statute is grounded in some power-conferring clause contained in Article I, Section 8, or elsewhere in the Constitution, and the further proposition (2) that some federal statutes will fail to be thus grounded. Why not say that Article I, Section 8, embodies the Framers' view of the entire set of powers justifiably held by unitary governments—and that state legislation, like federal legislation, is unconstitutional unless grounded in some clause of Article I, Section 8? The Tenth Amendment clearly precludes this weird interpretation of that section. "The powers not

delegated to the United States by the Constitution . . . are reserved to the States." In short, there are at least some types of legislation (such as laws regulating wholly intrastate activities) that the Constitution permits states to enact but disempowers the national government from enacting.[10]

More controversial is whether the national-power-limiting feature of the Constitution should be enforced by the U.S. Supreme Court or the lower federal courts (Moulton 1999; Yoo 1997). It would be quite possible and, arguably, quite legitimate to have a system of judicial review where Article I, Section 8, challenges to federal legislation were simply nonjusticiable. Indeed, during the years between 1937 and the *Lopez* case, the Supreme Court uniformly rejected all such challenges (Tribe 2000, 811-17), and some sophisticated constitutional thinkers argued that this was proper: the federal courts should simply defer to Congress on the question of whether a national statute fell within the terms of a constitutionally enumerated power, or so it was and still is claimed (Wechsler 1954; Choper 1980). But the more ambitious claim—that Article I, Section 8, is unbounded or bounded only by a proper understanding of the powers that a unitary national state would possess—is very hard to swallow.

The states, then, are clearly sovereign in the limited-national-power sense. Are they also sovereign in the constrained-national-power sense? This is not an easy question. To begin, the Constitution is colorably interpreted as lacking any (nonminimal) state sovereignty constraint. And even if that interpretation is rejected, it remains quite unclear how we ought to delineate the contours of the (nonminimal) constraint—how we should distinguish between permitted and prohibited uses of the powers laid out in Article I, Section 8.

A STATE SOVEREIGNTY CONSTRAINT?

Let me start with the first point. Places in the constitutional text where the states are explicitly accorded rights against the national government are few in number and relatively minimal in importance—notably, Article I, Section 9's prohibition of federal taxes on exports from any state and of federal preferences for the ports of one state over another; Article IV, Section 3's ban on the creation of new states through the division or merger of old ones; and various references to the state legislatures, implying that Congress cannot validly abolish them. Further, I see nothing unreasonable or plainly wrong in a reading of the Constitution that envisions these as the only such constraints. Indeed, such a reading was seemingly adopted by the Court in 1985, in the *Garcia* case.[11] The question in *Garcia* was whether the Fair Labor Standards Act (FLSA), a national statute that regulates the hours and wages of employees, could constitutionally be applied to certain state employees as well as the employees of private firms. *Garcia* answered the question in the affirmative, thus overruling an earlier decision, *National League of*

Cities v. Usery,[12] in which the Court had held that considerations of state sovereignty barred the application of the FLSA to state employees.

The reader might wonder why Congress has the constitutional authority to prescribe minimum wages and maximum hours even for private firms, let alone for states and state subdivisions. The answer is that the post–New Deal Court has consistently interpreted the commerce clause as empowering congressional regulation of intrastate activities that "substantially affect" interstate commerce (Tribe 2000, 811-24). It was clear in *Garcia* that the application of the FLSA to the state employees at issue in the case satisfied this well-established test—and this was sufficient for constitutionality, in the Court's view. *Garcia* declined to find, in the Constitution, a state sovereignty constraint that would warrant the judicial invalidation of statutes satisfying the "substantial effect" test. The Court explained:

Apart from the limitation on federal authority inherent in the delegated nature of Congress' Article I powers, the principal means chosen by the Framers to ensure the role of the States in the federal system lies in the structure of the Federal Government itself. . . . The States were vested with indirect influence over the House of Representatives and the Presidency by their control of electoral qualifications and their role in Presidential elections. . . . They were given more direct influence in the Senate, where each State received equal representation and each Senator was to be selected by the legislature of his State. . . .

. . . against this background, we are convinced that the fundamental limitation that the constitutional scheme imposes on the Commerce Clause . . . is one of process [that is, the federal political process] rather than one of result.[13]

The excerpt from *Garcia* just quoted appears to adopt the view that the Constitution lacks any state sovereignty constraints (beyond the explicit and minimal constraints set forth in Article I, Section 9, and in Article IV, which the *Garcia* Court mentioned only in passing and presumably did not mean to disparage). Congress is constitutionally permitted to exercise its commerce clause powers in a way that changes the structure of state government, sets the qualifications for state officers, and so forth; the states are not shielded from these outcomes by constitutional guarantees, but rather by the structure of the national political process, which makes such outcomes unlikely. Elsewhere, the *Garcia* Court seems to take a different and less striking view: namely, that a state sovereignty constraint does or may exist but is unenforceable by courts.[14] Either way, the judicial outcome is the same: the Court in *Garcia* held that no enforceable state sovereignty constraint barred the application of the FLSA to state employees, and it more generally suggested that considerations of state sovereignty would never (or almost never)[15] warrant judicial invalidation of those federal statutes that Article I, Section 8, empowered Congress to enact.

This is the backdrop for the anti-commandeering decisions, *New York* and *Printz*. The statutory provision struck down in *New York* basically required each state's legislature to en-act legislation providing for the disposal of low-level radioactive waste produced within that state. Crucially, the Court held that this provision was permissible under the substantial-effect test but nonetheless invalidated the provision as an unconstitutional "commandeering" of state legislatures. *Printz* extended *New York* by holding that the anti-commandeering doctrine protected the executive branch of state government as well as the state's legislature. The Brady Act, in relevant part, required certain state law enforcement officials to take "reasonable" steps to investigate the legality of pending gun sales. Such a requirement violated state sovereignty, or so the Court in *Printz* opined.

We held in *New York* that Congress cannot compel the states to enact . . . a federal regulatory program. Today we hold that Congress cannot circumvent that prohibition by conscripting the State's officers directly. The Federal Government may neither issue directives requiring the States to address particular problems, nor command the States' officers, or those of their political subdivisions, to administer or enforce a federal regulatory program. . . . such commands are fundamentally incompatible with our constitutional system of dual sovereignty.[16]

THE ANTI-COMMANDEERING DOCTRINE

What is commandeering? Paradigmatically, commandeering occurs when Congress imposes a duty of legislation upon state legislatures or a duty of enforcement upon the state executive branch. More generally, it seems, the Court in *Printz* and *New*

York means to preclude federal statutes that have the following characteristics: (1) the statutes are targeted at state legislative or executive officials, rather than being generally applicable both to private parties and to state officials; (2) the statutes impose coercive duties upon state legislative or executive officials (by contrast, for example, with statutes that merely require certain actions by these officials as a condition for state receipt of federal moneys); and (3) the statues impose affirmative duties on the state officials, duties of action, rather than negative duties, duties of inaction (Adler and Kreimer 1998, 74-95).

As for the constitutional status of the anti-commandeering rule, there are two possible readings of *New York* and *Printz*. According to the first reading, the anti-commandeering rule is a constitutional "constraint" (in the sense I have been discussing): a prohibition on targeted, coercive, and affirmative federal duties that is additional to, and separate from, the requirement that federal legislation be grounded in an Article I, Section 8, power. On this reading, the anti-commandeering rule is analogous to the First Amendment, or the explicit constraint on export taxes set out in Article I, Section 9. According to the second reading of *New York* and *Printz*, the anti-commandeering rule is not a separate such requirement but instead is an internal limitation on the scope of the commerce clause. On this reading, the substantial-effect doctrine is only one part of the test for deciding whether a statute is empowered by the commerce clause.

The full test runs as follows: the federal statute must (1) regulate an activity with a substantial effect on interstate commerce and (2) not constitute a commandeering of state officers.

I am inclined to adopt the first reading of *New York* and *Printz*; the anti-commandeering rule is best understood, I think, as a constraint on the commerce power rather than an internal limitation. The constraint view is better supported by the text of the commerce clause. The clause empowers Congress to "regulate Commerce . . . among the Several States," which (together with the necessary and proper clause of Article I, Section 8, Clause 18) leads to the substantial-effect test rather than the more complicated disjunctive test posited by the internal-limitation view. Further, the internal-limitation view gives rise to two structural problems that are avoided by the constraint view:

1. According to the internal-limitation view, if Congress is prohibited from exercising any of its Article I, Section 8, powers to impose affirmative, targeted, and coercive duties on the states (as presumably Congress is), then the no-commandeering rule shows up as a second clause in each of the Article I, Section 8, doctrines; this creates not only unnecessary complexity but also the risk that the substance of the anti-commandeering prohibition might vary from clause to clause within Article I, Section 8.

2. The powers set forth in Article I, Section 8, can be seen to embody or reflect prima facie justifications for

federal lawmaking—for example, the federal government is prima facie justified in regulating interstate activities, since such activities have multistate welfare impacts—which must be balanced against the countervailing considerations that are set forth elsewhere in the Constitution (for example, in the Bill of Rights) or are implicit in the Constitution's overall design, and which may render a particular instance of federal lawmaking unjustified, all things considered. The internal-limitation view muddies this understanding of constitutional powers by construing the commerce clause to incorporate both a prima facie justification for federal lawmaking (the existence of a substantial effect on interstate commerce) and one but not all of the countervailing considerations that may undermine a particular federal law.

I therefore interpret *Printz* and *New York* as (re)establishing an enforceable and nonminimal state sovereignty constraint. I say "(re)establishing" because some such constraint had been intermittently recognized by the Court during earlier periods of constitutional law, albeit not in the specific shape of the anti-commandeering rule. The pre–New Deal Court repeatedly invoked state sovereignty to invalidate federal taxation of state institutions or officers (Tribe 2000, 861-62, 866-67). State sovereignty was not an important consideration in the post–New Deal case law prior to *National League of Cities*. That case set forth a constraint (or perhaps an internal limitation on the commerce clause)

prohibiting federal action that impaired the states' ability to "structure integral operations in areas of traditional governmental functions" and that satisfied a few other criteria.[17] But the Court found it difficult to specify the content of the "traditional governmental function" constraint (Tribe 2000, 863-73), and *National League of Cities* was overruled by *Garcia*. A decade later, in *New York* and then *Printz*, the Court shifted course once more and established the anti-commandeering rule. These cases did not overrule *Garcia*, since the statute upheld there was not commandeering (the duties it imposed were generally applicable to state and private actors alike, rather than being targeted at the states), but *New York* and *Printz* did depart from the general view about state sovereignty articulated in *Garcia*, the view that the Constitution creates no enforceable (and nonminimal) state sovereignty constraint. Even if I am incorrect in construing the anti-commandeering rule as a constraint rather than an internal limitation on the scope of the commerce clause, *New York* and *Printz* remain highly significant cases since in either event they (re)introduce state sovereignty as a consideration that can prompt judicial invalidation of national statutes satisfying the substantial-effect test.

IS THE ANTI-COMMANDEERING DOCTRINE JUSTIFIED?

Are *New York* and *Printz* rightly decided? One line of criticism denies the existence of any state sovereignty constraint, beyond the constraints explicitly set forth in the text of the Constitution. This view, as I have already said, is a colorable one. The view is colorable because it flows from a colorable theory of constitutional interpretation, namely, textualism. The textualist insists that constitutional rights, powers, duties, constraints, and other elements of the legal structure that we call constitutional law derive from the text of the Constitution. More precisely, the textualist (as I am using that term) insists that constitutional rights, powers, duties, and so on derive from the text of the Constitution with a fairly high degree of clarity and determinacy—paradigmatically, by flowing from discrete and reasonably specific constitutional clauses (Bork 1990). A right, power, and so forth that cannot be linked to a discrete such clause—like the anti-commandeering rule or, more generally, any nonminimal state sovereignty constraint—is suspect.

I am skeptical of textualism, for reasons developed at length by the various scholars who have advanced non-textualist accounts of constitutional interpretation (Brest 1980; Dworkin 1977; Fallon 1987; Grey 1975; Perry 1982; Richards 1989). Some constitutional issues simply cannot be determinately resolved by the text of the Constitution. (For example, the fundamental, methodological debate between textualists and non-textualists cannot be thus resolved. Even if the Constitution were to contain a pro-textualism clause, the non-textualist could legitimately ask why the clause should be binding, and the textualist would

have to answer that question through general political and moral argument.) Many other constitutional issues are not, in fact, determinately resolved by the text of our Constitution. To give two famous examples: *Marbury v. Madison*[18] held that the Supreme Court had the power of judicial review, even though no discrete clause in the Constitution creates such a power; and the right of privacy recognized in *Griswold v. Connecticut*[19] was located by the Court in the "penumbra" of the Bill of Rights, since there is no separable language in the Bill of Rights or elsewhere from which a privacy right could be said readily to derive. Even those constitutional rights, powers, and so forth that do derive from separable constitutional clauses often are not *determinately* derivable. For example, the connection between existing free speech doctrine, or equal protection doctrine, and the language of the First Amendment, or the equal protection clause, is highly indeterminate and contestable.

If textualism is, indeed, an incorrect account of constitutional interpretation, why think that state sovereignty constraints are limited to those minimal constraints set forth in Article I, Section 9, and in Article IV? The Constitution, read as a whole, suggests that the states are political communities: they have "legislatures" (for example, Article I, Section 4) and "citizens" (for example, Article IV, Section 2), and their powers are guaranteed by the Constitution itself, rather than being delegated and revocable by Congress. States are vehicles for political participation and democratic self-governance; all this is a reasonable inference from the text of the Constitution and from constitutional history (Friedman 1997, 389-94; Jackson 1998, 2221; Merritt 1988, 7-8; McConnell 1987, 1507-11; Rapaczynski 1985, 395-408; Shapiro 1995, 139). Imagine a federal law that pursues a legitimate federal end (thus falling within an Article I, Section 8, power) and does not run afoul of the explicit state sovereignty constraints but pursues its legitimate federal end in a way that subverts—deeply subverts—the character of states as political communities. (For example, imagine a federal law that requires Louisiana citizens to vote in favor of amending their state constitution to eliminate a provision that has hindered commercial ties between Louisiana and other states.) Why insist that such a law is constitutionally valid? Assume the *Garcia* Court was correct in its claim that states are well represented in the national political process (Wechsler 1954). It does not follow that the national political process is constitutionally unconstrained, qua state sovereignty. Presumably, the states are given a special role in the national political process just because they are sovereign, and the recognition of an implicit, nonjusticiable state sovereignty constraint would not function to truncate the national political process.

The key word in the last sentence is "nonjusticiable." A justiciable—judicially enforceable—state sovereignty constraint would truncate the national political process, since the question of whether a given statute violated that constraint would be

finally resolved by the Supreme Court rather than Congress. *Garcia's* political-process argument is best seen as an argument for the unenforceability of state sovereignty constraints rather than for their nonexistence. But is the argument, thus understood, a persuasive one? I think not. The Constitution does indeed structure the national political process in a way that is protective of states. Yet the most salient such feature—the election of senators on a state-by-state basis—does not protect state institutions. Rather, it serves to advance the shared interests of those persons who reside in each state; it makes each such collectivity a potent "interest" group (Kramer 2000, 221-27). If a senator can maximize the satisfaction of his constituents' interests through federal legislation that interferes with state governments—for example, by commandeering state officers, as did the Brady Act—he will vote in favor of that legislation.[20] Other constitutional provisions give state legislators some role in national politics, for example, in designing congressional electoral districts. Here, too, it is questionable whether the states qua political communities are significantly protected (Kramer 2000, 226-27). First, the role of state legislators in shaping the national government has significantly diminished over the last century; state legislators no longer choose senators (as they did prior to the Seventeenth Amendment) and, as a result of the Court's voting rights jurisprudence, are much less free to shape electoral districts. Second, a state legislator will presumably use his various constitutionally allocated powers to maximize the satisfaction of *his* constituents' interests and therewith his own chances of reelection. Whether a reelection-maximizing state legislator is likely to advance, or impair, state sovereignty is an open question.

I thus believe that *Printz* and *New York* were correct to recognize *some* enforceable state sovereignty constraint not derivable from discrete constitutional clauses.[21] The cases are, on this level, rightly decided. But they remain vulnerable to a different, less sweeping criticism, namely, that considerations of state sovereignty justify some enforceable rule other than an anti-commandeering rule (Jackson 1998, 2246-59).

ALTERNATIVE FORMULATIONS
FOR A STATE SOVEREIGNTY
CONSTRAINT

To begin, there is plenty of evidence that the Framers of the Constitution intended to recognize sovereign states—genuine political communities, not merely subdivisions of the national government—but no strong evidence that they intended to implement notions of state sovereignty through an anti-commandeering rule. The putative historical case for that rule, set forth by the Court in *Printz*, is unpersuasive (Caminker 1995, 1042-50; 1997, 209-12). To be sure, the anti-commandeering rule would be constitutionally justified, even absent strong textual or historical grounding, if it were the case that the concept of state sovereignty implied such a rule; but this is not the case, as Professor Seth Kreimer and I recently argued

at length in an article entitled "The New Etiquette of Federalism: *New York, Printz* and *Yeskey*" (Adler and Kreimer 1998). We there tried to show that the distinctions central to the anti-commandeering rule— between permissible negative duties and impermissible affirmative ones; between the permissible enactment of generally applicable laws and the impermissible targeting of the states; between permissible encouragement of state officials to take action and the impermissible coercion of such officials; between the permissible imposition of targeted, coercive, affirmative duties on state judges and the impermissible imposition of such duties on state legislators and executive officials—are not *relevant* distinctions in light of federalism values and, specifically, in light of the states' status as political communities.

Consider the affirmative-negative distinction. The anti-commandeering rule prohibits the federal government from coercing state legislators or executive officials to enact or enforce a particular law, but it does not prohibit the federal government from coercing state legislators or executive officials to refrain from enacting or refrain from enforcing a law. Why the difference? In either event, the state officials and, derivatively, the state citizenry are deprived of a policy choice. Absent federal intervention, the state may choose between regulating a given activity and leaving it unregulated. Impermissible federal commandeering deprives the state of the deregulatory option; the permissible imposition of negative federal duties deprives the states of the regulatory option. But the concept of state sovereignty is not biased toward deregulation; each type of federal intervention reduces the state's vitality and autonomy as a political community. Kreimer and I flesh out this analysis in "The New Etiquette" and present parallel critiques of the coercion-encouragement, targeted–generally applicable, and judge-legislator or executive distinctions.

What are the alternatives to the anti-commandeering rule? Consider some possibilities. First, the Supreme Court and lower federal courts might simply decide, on a case-by-case basis, whether a particular federal statute seriously undermined state sovereignty or political community; the concepts of state sovereignty and political community could play a direct role in constitutional adjudication, rather than being translated into doctrinal rules like the anti-commandeering rule or *National League of Cities*' "traditional governmental function" rule. Such rules are more determinate, and easier to apply, than the underlying concepts, but precisely for that reason the rules are not completely faithful to the concepts; some federal statutes that are genuinely violations of state sovereignty will be permissible under a given rule, and vice versa. Second, the Court could put in place a rule different from the anti-commandeering rule. The subsequent history of *National League of Cities* impeaches the "traditional governmental function" rule, but it is hardly the case that this is the only rule-based alternative to *Printz* and *New York*. Some commentators have

suggested that the Court should invalidate federal statutes that change the structure of state governments, as opposed to statutes that merely impose duties on (or otherwise induce action or inaction by) state officials (Tribe 2000, 912-20). Paradigmatic would be federal statutes (enacted under the commerce clause, as opposed to Congress's special power to enforce the Fourteenth and Fifteenth Amendments) that specified state voting qualifications or electoral districts, the size of the state legislature, the procedures for legislation, or the separation of powers between the legislature and the state's executive branch (Merritt 1988, 37-55).

Perhaps the structural-nonstructural distinction would prove as ineffable as the distinction between traditional and nontraditional state functions. If so, a more specific rule or set of rules might be crafted that distinguished between those processes and institutions that are central to the democratic self-governance of the state (the voting process, the legislature) and those processes and institutions that are less central. Consider, for example, a doctrine that prohibited Congress from imposing any duties (positive or negative) on state legislators, on the state governor (insofar as he or she has a role in the legislative process), or on state voters but permitted the imposition of any duties (positive or negative) on state enforcement officials or judges. Such a rule would be no more difficult to apply than the anti-commandeering rule; it would cohere with the supremacy clause (since the state officials who apply state law to particular cases—that is, enforcement officials or judges—would in any case of conflict between federal and state law give effect to the federal law); and it would better effectuate the underlying concept of state sovereignty than the anti-commandeering rule, since it would leave the state's legislative process entirely unconstrained by federal statutory law.

I believe, then, that the Court's adoption of the anti-commandeering rule in *Printz* and *New York* was mistaken; but let me also emphasize that this was not an obvious or clear error. *Printz* and *New York* are not only significant decisions, for reinstating a nonminimal state sovereignty constraint within enforceable constitutional doctrine. They are also hard decisions, hard because the doctrinal specification of state sovereignty is subtle and difficult—as the tortuous path from the immediate post–New Deal period, to *National League of Cities*, to *Garcia*, and finally to *Printz* and *New York* demonstrates. Note that there has been no comparable vacillation in defining the basic structure of many other constitutional doctrines, such as equal protection doctrine (which since the New Deal has been grounded on the prohibition against discrimination) or free speech doctrine.

Is the game worth the candle? Does the vacillation amount to a persuasive argument for the non-enforcement of the state sovereignty constraint—an argument more cogent than the political-process argument sketched in *Garcia*—namely, that the Supreme Court is incompetent to specify the content of state sovereignty? I think not. The issue is not absolute but relative competence (Komesar 1994), and I see no reason why Congress is best positioned to decide the hard issues posed in the anti-commandeering cases. The Court should, I suggest, continue to struggle with the meaning of state sovereignty; and the decisions in *Printz* and *New York* mean that the Court will continue thus to struggle, at least for now.

Notes

1. 505 U.S. 144 (1992).
2. Id. at 161.
3. 521 U.S. 898 (1997).
4. 120 S. Ct. 666 (2000).
5. Id. at 672. An important recent case closely related to *New York*, *Printz*, and *Condon* is *Alden v. Maine*, 527 U.S. 706 (1999), in which the Court grounded so-called sovereign immunity doctrine—a doctrine that shields the states from lawsuits—in unwritten constitutional principles of state sovereignty rather than in the text of the Eleventh Amendment. Space limitations prevent me from discussing in this article sovereign immunity doctrine and its interesting connections to the anti-commandeering doctrine.
6. 514 U.S. 549 (1995).
7. 120 S. Ct. 1740 (2000).
8. 517 U.S. 44 (1996).
9. 527 U.S. 706 (1999).
10. See, for example, *Morrison*, 120 S. Ct. at 1754 ("The Constitution requires a distinction between what is truly national and what is truly local.... The regulation and punishment of intrastate violence that is not directed at the instrumentalities, channels, or goods involved in interstate commerce has always been the province of the States.").
11. *Garcia v. San Antonio Metro. Transit Auth.*, 469 U.S. 528 (1985).
12. 426 U.S. 833 (1976).
13. *Garcia*, 469 U.S. at 550-51, 554.
14. See id. at 547.
15. See id. at 556.
16. *Printz*, 521 U.S. at 935.
17. *Garcia*, 469 U.S. at 537.

18. 5 U.S. (1 Cranch) 137 (1803).

19. 381 U.S. 479 (1965).

20. More precisely, senators can be predicted to be responsive to the politically mobilized or organized segments of the state citizenry, rather than to the state citizenry as a whole. This qualification does not change the basic point here, that the state-by-state election of senators does not function to safeguard the sovereignty of state governments.

21. I do not have the space here to fully defend this view. I have just sketched a rebuttal to *Garcia*'s argument for the nonjusticiability of state sovereignty constraints; but there are other plausible arguments for non-justiciability (Kramer 2000), and a full defense of the claim that such constraints should be judicially enforced would need to rebut these arguments.

References

Adler, Matthew D. and Seth F. Kreimer. 1998. The New Etiquette of Federalism: *New York*, *Printz* and *Yeskey*. *Supreme Court Review* 1998:71-143.

Bork, Robert. 1990. *The Tempting of America: The Political Seduction of the Law*. New York: Free Press.

Brest, Paul. 1980. The Misconceived Quest for the Original Understanding. *Boston University Law Review* 60:204-38.

Caminker, Evan H. 1995. State Sovereignty and Subordinacy: May Congress Commandeer State Officers to Implement Federal Law? *Columbia Law Review* 95:1001-89.

———. 1997. Printz, State Sovereignty, and the Limits of Formalism. *Supreme Court Review* 1997:199-248.

Choper, Jesse H. 1980. *Judicial Review and the National Political Process*. Chicago: University of Chicago Press.

Dworkin, Ronald. 1977. *Taking Rights Seriously*. Cambridge, MA: Harvard University Press.

Fallon, Richard H., Jr. 1987. A Constructivist Coherence Theory of Constitutional Interpretation. *Harvard Law Review* 100:1189-286.

Friedman, Barry. 1997. Valuing Federalism. *Minnesota Law Review* 82: 317-412.

Gardbaum, Stephen A. 1994. The Nature of Preemption. *Cornell Law Review* 79:767-815.

Grey, Thomas C. 1975. Do We Have an Unwritten Constitution? *Stanford Law Review* 27:703-18.

Hills, Roderick M., Jr. 1998. The Political Economy of Cooperative Federalism: Why State Autonomy Makes Sense and "Dual Sovereignty" Doesn't. *Michigan Law Review* 96:813-944.

Jackson, Vicki C. 1998. Federalism and the Uses and Limits of Law: Printz and Principle? *Harvard Law Review* 111:2180-259.

Komesar, Neil K. 1994. *Imperfect Alternatives: Choosing Institutions in Law, Economics, and Public Policy*. Chicago: University of Chicago Press.

Kramer, Larry D. 2000. Putting the Politics Back into the Political Safeguards of Federalism. *Columbia Law Review* 100:215-93.

McConnell, Michael W. 1987. Federalism: Evaluating the Founders' Design. *University of Chicago Law Review* 54: 1484-512.

Merritt, Deborah Jones. 1988. The Guarantee Clause and State Autonomy: Federalism for a Third Century. *Columbia Law Review* 88:1-78.

Moulton, H. Geoffrey. 1999. The Quixotic Search for a Judicially Enforceable Federalism. *Minnesota Law Review* 83:849-925.

Perry, Michael J. 1982. *The Constitution, the Courts and Human Rights*. New Haven, CT: Yale University Press.

Rapaczynski, Andrzej. 1985. From Sovereignty to Process: The Jurisprudence of Federalism After Garcia. *Supreme Court Review* 1985:341-419.

Richards, David A. J. 1989. *Foundations of American Constitutionalism*. New York: Oxford University Press.

Rubin, Edward L. and Malcolm Feeley. 1994. Federalism: Some Notes on a National Neurosis. *UCLA Law Review* 41:903-52.

Sager, Lawrence Gene. 1978. Fair Measure: The Legal Status of Underenforced Constitutional Norms. *Harvard Law Review* 91:1212-64.

Shapiro, David L. 1995. *Federalism: A Dialogue*. Evanston, IL: Northwestern University Press.

Tribe, Laurence H. 2000. *American Constitutional Law*. 3rd ed. Vol. 1. New York: Foundation Press.

Wechsler, Herbert. 1954. The Political Safeguards of Federalism: The Role of the States in the Composition and Selection of the National Government. *Columbia Law Review* 54:543-60.

Yoo, John C. 1997. The Judicial Safeguards of Federalism. *Southern California Law Review* 70:1311-406.

State Autonomy in Germany and the United States

By DANIEL HALBERSTAM and RODERICK M. HILLS, JR.

ABSTRACT: Both the United States and the Federal Republic of Germany have mechanisms by which their component jurisdictions—states or *Länder*—can either implement federal law or resist such implementation. The authors describe the different constitutional mechanisms by which the two federal regimes induce state cooperation and protect state autonomy. They then offer some speculations as to how such constitutional rules might affect cooperative federalism in the two nations, arguing that the German system provides more categorical and therefore more secure protection of the *Länder*, whereas the U.S. system provides for a more flexible system of cooperative federalism. This flexibility of the U.S. system, the authors suggest, allows for vertical competition between the federal government and the states, which may provide a valuable tool to combat inefficiency in policy implementation.

Daniel Halberstam is assistant professor of law at the University of Michigan Law School, specializing in U.S. constitutional law and European Union law. He clerked for Justice David H. Souter of the U.S. Supreme Court and Judge Patricia M. Wald of the Court of Appeals for the D.C. Circuit, served as judicial fellow to Judge Peter Jann of the European Court of Justice, and was attorney advisor in the Office of Legal Counsel at the U.S. Department of Justice.

Roderick M. Hills, Jr., is professor of law at the University of Michigan Law School, specializing in U.S. constitutional law, local government law, the law of federalism and intergovernmental relations, and land-use regulation. Prior to joining the Michigan faculty, he clerked for Judge Patrick Higginbotham of the U.S. Court of Appeals for the Fifth Circuit and practiced law in Colorado.

I N his dissent in the 1995 decision of *Printz v. United States*,[1] Justice Breyer embarked on a rare judicial excursion into comparative constitutional law. *Printz* held that the federal government could not require state governments' executive officials to regulate private persons according to federal standards. The decision extended the 1992 holding of *New York v. United States*,[2] which held that the federal government could not commandeer the state legislature by requiring the state to enact a program for the storage of privately generated nuclear waste. Thus, after *New York* and *Printz*, state governments may refuse to comply with the federal government's commands that state and local governments regulate private persons according to federal standards. We will call this power of state and local governments the "*Printz* entitlement."

In his criticism of the *Printz* entitlement, Justice Breyer argued that the experience of other federal regimes showed that it was not necessary for protecting federalism. As Justice Breyer observed, "The federal systems of Switzerland, Germany, and the European Union, for example, all provide that constituent states, not federal bureaucracies, will themselves implement many of the laws, rules, regulations, or decrees enacted by the central 'federal' body."[3] As Justice Breyer observed, these federal regimes give their component states the power but also the obligation to execute federal policy "because they believe that such a system interferes less, not more, with the independent authority of the 'state,' member nation, or other subsidiary government, and helps to safeguard individual liberty as well."[4] This comparison with foreign constitutional regimes led Justice Breyer to ask the majority a pointed question: "Why, or how, would what the majority sees as a constitutional alternative—the creation of a new federal . . . bureaucracy, or the expansion of an existing federal bureaucracy—better promote either state sovereignty or individual liberty?"[5]

This article attempts to take up Justice Breyer's question by comparing U.S. and German constitutional rules regarding state autonomy. In part 1 of this article, we will lay out some of the essential U.S. and German constitutional doctrines that define how cooperative federalism operates in the two regimes. In part 2, we will suggest that one can fruitfully compare the U.S. and German systems of cooperative federalism to evaluate how each set of constitutional entitlements to states (or *Länder*) affects how these component governments implement policies of the federal government. Although differences in political culture make such comparisons hazardous, we will tentatively suggest ways in which (1) the German system provides greater protection for state independence in implementing federal law but (2) the U.S. system avoids some of the problems of inefficiency familiar from the German experience.

I. COOPERATIVE FEDERALISM: GERMAN AND AMERICAN SYSTEMS COMPARED

According to an oft-repeated cliché, the German and American systems of federalism are radically different from each other. The Germans divide power between federation and *Länder* vertically, giving the federation the primary prerogative of enacting legislation and the *Länder* the prerogative of executing such legislation. By contrast, the U.S. Constitution is said to divide powers horizontally, giving the federal government and the states separate legislative jurisdictions in which each can enact and execute their own distinct policies free from interference from the other.

This conventional contrast between the German and American systems of federalism, however, is misleading. At least since the U.S. Supreme Court decided *Wickard v. Filburn*[6] in 1942, the U.S. Constitution has not reserved much exclusive jurisdiction to state governments to legislate free from federal interference. Moreover, since the New Deal, the U.S. government has enlisted the states to play the primary executive role in implementing dozens of important federal programs, including unemployment insurance, poverty assistance, environmental protection, worker health and safety, public housing, community development, maintenance and construction of interstate highways, and so on. This is not to say that the German and American systems of cooperative federalism do not differ in important ways. Indeed, there are three salient differences that merit discussion.

First, the Grundgesetz (the German Constitution, or Basic Law) provides for the formal representation of state governments in the federal legislative process through the Bundesrat. Each *Land* government sends members of its cabinet to represent the interests of the *Land* in the Bundesrat. As these officials are simultaneously delegates to the Bundesrat and officers of the *Land* government and can be instructed and recalled by the *Land* government, their representation of *Land* interests is more direct than the U.S. senator's representation of state interests even prior to the ratification of the Seventeenth Amendment, when senators were chosen (but not instructed or recallable) by state legislatures. In return for this closer representation of the *Länder* governments in the Bundesrat, however, the German framers of the Grundgesetz who favored federalism had to limit the jurisdiction of the Bundesrat (Golay 1958, 50). The Bundesrat does not have the same capacity as the U.S. Senate to stop federal legislation but instead can veto only those laws that affect the administrative duties of the *Länder*.

Since the ratification of the Seventeenth Amendment (and probably before then as well), the American states have lacked any such direct and formal power to veto collectively federal laws imposing administrative duties on states. The *Printz* entitlement, however, gives them an analogous power: the power of individual states to refuse to implement federal statutes within that state's borders. The *Printz* entitlement could be characterized as a more individualistic version of the Bundesrat: whereas the Bundesrat gives the *Länder* the power *collectively* to veto federal imposition of administrative duties on the *Länder*, the *Printz* entitlement gives each *individual* state a similar power to veto federal administrative duties. One could regard these two regimes as legal formalizations of the individual and collective strategies of "political localism" described by Edward Page (1991, 42-44).

The second respect in which the German and U.S. constitutional rules regarding cooperative federalism differ is that, apart from those areas enumerated in Article 87 in the Grundgesetz in which the federation must maintain its own implementing bureaucracy, the Grundgesetz gives the *Länder* a monopoly on the implementation of federal law, either as the agents of the federation or as a matter of their own concern. The federation can take measures to ensure that the *Länder* execute federal laws faithfully, but, when the *Länder* execute such laws as a matter of their own concern, the measures available to the federation are strictly limited by Grundgesetz Article 84. In particular, the federation cannot create its own federal field offices or send commissioners to any but the highest *Länder* authorities without the consent of the Bundesrat.

The United States gives Congress a different weapon by which to induce faithful state implementation of federal law. Since at least *McCulloch v. Maryland*,[7] the United States has the constitutional power to create an unlimited array of federal agencies to implement federal law. Under no obligation to involve the states at all in the implementation of federal laws, Congress may bypass the states entirely if they do not carry out federal laws in the manner demanded by Congress, using agencies designed according to Congress's specifications. In addition, Congress may condition a state's continued ability to regulate in a given area on that state's assistance in the implementation of federal regulatory policies.[8] Thus Congress can secure state cooperation whenever (1) Congress can make a credible threat to preempt state law by creating a federal agency to regulate a field in place of the states unless the states regulate according to federal standards and (2) state politicians value the right to continue the state's regulatory presence in the preemptible field more than they dislike the conditions that Congress places upon their continued presence in that field. Finally, Congress may also condition a state's receipt of federal funds on that state's regulating according to federal standards and will secure state assistance as long as state politicians value the federal funds more than they dislike the federal conditions (Hills 1998).

A third difference between the U.S. and German systems of federalism is that the *Länder* have much more limited capacity to initiate their own tax and regulatory policies absent federal authorization, because the German doctrine of field preemption is broader than the analogous American doctrine. Article 72(1) of the Grundgesetz provides that *Länder* may exercise concurrent powers "only so long as and to the extent that the federation does not exercise its right to legislate." This provision has been construed to forbid the *Länder* from imposing taxes that are also imposed by the federation (Isensee and Kirchhof 1990). As a result, Article 106 of the Grundgesetz precisely specifies the taxes that each level of government can impose, leaving the *Länder* with the relatively unimportant sources of revenue enumerated in Article 106(2) (Currie 1994, 53-54).

This is not to say that the *Länder* are financially impoverished, because Article 106(3) provides that revenue from income, corporation, and sales taxes shall be shared by both the federation and the *Länder*. Such taxes are imposed only with the consent of both *Länder* (through the Bundesrat under Grundgesetz Article 105(3)) and federation, however, with the result that no single *Land* can generate much revenue through its own solitary efforts. Aside from the strict limit on taxing authority, the *Länder* are fiscally hobbled by Article 107(2) of the Grundgesetz, which imposes a requirement of *Finanzausgleich*, or financial equalization between rich and poor *Länder*, requiring wealthy *Länder* to provide financial assistance to poorer *Länder* to ensure substantial equality of living conditions and state resources (Larsen 1999). Both provisions limit the capacity of *Länder* to generate own-source revenue or, if they can generate such revenue, to retain it. In the United States, by contrast, states are permitted to levy any tax concurrently with the federal government so long as the federal government does not expressly preempt such taxation and so long as the tax complies with fairly lenient constitutional limits (for example, the tax must not be legally incident on, or discriminate against, a federal agency and must not discriminate against or unduly burden interstate or international commerce). As a result, states have much more flexibility to come up with and retain extra money through state-imposed taxes in the United States than the *Länder* do in Germany.

In the U.S. system, aside from greater powers of concurrent taxation, the states also have greater capacity than the *Länder* have in Germany to regulate private activity when federal law does not expressly preempt such law. This is not to say that there is no implied or field preemption in U.S. jurisprudence. However, the U.S. Supreme Court strains to avoid constructions of federal law that result in the preemption of state law, with the result that states can frequently regulate activities even when those activities are already subject to comprehensive and pervasive federal regulatory schemes.[9] By contrast, Article 72(1) of the Grundgesetz bars the *Länder* from regulating in fields where the federation has exercised its right to legislate, which appears to imply a broader notion of field preemption. The *Länder* can thus be ousted from regulating in a field simply by the fact that the federation enacted a statute that also regulates such a field. Indeed, until the constitutional amendments of 1994, *Länder* were barred from regulating as soon as the federation commenced its lawmaking process. Even under the new version of Article 72(1), the federal law need only be enacted as law and need not have become effective to preempt *Land* legislation in the area (Degenhart 1996). As a result, it may be more difficult for *Länder* than for American states to supplement federal regulatory schemes with their own more activist versions of such regulation.

II. THE PRACTICAL EFFECTS OF DIFFERENT CONSTITUTIONAL STRUCTURES

We will suggest that two general consequences plausibly follow from the differences in constitutional structure. We stress that these are tentative hypotheses that can be confirmed only through more careful empirical work. Indeed, it is quite possible that the effects of, for example, the political culture or the political party system overpower any appreciable effects of constitutional structure. To the extent that the constitutional structure has practical effects, however, we speculate that (1) the U.S. system of federalism is likely to provide states with less effective protection from the federal government than the Grundgesetz provides to the *Länder* but (2) the German protections for the *Länder*

arguably impose a greater cost than the American system in terms of efficient and flexible administration of national laws.

Our first hypothesis is that the *Printz* entitlement is likely to be less effective in protecting state autonomy than the structures created by the Grundgesetz. There are two reasons for this inference. First, the *Printz* entitlement will provide little practical benefit to state governments if the federal government can easily bypass the state governments by federalizing activities using purely federal agencies. In such a case, as several scholars have noted, the state governments would enjoy a useless autonomy, because their fields for autonomous activity would be preempted. Justice Breyer seems to endorse this view when he suggests that the alternative to commandeering is "the creation of a new federal . . . bureaucracy, or the expansion of an existing federal bureaucracy."[10] The *Printz* entitlement poses no direct obstacles to such bypass of the states and preemption of state law. By contrast, Articles 83- 86 of the Grundgesetz give the *Länder* the right and duty to administer all federal policies not enumerated in Article 87, making it impossible for the federal government to bypass the *Länder*.

Second, the *Printz* entitlement gives states only an individual rather than collective veto: each state has the power to refuse to implement federal regulation of private persons within its own borders. The exercise of such a power by a single state is likely to be politically difficult because, by declining to implement federal policy, the state's voters would forfeit federal grant revenue while still paying the same federal taxes that would finance the federal program in acquiescing states. The payment of federal taxes for the benefit of neighboring states is not likely to be a political winner (Baker 1995). By contrast, the Grundgesetz gives the *Länder* a collective veto over federal policy in the form of the Bundesrat: if the *Länder* exercise this veto, then the federal policy is not implemented in any *Land*. The *Länder* that oppose a federal policy through the Bundesrat, therefore, need not fear that the policy will give a competitive advantage to those *Länder* that do not oppose it. In this sense, the Bundesrat functions as something like a legally protected cartel of the *Länder* from which defection is impossible.

We do not wish to overstate the barriers to the effective use of the *Printz* entitlement. The states have some compensating legal advantages that may mitigate the risk that the federal government will implement federal laws with federal agencies whenever states exercise their *Printz* entitlement. In particular, field preemption in the United States appears to be narrower than German field preemption with the consequence that, compared to the German *Länder*, states under the U.S. Constitution appear to retain broader powers to initiate policies that supplement federal laws and federal revenues even when Congress is deadlocked over controversial policy proposals.[11]

The states may exploit this power to initiate programs as a practical means to counteract Congress's constitutional authority to federalize policy areas. For example, before Congress generates enough political will to legislate in any given area, states may step into the field with their own policy proposals. One result is that state policy initiatives may be quite influential in the federal lawmaking process by providing the initial impetus and sometimes even blueprint for federal action (Elliot, Ackerman, and Millian 1985). To bypass or overrule the states, not only must Congress often demonstrate that its proposed regulatory scheme is politically desirable, but it must do so by arguing specifically against the continued existence of active state regulation.

It is not surprising, therefore, that when Congress enters new policy areas, the resulting federal statutes pay substantial deference to the existing state schemes and often carve out a special place for them in the federal scheme. Consider, for instance, the Clean Air Act's accommodation of California's more stringent automobile emission standards[12] or the federal Unemployment Insurance program's accommodation of experience rating, largely in deference to Wisconsin's use of the device (Larson and Murray 1955, 185, 199-200). Likewise, federal enforcement costs money. Because state taxes are usually more popular than federal taxes (Wright 1988, 136-37), Congress will have considerable incentive to make concessions to state officials simply to get control over state matching funds that would be lost if states declined federal grants. Consider, for instance, the considerable concessions that the Social Security Administration made to induce California to place state revenue in the federal Supplemental Security Income program (Derthick 1990, 105-9). The *Printz* entitlement, at a minimum, prevents Congress from simply taking over the states' bureaucratic structures cost-free for its own policy programs. Instead, Congress either has to undergo the political risk and fiscal expense of creating its own structures or must pay the state governments a grant acceptable to them in return for the states' services (Hills 1998).

Nevertheless, one might respond that this description of the *Printz* entitlement rests on empirical assumptions too tentative to justify confidence that the entitlement will protect state autonomy as effectively as German law does. How can one be sure that the vagaries of intergovernmental deal-making will ensure that the states will be left with enough discretion to implement federal law? Perhaps Congress will bypass states and use federal agencies even when it is inefficient to do so, simply because Congress has a self-interested desire to monopolize patronage or credit-taking opportunities (Chubb 1985, 284-85; Conlan 1988, 38; Anton 1989, 111). By contrast, German federalism gives the *Länder* the surer protections of a constitutional entitlement to administer federal statutes and a collective rather than individual veto over federal mandates (Halberstam forthcoming). In short, it seems hard to argue with the conclusion that German law protects state autonomy more reliably than U.S. federalism does.

This extra protection of federalism, however, comes at a price. Our second hypothesis is that, when compared to the U.S. system of cooperative federalism, the German system tends to produce what Fritz Scharpf (1987) has described as a "joint decision trap"—the tendency in German federalism to require consent from multiple actors for political action, resulting in the obstruction of clear and effective policymaking. By giving the *Länder* a collective veto (through the Bundesrat) and a monopoly (through Articles 83-86 of the Grundgesetz) over the implementation of federal law, the German system locks the two levels of government—*Länder* and federation—into a position in which neither can dispense with the other in executing any policy of significance (Halberstam forthcoming). This collective veto over federal lawmaking gives the *Länder* far greater capacity to hold federal lawmaking hostage to their demands for policy concessions or simply for more revenue, even when this is not justified by their superior regulatory performance. Consider, for instance, the recent successful efforts of three *Länder* to demand large ad hoc grants in return for their Bundesrat votes in favor of *Steuerreform*—tax reform generally favored by both the Christian Democratic Union and Christian Social Union, on the one hand, and the Social Democratic Party, on the other (Lambsdorff 2000; Bayer et al. 2000). The federation, therefore, must enter into lengthy, complex, and publicly invisible negotiations with the byzantine networks of appointed and elected officials of the *Länder* to secure passage and faithful implementation of the law (Leonardy 1991).

The U.S. system of intergovernmental relations mitigates this obstacle to national legislation by not giving state governments any legal monopoly over the power to implement national laws and by allowing each state to withhold its implementing services separately rather than collectively through the individual exercise of the *Printz* entitlement. With the states' lack of any monopoly on implementation, the upper limit of money and discretion for which a state can bargain is determined not by constitutional procedure but by the opportunity costs that the federal government faces by forgoing state services—namely, the creation of a potentially inefficient federal agency, which might become an embarrassment to Congress and result in the loss of the matching funds that the state government would otherwise supply (Hills 1998). So, for instance, the Occupational Safety and Health Act (OSHA) is administered in roughly half the states by federal personnel and in the other half by state officials, and there are intense political controversies within individual states about the relative performance and cost of federal and state administrators.[13] We suggest that this ad hoc method of determining the state role in implementing federal legislation mitigates the joint decision trap faced by the German federation while still preserving a significant role for states in implementing (and resisting) federal policy.

A second potential cost of the German system of federalism is that the assignment of implementation duties to the *Länder* is remarkably inflexible. The responsibilities of federation and *Länder* bureaucracies are defined ex ante by the Grundgesetz; thus the German system does not allow for greater or fewer enforcement responsibilities to be allocated to the *Länder* based on any *Land*'s track record of enforcement. This rigidity may prevent more generally what Albert Breton (1996) calls "vertical competition," that is, competition between the state and federal bureaucracies to determine which level of government can administer a function more efficiently (233-39). The essential idea underlying Breton's theory is that the performance of one level of government in delivering services in one jurisdiction can serve as a benchmark for citizens to appraise how well another level of government is delivering the same services in another jurisdiction. For instance, California residents might evaluate how well the California government is performing safety inspections in the workplace by examining the performance of the federal Occupational Safety and Health Administration in conducting safety inspections in, say, Arizona. Breton's theory of vertical competition is not merely an ideal theory: with some important qualifications, the federal courts use the federal government's enforcement of OSHA as a benchmark for assessing whether states maintain adequate staffing when implementing OSHA.[14]

One might argue, then, that the Grundgesetz's constitutional division of labor inflexibly prevents citizens from gaining information about the relative competence of the different levels of government by observing their performance and withdrawing responsibility from inefficient agencies. The need for vertical competition might be especially great in Germany given that bureaucratic section heads (*Referenten*) in charge of implementing federal policy tend to be overly risk averse and hostile to efficiency-promoting reform (Mayntz and Scharpf 1975, 69-76). The degree to which *Länder* politicians will combat these bureaucratic tendencies may be uneven. In Schleswig-Holstein, for instance, Minister-President Heide Simonis has been locked in an intense political battle with public school teachers in an effort to deprive them of civil servant status. But politicians in other *Länder* may not exert this sort of effort against powerful interests, especially given that *Finanzausgleich* ensures that some *Länder* can force other *Länder* to pay for the inefficiencies in their bureaucracy (Larsen 1999, 467-69).

In sum, contrary to conventional wisdom, the U.S. and German systems of federalism both enlist component jurisdictions to implement national policies. The difference between the two regimes is not whether but how the enlisting occurs. There is reason to believe that the structure of German intergovernmental relations has some costs that the American system avoids, such as potential ineffi-ciencies of collaborative decision making and diminished possibilities for checking inefficiencies in policy implementation through vertical competition. Conversely, the German system may better protect the significance of the *Länder* by providing categorical and collective protection within the constitutional structure. If elected federal legislators have a self-interested bias in favor of centralized administration, then the U.S. system may inadequately protect the states' role in administering federal law. While the Grundgesetz eliminates the danger of the underuse of the *Länder* posed by such perverse incentives, it appears to do so with a cleaver rather than a scalpel, imposing *Länder* implementation even when such a system might be excessively costly. The challenge, in this case, would be to discover a mechanism for eliminating federal politicians' perverse incentives to underuse subordinate jurisdictions without eliminating some of the flexibility of ad hoc arrangements characteristic of the U.S. system.

Notes

1. 521 U.S. 898 (1997).
2. 505 U.S. 144 (1992).
3. *Printz v. United States*, 521 U.S. 898, 976 (Breyer, J., dissenting) (citations omitted).
4. Id. at 976-977 (citations omitted).
5. *Printz*, 521 U.S. at 977-78.
6. 317 U.S. 111 (1942).
7. 17 U.S. (4 Wheat.) 316 (1819).
8. *New York*, 505 U.S. at 167-69.
9. See, for example, *Cippillone v. Liggett*, 505 U.S. 504 (1992).
10. *Printz*, 521 U.S. at 978.

11. As Susan Rose-Ackerman (1980) has noted, state politicians might hang back, waiting for others to take successful risks that the latecomers can then imitate. But, in practice, the advantages of being the first to succeed with a policy seem sufficient incentive for ambitious state politicians to engage in creative policymaking in order to make a national name for themselves (Sabato 1983; Beamer 1999).

12. Codified at 42 U.S.C.A. § 7543(b)(1).

13. See, for example, Weinstein 1988.

14. *A.F.L.-C.I.O. v. Marshall*, 570 F.2d 1030, 1038 (D.C. Cir. 1980) (suggesting that the federal Department of Labor's staffing levels for safety inspectors can constitute a benchmark for state staffing levels if the former follow a "coherent plan").

References

Anton, Thomas J. 1989. *American Federalism and Public Policy: How the System Works.* New York: Random House.

Baker, Lynn. 1995. Conditional Federal Spending After *Lopez. Columbia Law Review* 95:1911-89.

Bayer et al. 2000. Da habe ich Ja gesagt. *Der Spiegel* 2000(29):22-28.

Beamer, Glenn. 1999. *Creative Politics: Taxes and Public Goods in a Federal System.* Ann Arbor: University of Michigan Press.

Breton, Albert. 1996. *Competitive Governments: An Economic Theory of Politics and Public Finance.* New York: Cambridge University Press.

Chubb, John. 1985. Federalism and the Bias in Favor of Centralization. In *The New Direction in American Politics,* ed. John Chubb and Paul Peterson. Washington, DC: Brookings Institution.

Conlan, Timothy. 1988. *New Federalism: Intergovernmental Reform from Nixon to Reagan.* Washington, DC: Brookings Institution.

Currie, David P. 1994. *The Constitution of the Federal Republic of Germany.* Chicago: University of Chicago Press.

Degenhart, Christoph. 1996. Art. 72 GG Kommentar. In *Grundgesetz: Kommentar,* ed. Michael Sachs. Munich: C. H. Beck.

Derthick, Martha. 1990. *Agency Under Stress: The Social Security Administration in American Government.* Washington, DC: Brookings Institution.

Elliot, E. Donald, Bruce Ackerman, and John C. Millian. 1985. Toward a Theory of Statutory Evolution: The Federalization of Environmental Law. *Journal of Law, Economics, & Organization* 1:313-40.

Golay, John Ford. 1958. *The Founding of the Federal Republic of Germany.* Chicago: University of Chicago Press.

Halberstam, Daniel. Forthcoming. Comparative Federalism and the Issue of Commandeering. In *The Federal Vision,* ed. Kalypso Nicolaidis and Robert Howse. Oxford: Oxford University Press.

Hills, Roderick M. 1998. The Political Economy of Cooperative Federalism: Why State Autonomy Makes Sense and "Dual Sovereignty" Doesn't. *Michigan Law Review* 96:801-944.

Isensee, Joseph and Paul Kirchhof. 1990. *Handbuch des Staatsrechts.* Heidelberg: C. F. Müller.

Lambsdorff, Otto Graf. 2000. Föderaler Kuhhandel verdirbt die Sitten. *Frankfurter Allgemeine Zeitung,* 19 July.

Larsen, Clifford. 1999. States Federal, Financial, Sovereign, and Social: A Critical Inquiry into an Alternative to American Financial Federalism. *American Journal of Comparative Law* 47(Summer):429-88.

Larson, Arthur and Merrill G. Murray. 1955. The Development of Unemployment Insurance in the United States. *Vanderbilt Law Review* 8:181-217.

Leonardy, Uwe. 1991. The Working Relationships Between Bund and Länder in the Federal Republic of Germany. In *German Federalism Today,* ed. Charlie

Jeffery and Peter Savigear. Leicester: Leicester University Press.

Mayntz, Renate and Fritz Scharpf. 1975. *Policymaking in the German Federal Bureaucracy.* New York: Elsevier.

Page, Edward C. 1991. *Localism and Centralism in Europe.* New York: Oxford University Press.

Rose-Ackerman, Susan. 1980. Risk Taking and Reelection: Does Federalism Promote Innovation? *Journal of Legal Studies* 9:593-619.

Sabato, Larry. 1983. *Goodbye to Good-Time Charlie: The American Governorship Transformed.* 2d ed.

Washington, DC: Congressional Quarterly Press.

Scharpf, Fritz. 1987. The Joint-Decision Trap: Lessons from German Federalism and European Integration. In *Law and State: A Biannual Collection of Recent German Contributions to These Fields.* Tübingen: Institute for Scientific Cooperation.

Weinstein, Henry. 1988. Prop. 97 Gives State Task of Restoring Funds for Cal/OSHA. *Los Angeles Times,* 10 Nov.

Wright, Deil. 1988. *Understanding Intergovernmental Relations.* 3d ed. Belmont, CA: Wadsworth.

Did the Oklahoma City Bombers Succeed?

By JORDAN STEIKER

ABSTRACT: The worst case of domestic terrorism in our country's history, the bombing of the Alfred P. Murrah Federal Building in Oklahoma City, led to the enactment of a landmark antiterrorism statute. Not surprisingly, several of the statute's provisions strengthen federal power in extraordinary and unprecedented ways to counter the threat of terrorism. But other provisions radically restrict the ability of federal courts to enforce the federal constitutional rights of state prisoners. How could Congress miss the apparent irony of responding to the destruction of a federal courthouse with its own assault on federal judicial power? This article argues that the role of federal habeas corpus has changed substantially over the past three decades. Whereas federal habeas had emerged during the Warren Court as a general forum for supervising state court compliance with constitutional norms, it has now become primarily a forum for death penalty litigation. Congress appears to have recognized this transformation, and the antiterrorism statute confirms that Congress views federal habeas through the lens of the death penalty rather than the lens of federalism. This article explores the costs of the "capitalization" of habeas and the subtle relationship between federalism, federal habeas, and the death penalty.

Jordan Steiker is the Cooper K. Ragan Regents Professor of Law at the University of Texas School of Law. He has written extensively on capital punishment and federal habeas corpus. He has also worked with state legislative committees addressing death penalty issues in Texas, and he codirects the capital punishment clinic at the University of Texas School of Law.

ON 19 April 1995, a massive bomb placed in a rental truck exploded in downtown Oklahoma City, ripping apart the Alfred P. Murrah Federal Building and killing 168 people inside. Timothy McVeigh and Terry Nichols were subsequently convicted for their involvement in the bombing and sentenced to death and to life imprisonment, respectively. McVeigh apparently planned the attack as some sort of revenge for the federal government's siege of the Branch Davidian compound in Waco, Texas, two years before.

Within days of the first anniversary of the Oklahoma City bombing (and the third anniversary of the Waco catastrophe), Congress enacted the Anti-Terrorism and Effective Death Penalty Act (AEDPA). Much of the AEDPA expands federal power in extraordinary ways. On the immigration side, the AEDPA makes it easier to remove aliens suspected of terrorism and to exclude persons with ties to alleged terrorist organizations from entering the United States or receiving financial support. On the domestic side, the legislation continues the movement toward the federalization of crime and toward the enhancement of federal law enforcement powers. Federal law enforcement officers now account for nearly 10 percent of all law enforcement officers nationwide (Strossen 1997), and the number of offenses within the federal criminal justice system has never been greater.

In many respects, then, the congressional response to the Oklahoma City bombing was to advance precisely the agenda that McVeigh and Nichols apparently feared: to expand and nurture the ever growing federal criminal machinery. For conservative dissenters whose rallying cries are Ruby Ridge and Waco, the AEDPA reinforces fears about the lurking threat of jackbooted government thugs.

At the same time that Congress fed the federal leviathan, though, it radically curtailed federal judicial power to grant federal habeas corpus relief to state prisoners. In addition to imposing a new limitations period for filing federal habeas petitions and restricting the availability of successive petitions, the AEDPA altered the most central feature of the federal habeas statute: the substantive standard for granting relief.[1] Prior to the AEDPA, the governing statutory language was quite bare, authorizing habeas relief for inmates held in violation of the Constitution, laws, or treaties of the United States. The federal courts had construed this language as requiring federal courts to undertake de novo review of state court determinations of federal law.[2] Under the AEDPA, however, federal courts are required to focus not on the federal lawfulness of an inmate's custody but, rather, on the state court's resolution of an inmate's federal constitutional claims. A habeas court can grant relief only if a state court's decision rejecting the merits of an inmate's claims is contrary to, or an unreasonable application of, clearly established federal law. The net effect of this change is to require the federal courts to leave unredressed reasonable but wrong state court legal determinations concerning the federal constitutional rights of state prisoners.[3]

For those interested in the theory and practice of American federalism, the AEDPA presents an enormous puzzle. On the one hand, the AEDPA abundantly illustrates Congress's willingness to augment the size, power, and significance of the federal law enforcement bureaucracy. In this respect, the AEDPA is of a piece with other statutes that move ever closer to establishing a general congressional police power. On the other hand, the habeas provisions appear to honor the finality concerns of state criminal justice systems and the comity concerns of state courts. In this light, the habeas reforms of the AEDPA seem to be one of the very few examples of congressional respect for the notion of limited federal government.

One crass explanation for the AEDPA's apparent schizophrenic attitude toward federalism is to insist that Congress is much more concerned with its own power than with federal power generally. To borrow from Justice O'Connor's critique in a federalism case,[4] Congress's underdeveloped capacity for self-restraint is simply not implicated in battles involving the power of the federal judiciary vis-à-vis states; or, to put it more bluntly, Congress is quite comfortable embracing federalism-based limits on the judiciary that it would never impose on itself.

Though likely true, this explanation fails to capture a related but importantly distinct phenomenon: in contemporary political discourse, the debate over the scope of federal habeas is less about federalism than it is about the death penalty. This fact is obviously reflected in the title of the legislation itself, and given that the most significant reforms of

the AEDPA apply equally to death and non-death penalty cases, one wonders why the legislation is not called something like the "Anti-Terrorism and Anti-Federal Habeas Act."

It should not be surprising, though, that the congressional response to domestic terrorism—even terrorism inspired by those critical of expansive federal power (though I do not argue that McVeigh and Nichols were themselves committed to some version of federalism)—is to ensure the viability of the death penalty. The most extreme crimes in this country invariably ignite calls for a more robust death penalty, and Congress has not shied away from affirming its commitment to the ultimate punishment. At the symbolic level, Congress continues to increase the number of federal offenses punishable by death, though the federal death penalty remains an insignificant part of the death penalty machinery nationwide (with considerably less than 1 percent of death row inmates produced by federal prosecutions) (NAACP 2000, 122-23).[5] The habeas reforms, on the other hand, are likely to have a real impact on the effectiveness of the death penalty, if that is measured in terms of the ability of states to carry out executions and to do so in an expeditious fashion.

THE CAPITALIZATION OF FEDERAL HABEAS CORPUS

The most interesting question, then, is not about the apparent irony of Congress's destroying federal habeas in response to the destruction of a federal courthouse. Rather, it is how the debate about federal habeas became a debate about the death penalty. It has not always been so. Federal habeas first attracted significant public debate during the 1960s, when the federal courts first assumed a significant role in regulating state criminal justice systems. Prior to the 1960s, federal habeas for state prisoners was relatively inconsequential as a practical matter because the range of federal rights enforceable in state proceedings was extremely limited. Until the United States Supreme Court began to apply the Bill of Rights against the states via the due process clause, state prisoners seeking relief in federal court could challenge state practices only on the ground that the latter were so unfair or arbitrary as to deny due process. When the Court made clear in 1953 that the legal claims of state prisoners should be addressed de novo on federal habeas, Justice Jackson complained of a "haystack" of petitions[6] that in today's terms looks like an anthill; the 541 petitions filed in 1951 had become 12,000 by 1990 (Mecham 1991).

As the Supreme Court "constitutionalized" criminal procedure in the 1960s and extended to state prisoners virtually all of the protections of the Fourth, Fifth, Sixth, and Eighth Amendments, the scope and availability of federal habeas became extremely consequential. For many state inmates, the Court's declaration of new rights occurred after their convictions had already become final, so vindication would have to come, if at all, in postconviction proceedings. Because a large number of states did not offer comprehensive postconviction remedies, these inmates brought their claims, often pro se, directly to federal court via federal habeas corpus. The disruption to state criminal justice systems was substantial, as the federal courts retroactively enforced many (though not all) of the constitutional guarantees that had recently been extended to state prisoners.

By the late 1960s and early 1970s, federal habeas seemed like an essential component of the Warren Court "revolution" in federalizing criminal procedure. But by the late 1970s and to the present day, the typical beneficiary of federal habeas had changed dramatically. Over the past quarter-century, the courts' relatively solicitous attitude toward pro se filings during the Warren Court era has given way to more sporadic and cursory review. The increasing reluctance to vindicate the claims of pro se petitioners is reflected in part by the enormous growth of intricate procedural obstacles to federal habeas review (Steiker 1998). Exhaustion, procedural default, and nonretroactivity rules make it extremely unlikely for uncounseled petitioners to receive "merits" review of their underlying constitutional claims (much less relief). At the same time, in the past two decades Congress established an unprecedented right of court-appointed counsel for state death row inmates challenging their conviction or sentence on federal habeas. As a result of these two developments, virtually all of the meaningful contemporary federal habeas litigation involves capital defendants represented by federally funded lawyers.

Moreover, a good portion of the litigated claims in federal habeas concerns doctrines unique to capital punishment law under the Eighth Amendment. When the Court first subjected state death penalty schemes to federal constitutional scrutiny in the early 1970s, the popular perception was that the Court was deciding the constitutional rightness or wrongness of the death penalty as a punishment. In 1976, though, the Court made clear that the death penalty was a permissible punishment so long as states developed adequate systems for ensuring its reliable and equitable administration.

The notorious subsequent history reveals the development of extremely intricate, difficult-to-apply doctrines that have plunged states and petitioners into a morass of confusing litigation concerning states' obligations in their administration of the death penalty (Steiker and Steiker 1995, 371-403). The most conspicuous example of how the Court's substantive Eighth Amendment jurisprudence has generated protracted litigation is in the Court's insistence that states channel or guide sentencer discretion to ensure evenhanded, consistent treatment of capital defendants while also insisting that states permit sentencers to exercise unbridled, uncircumscribed discretion to withhold the death penalty based on "individualized" (usually mitigating) factors. Over the past 20 years, literally dozens of cases in the United States Supreme Court (and hence hundreds of cases in the lower federal courts) have involved challenges to state schemes on the grounds that they provide either insufficient guidance or insufficient discretion (or both) to capital sentencers.

Federal habeas, then, has become less a broad forum for enforcing the federal rights of state prisoners generally than the inevitable battleground for enforcing or overturning state death sentences and elaborating the meaning of the Eighth Amendment in capital cases. The drafters of the AEDPA undoubtedly understood this when they equated "effective death penalty" with diminished federal habeas corpus.

Should we embrace the "capitalization" of federal habeas, and what are its costs? First, we should recognize that by shaping federal habeas doctrines with death row inmates as the norm, both the Court and Congress have put federal habeas out of the reach of virtually all noncapital inmates. The new one-year filing deadline imposed by the AEDPA,[7] for example, is simply not suited to the typical indigent, pro se, non-death-sentenced inmate, especially when viewed in light of the Court's strict procedural default and exhaustion requirements.

One could make a case that the old federalism model of federal habeas is no longer viable and that the practical unavailability of federal habeas in noncapital cases is entirely justified. On this view, the strongest arguments for federal supervision over state court adjudication of federal rights have diminished or disappeared entirely.

For example, it was commonly asserted in the 1960s that the federal courts would have greater expertise in applying the criminal procedure provisions of the Bill of Rights against the states at least in part because federal courts had been applying such protections in federal criminal cases for almost two centuries. Now, though, state courts have had almost four decades of experience with constitutional criminal procedure and in fact are more likely to address such issues on a routine basis.

Moreover, the claim that state courts are particularly hostile toward federal rights made more sense in the context of the general legal upheaval wrought by the Warren Court. By the mid-1960s, the Warren Court legacy had come to include not just incorporation and a newly expansive view of the rights of criminal defendants but also the recognition of privacy rights and more expansive speech rights, a greater commitment to separation between church and state, and, above all, an attack (albeit restrained) against legally enforced segregation in schools and other institutions. Today, the Rehnquist Court does not represent the same sort of threat to localist concerns, and the ideological divide between federal and state judges is more complicated and nuanced than the Warren Court models would suggest. Indeed, many state courts have provided greater rights than those required by the federal constitutional floor.

These arguments, though, prove too much. They do not explain the current state of affairs in which uncounseled state inmates have a legal right but no genuine opportunity to seek habeas relief in federal court. The prospect that vindication of constitutional rights depends entirely on the fortuity of having the means to secure counsel runs counter to basic democratic and egalitarian commitments in our law. Perhaps the altered legal and structural landscape of the present era invites reexamination of the central premises of federal habeas (and reevaluation of the virtues and vices of federalism in this context), but the new landscape hardly justifies preserving on paper rights we are unwilling to make effective.

On the capital punishment side, the costs are slightly different. Death row inmates have lawyers, and the gatekeeping doctrines that essentially bar noncapital inmates do not completely shut the door to capital petitioners. To make the death penalty more effective, Congress chose to restrict rather than eliminate federal habeas review. Whatever one's view about the optimal level of federal review, this choice has distinctive costs.

FEDERAL HABEAS CORPUS, FEDERALISM, AND THE DEATH PENALTY

Most obviously, litigants on federal habeas spend extraordinary and disproportionate resources determining whether the federal courts can reach the merits of federal claims. Although the court-driven and congressional reforms of habeas impose significant procedural obstacles to relief, the reforms are invariably accompanied by intricate exceptions. As a result, instead of litigating, for example, whether an inmate's counsel performed below constitutionally mandated minimum standards, the parties debate whether the inmate adequately preserved the claim in state court and, if not, whether exceptional circumstances ("cause and prejudice" or "miscarriage of justice") nonetheless justify reaching the merits of the claim. The efficiency secured by such reforms is not to be found in the preservation of scarce federal judicial resources, as it is clear from published opinions that federal judges must spend no less time (and considerably more intellectual energy) navigating the maze of procedural rules than they would interpreting the underlying constitutional norms.

An outside observer of the American system of appeals and postconviction remedies in criminal cases, particularly our apparatus for entertaining the constitutional claims of state prisoners, would likely be astonished. We appear to have an unparalleled taste for expensive procedural safeguards and yet an extraordinary reluctance to have those safeguards make a difference in terms of constitutional norm enforcement. We want to nod in the direction of the Great Writ (and are willing to bear great administrative costs in doing so), but, at the end of the day, we want our executions to be carried out as well. To borrow from the old saw about our nation's capital (combining southern efficiency and northern charm), contemporary federal habeas combines southern efficiency and (when it comes to the death penalty) southern charm.

In addition, by slowly closing but not fully shutting the door to federal habeas review, Congress has managed to preserve the appearance of extensive federal supervision over state death penalty practices even though in fact the scope of federal remedies has become quite limited. As most lawyers know, federal habeas courts do not revisit a sentencer's ultimate decision to sentence an inmate to death rather than imprisonment. But as most lawyers do not know (unless they are involved in federal habeas practice), the federal courts also no longer decide whether the processes leading to an inmate's sentence were constitutional. That is the question that the United States Supreme Court asks in the extremely rare cases it chooses to hear on direct review. Instead, in accordance with the modifications of habeas to enhance the death penalty system's effectiveness, the habeas court asks whether the Supreme Court had previously made clear what the Constitution requires and, if so, whether the state court unreasonably departed from such clear commands.

Supporters of the death penalty, including prosecutors and executive officials, routinely insist that they (and therefore we) should be more comfortable with the punishment because of the numerous layers of searching review. But it is neither true nor fair to insist, as most proponents do, that two sets of courts have exhaustively scoured the record looking for error. In short, the very existence of federal habeas, even in its increasingly truncated form, unjustifiably alleviates anxiety about the accuracy of state court capital proceedings.

Ultimately, these considerations suggest that federal habeas should either be eliminated or revived. If, in the end, robust federal habeas review treads excessively on legitimate state law enforcement interests, we should not continue to erect expensive, time-consuming obstacles to such review simply to indulge the fiction that state prisoners have a meaningful opportunity to vindicate federal constitutional claims. If, on the other hand, federal enforcement of federal law contributes sufficiently to the protection of constitutional norms to justify bearing those costs, we should resist efficiency-based reforms such as those found in the AEDPA.

As I have argued elsewhere, productive federal habeas reform should take account of the hybrid nature of the federal habeas remedy: federal habeas provides both an appellate forum for record legal claims litigated in state court and an original forum for nonrecord claims that often require additional factual development (Steiker 2000, 1728). By disaggregating these appellate and original functions, and insisting the record claims be resolved soon after direct review (perhaps in the federal courts of appeals rather than the federal district courts), federal habeas could significantly reduce the finality and comity costs of the status quo. At the same time, the central resource-consuming and norm-defeating procedural obstacles of current habeas law, such as the nonretroactivity and reasonableness-review doctrines, could be withdrawn, allowing for both timely and meaningful federal resolution of federal claims.

These sorts of changes are unlikely to emerge unless the United States Supreme Court and Congress swap their current orientations toward federal habeas. Unlike Congress, the Court is well aware of the federalism implications of federal habeas, and the Court's decisions routinely and self-consciously locate the debate surrounding the proper scope of habeas within a larger dialogue on federalism. Given this focus, it is not surprising that the Court seems more attentive to the costs rather than the benefits of the federal enforcement of federal rights. If the Court were to recognize, though, that federal habeas has become primarily a capital punishment forum, it could recalibrate federal habeas in light of the goals of its capital punishment jurisprudence.

One prominent theme in that jurisprudence is the requirement of heightened reliability in capital cases (Steiker and Steiker 1995, 379). That commitment should not tolerate the deferential review reflected in the current nonretroactivity and reasonableness-review doctrines. Heightened reliability should encompass not only the procedures states must adopt in capital prosecutions but also the mechanisms in federal court for ensuring that states honor the principle.

Congress, on the other hand, should think of federal habeas not solely in terms of the death penalty but also in terms of federalism. Congress's high regard for its own responsibility in enforcing civil rights law should extend beyond the usual contexts to the area of criminal justice. Just as Congress recognizes that national resources are often necessary to fulfill national antidiscrimination commitments (to guarantee equality for women and for racial and religious minorities), it should recognize the role of the federal courts in securing compliance with the protections for criminal defendants embedded in the Bill of Rights and the Fourteenth Amendment.

To answer the question raised by this article, the Oklahoma City bombers did not succeed. Federal law enforcement power grew in the wake of the bombing, and the bombers' terroristic act offered poignant support for such expansion. Martyrdom has been shifted, or at least shared, as the victims of Oklahoma City are now inextricably linked to the Waco tragedy. But the political reaction to Oklahoma City embodied in the AEDPA should at least prompt us to assess the complicated relationship between federal habeas, capital punishment, and federalism. Congress and the Court should revisit the current state of federal habeas with a clearer picture of what federal habeas accomplishes (or fails to accomplish) and at what cost. The pure federalism paradigm that captured a particular moment in history should be reexamined to determine what role, if any, federal courts should play in securing federal constitutional rights, with special attention to the practical significance that

habeas review holds for the implementation of the Court's death penalty law.

Notes

1. See Pub. L. No. 104-132 § 104, 110 Stat. 1214, 1218-19 (codified at 28 U.S.C. § 2254(d)).

2. See, for example, *Brown v. Allen*, 344 U.S. 443, 503-08 (1953) (opinion of Justice Frankfurter) (articulating de novo standard).

3. See *Williams v. Taylor*, 526 U.S. 1050 (1999) (construing new standard of review under the AEDPA).

4. See *Garcia v. San Antonio Metropolitan Transit Ass'n*, 469 U.S. 528, 588 (1985) (O'Connor, J., dissenting).

5. NAACP 2000 indicates that 24 of 3691 death row inmates were sentenced to death in federal (nonmilitary) proceedings; an additional 7 death row inmates were sentenced in federal military proceedings.

6. See *Brown v. Allen*, 344 U.S. 443, 537 (1953) (Jackson, J., concurring in the result).

7. See 28 U.S.C. § 2244(d)(1) (new limitations provision).

References

Anti-Terrorism and Effective Death Penalty Act. Pub. L. No. 104-132. 110 Stat. 1214 (codified in scattered titles of U.S.C. (Supp. IV 1998)).

Mecham, Ralph L. 1991. *Annual Report of the Director of the Administrative Office of the United States Courts.* Washington, DC: Administrative Office U.S. Courts.

NAACP (National Association for the Advancement of Colored People). Legal Defense and Education Fund Inc. 2000. *Death Row, U.S.A.* New York: NAACP.

Steiker, Carol and Jordan M. Steiker. 1995. Sober Second Thoughts: Reflections on Two Decades of Constitutional Regulation of Capital Punishment. *Harvard Law Review* 109:355-438.

Steiker, Jordan. 1998. Restructuring Post-Conviction Review of Federal

Constitutional Claims Raised by State Prisoners: Confronting the New Face of Excessive Proceduralism. *Legal Forum* 1998:315-47.

———. 2000. Habeas Exceptionalism. *Texas Law Review* 78:1703-30.

Strossen, Nadine. 1997. Symposium: Justice and the Criminal Justice System, the Fifteenth Annual National Student Federalist Society Symposium on Law and Public Policy—1996: Panel VI: Feds Fighting Crime: When and How: Criticism of Federal Counter-Terrorism Laws. *Harvard Journal of Law and Public Policy* 20:531-41.

Book Department

INTERNATIONAL RELATIONS AND POLITICS

ASCHER, WILLIAM. 1999. *Why Governments Waste Natural Resources: Policy Failures in Developing Countries.* Pp. ix, 333. Baltimore, MD: Johns Hopkins University Press. $59.00. Paperbound, $17.95.

This book attempts to answer two important questions: why governments in developing countries waste natural resources, and what can be done about it. Obviously, natural resources can be squandered by private and communal resource users as well as by government agencies even when policy failures are not apparent. However, Ascher's attention to faulty natural-resource policies of governments is well placed since governments have the responsibility to oversee the use of resources and to protect them from abuse. Based on the premise that poor resource practices are largely caused by government policies, Ascher proposes a theory to explain why government officials in developing countries often induce and engage in unsound natural-resource policies.

The gist of the theory is that government officials adopt such policies in order to pursue various political and economic objectives. Promoting development initiatives, redistributing wealth, and capturing revenues for the central treasury are among the most important objectives. Others include creating rent-seeking opportunities for supporters, capturing and maintaining discretion over the financial flows involved in resource exploitation at the expense of competing government agencies, and evading accountability through reliance on low-visibility resource maneuvers.

Ascher identifies an elaborate list of broad categories of natural-resource policy failures, which include price distortions, externalities, insecurity of property rights, uncertainty, direct state misexploitation, and absence of accountability. After a detailed discussion of how these policy failures are related to the political and economic objectives pursued by government officials, Ascher provides extensive empirical support for his theory by presenting 16 case studies, all chosen for the importance of the resources involved. The cases support Ascher's proposition that faulty resource policies are related to the political and economic objectives of government officials. In addition, the cases reveal that, in most instances, governments failed to attain their developmental and redistributive objectives, which are part of the reason why they adopt faulty natural-resource policies.

On the basis of the findings and his conviction that, under conditions of perfect information, competition, and secure property rights, the market mechanism sets input and output prices in a manner such that private and societal interests converge, Ascher proposes a number of policy recommendations. He suggests that governments (1) restore nongovernmental resource control while fostering competition, secure property rights, and the availability of information; (2) restructure resource exploitation by state agencies in order to ensure that they are accountable and apply appropriate rates and methods; (3) manage externalities in such a way that private resource exploiters bear the indirect costs to society and are rewarded for providing benefits to society; and (4) separate the objectives of distributional equity from the production process in order to promote efficiency.

Many readers are not likely to share Ascher's notion of what constitutes optimal resource policies that maximize societal benefits. He defines optimal policies in terms of dynamic efficiency. The technical problems of identifying input and output prices that represent dynamic efficiency aside, efficiency considerations rarely account for distributional issues. Furthermore, policies that are geared to advancing efficiency only are not always the best policies.

Ascher's suggestion to exclude issues of distribution from defining best resource practices is certain to concern many readers. He considers distributional equity to be "extraordinarily important." However, he views it to be a matter of value, and he believes that distribution policies should be pursued at the level of central budgeting and outside the production process. It is doubtful that issues of poverty alleviation and distributive equity would be effectively addressed through budgets in an era of globalization. Global competition has exerted pressure on governments to lower their tax rates, and conditionalities set by the IMF- and World Bank–sponsored Structural Adjustment Programs have forced governments to restrict budgetary expenditures.

A healthy balance between the goals of safeguarding resources and meeting the developmental needs of people in developing countries is essential for appropriate management of resources.

Striking such a balance is not likely to be attainable without addressing the issues of poverty and maldistribution of income. Thus what is needed is theories and policy options that safeguard natural resources without neglecting the goals of poverty alleviation and distributive equity. This book does not quite strike the necessary balance, but it contributes considerably to the search for theories that strike the balance. The richness of the cases and the meticulous analysis of the evidence are among the many strengths of the book from which readers will greatly benefit.

KIDANE MENGISTEAB

Old Dominion University
Norfolk
Virginia

DESCH, MICHAEL C. 1999. *Civilian Control of the Military: The Changing Security Environment*. Pp. xiii, 184. Baltimore, MD: Johns Hopkins University Press. $34.95.

Through his work with the John M. Olin Institute of Strategic Studies, his organizing of conferences, and his stimulation of others' thinking, there would scarcely be a more influential scholar of civil-military relations than Michael C. Desch even if he had not written this summation of his ideas. With *Civilian Control of the Military*, Professor Desch assures his place at the top of this field.

The book offers the most persuasive theory of the structural determinants of civilian control that I have found. It is of great current interest because of its cogent explanation of the deterioration of civilian control in the United States since the end of the Cold War, but in addition Desch applies his theory to a wide range of specific situations including the transition from the Soviet Union to the Russian Federation of Republics, the German

Empire during World War I, France during the Algerian crisis, and Brazil, Argentina, and Chile from the 1960s to 1990s.

Desch presents the essentials of civilian control simply: "The best indicator of the state of civilian control is who prevails when civilian and military preferences diverge. If the military does, there is a problem; if the civilians do, there is not." He then explores the effects upon civilian control of four possible situations in which a state might find itself: a high external threat to its interests combined with a low internal threat to its stability; a low external threat combined with a high internal threat; high threats both external and internal; low threats both external and internal.

He posits, and his historical case studies seem to confirm, that civilian control tends to be most secure when there is a high external and low internal threat. In response to the high external threat, the interests of civilian and military leaders converge, and there also is likely to be maximum cohesiveness within each group. Thus during World War II and the Cold War, the American civilian leadership could reliably count on the military's doing what it wished. During World War II, there were many instances of civilian-military disagreement, for example, over the invasion of French North Africa; but there was never a question of the effectiveness of civilian control. During the Cold War, in spite of military discontent with much civilian decision making, particularly concerning Vietnam, civilian control also functioned effectively. The same pattern prevailed in the Soviet Union.

Since the end of the Cold War, in contrast, with the United States experiencing low levels of threat both externally and internally, civilian control has been less assured. External threats have not disappeared, but as they present themselves at a less acute level, the military feels freer to act in its own bureaucratic interest and to resist civilian control. Desch stresses that he is not envisaging military resistance on anything like the scale of a coup d'état. What has already occurred, however, is that the military has asserted a policymaking role in decisions on when to use military force, and sometimes in relation to its own administration, that is foreign to the American tradition of civilian control. It has done so in asserting abstract principles of when to go to war, as in the Powell Doctrine, and in specific situations, as when General Colin L. Powell, as chairman of the Joint Chiefs of Staff, led military resistance to intervention in Bosnia that delayed action there, with the military subsequently dragging its feet on the arrest of war criminals.

The current Russian situation is not altogether dissimilar. But there the lack of a democratic tradition of civilian control along with much more severe internal threats to the state—as in Chechnya—have led to occasional outright defiance of the civilian leadership by the military.

Germany in World War I, like France in the 1950s and Japan between the world wars, presents an instance of high threats externally and internally. In such cases, where the structural pattern of external as opposed to internal threats is indeterminate—they roughly balance out—Desch believes that the doctrine embraced by the military tends to shape responses to civilian control. During the mid to late years of World War I, for example, until remarkably close to the end, the German military believed Germany was winning the war and thus controlling the external threat, but the military's doctrine of the necessity to wage total war created a perception of a severe internal threat to the requisite unity; so the military responded by rejecting civilian control and establishing a military dictatorship.

In a situation of low external but high internal threats, such as the military leaders of Brazil, Argentina, and Chile believed they faced at various times in the 1960s and 1970s, the military, particularly in states without a tradition of civilian control, is especially likely to follow the path of throwing over the traces of civilian control altogether.

From these patterns, Desch draws prescriptions for policymakers. Most important, he concludes that a key to maintaining civilian control in any state is to keep the military focused on external missions. In the United States, even without an external threat of the magnitude of World War II or the Cold War, there remain plenty of external problems on which civilians should encourage the military to focus. In Desch's judgment, to bring the military into internal matters, such as drug enforcement, is to tempt the military into internal political entanglements that jeopardize civilian control.

Desch also believes that current trends toward yet more sophisticated military technologies may ease civil-military problems by stimulating a higher level of military professionalism while also bringing civilian and military technologists closer together and, in addition, encouraging a military focus on external threats.

Altogether, this is one of those rich, complex books that no review can plumb adequately. It must be read by anyone concerned with civil-military relations, American or global.

RUSSELL F. WEIGLEY

Temple University
Philadelphia
Pennsylvania

KATZ, MARK N. 1999. *Reflections on Revolutions.* Pp. ix, 146. New York: St. Martin's Press. $39.95.

Mark Katz has given us a unique contribution to the literature on revolutions. I say this in a positive sense despite many reservations concerning the book. Katz rereads selected theorists of revolutions, extracting from each an idea that can be useful in thinking about revolutions in the post–Cold War era. This is an intelligent format for a volume of reflections, and Katz is looking at revolutions in a fresh way.

The first chapter of part 1, "Class and Revolution," nicely summarizes Barrington Moore, and the next chapter usefully calls our attention to the conservatism of postrevolutionary regimes, which Abdallah Laroui handled with the concept of embourgeoisement. In part 2, "Nationalism and Revolution," there are many interesting empirical observations: Katz builds on Liah Greenfield in chapter 3 to raise good points about the fragility of civic nationalism, and asks, What if the United States declined as a great power? The fourth chapter extends T. R. Gurr's notion of relative deprivation from its economic context to a political one to explain secessionist movements, with real insights into when governments are likely to oppose or allow secession. Chapter 5, which opens part 3, "Democracy and Revolution," looks at the debate on the future of revolutions. It considers the work of Jeff Goodwin, who relies on a political (state-centered) analysis to argue that the era of revolutions is ending, and Eric Selbin, who draws on political economic arguments to call it far from over. We are treated to the interesting notion that democracy will "evolve" or change, especially as more democratic states come into existence, however imperfectly. Katz concludes that revolutions are neither over nor likely to remain the same but may have entered a new phase, largely taking the form of secessionist movements. The last chapter assesses the errors of Jeane Kirkpatrick's thesis about the superiority of authoritarian over totalitarian regimes as incubators of democracy and ends with a liberal plea for the United States to encourage democracy in the Middle East in order to avoid Islamic fundamentalism.

I had many mental reservations as I read this book. In general, Katz creatively extends the theorists he works with, drawing out their lessons in ways that they did not, but not always providing a subtle theoretical explanation for the patterns he observes. For Katz, neither economic nor cultural analysis comes easily. The book offers a very political-science view of power, in which politics operates without reference to culture, inside a modernizationist take on development, in which culture is seen mostly as religion and tradition. At every turn, Katz emphasizes the political in a highly formal, almost hyperrationalist way, at the expense of the economic and the cultural, privileging the state over civil society (for all his interest in democracy). Perhaps befitting an expert on Soviet foreign policy, there is a top-down, *Realpolitik* view of the world, and an aversion to Marxism, seen mainly as Marxism-Leninism. Therefore he sees 1989-91 as the great divide and falsifier of most existing theories of revolution (ignoring the "fourth generation" theorizing of Goodwin, Selbin, Timothy Wickham-Crowley, and me, among others). Katz sees revolutions only as "destructive and futile," missing the possibility that revolutions may take a nonviolent, democratic form and, in fact, have done so, in May 1968 France, Allende's Chile, Iran, and Chiapas (strikingly absent from the volume). He does raise the possibility of a "democratic revolution," but only in the sense of politically reforming a democracy by non- democratic means, as in Eastern Europe in 1989.

Overall, this is a very different kind of book in the literature on revolutions, not really to my taste, but perhaps more to the taste of political scientists and many of the readers of this journal.

JOHN FORAN

University of California
Santa Barbara

LEVERING, RALPH B. and MIRIAM L. LEVERING. 1999. *Citizen Action for Global Change: The Neptune Group and the Law of the Sea.* Pp. xx, 189. Syracuse, NY: Syracuse University Press. $45.00. Paperbound, $19.95.

The Third United Nations' Conference on the Law of the Sea (UNCLOS III) is a good illustration of Max Weber's dictum that politics is the slow boring of hard boards. Following the relatively unsuccessful negotiations in UNCLOS I (1958) and II (1960), UNCLOS III lasted for a period of nine years (1973-82). The negotiated agreement that emerged from the conference in 1982, and which finally became international law in 1994, established a new system of international governance of the oceans through such provisions as uniform 12-mile territorial seas; 200-mile economic resource zones for coastal states; and mechanisms for the peaceful resolution of disputes. This book gives us a description and an analysis of the role of nongovernmental organizations (NGOs), especially of the so-called Neptune Group (NG) in what is arguably one of the most significant developments in international law.

Composed of eight chapters, the bulk of *Citizen Action* is a history and memoir written by Miriam Levering, a key activist in the NG who died before the manuscript was completed, and her son, the political scientist Ralph Levering. The latter also wrote helpful introductory chapters and a valuable concluding one that summarizes the key lessons learned from the NG's experience with UNCLOS

III and that relates the experience to the literature on international relations and social movements. Information from interviews with 58 conference delegates, U.S. officials, and NGO participants adds important outsider views of the NG and its effectiveness.

"Neptune Group" was the name UNCLOS III delegates gave to two collaborating NGOs at the conference: the Ocean Education Project (OEP), founded by Miriam Levering and her husband Sam with the help of the United World Federalists and Quakers; and the United Methodist Law of the Sea Project (UMLSP), founded as a working committee of the United Methodist church. The networks out of which these two organizations emerged were crucial for their survival and ultimate success. With only a small cadre of staff and volunteers, the NG took on the daunting task of trying to influence four sets of actors: conference participants; three different presidential administrations; a changing U.S. Congress; and the American public.

Many of the conference delegates interviewed saw the NG's work as highly effective. Collaborating with the relatively favorable Nixon-Ford and Carter administrations, the NG was able to use an insider strategy at the conference. Quickly shifting from advocacy to a problem-solving approach, the NG looked for ways to help the delegates reach an agreement that would be fair to all. NG members found that they could help by building trust and credibility and assuming the role of honest brokers, helping behind the scenes to provide accurate information and facilitating communication and compromise between the delegates. The detailed discussion of the NG's successful activities is must reading for students of NGOs and social movements. It would have been helpful if the concluding chapter also included a systematic summary of the successful negotiation methods used at the conference.

The NG faced tougher times with the Reagan administration and a more conservative Congress. The authors chronicle how the NG helped protect the UNCLOS III negotiations from derailment through its advocacy work on Capitol Hill. In addition, Levering and Levering give us a fascinating account of the NG's coordinated domestic and international strategies.

This is an engaging, readable book about what NGOs actually do. NGO activists and graduate and upper-level undergraduate students will find it an informative and enjoyable read. Accompanied by some background reading on UNCLOS III, *Citizen Action* is ideal for courses on international relations, NGOs, or social movements and is a welcome addition to the literature.

RON PAGNUCCO

College of St. Benedict
St. Joseph
Minnesota

LIJPHART, AREND. 1999. *Patterns of Democracy: Government Forms and Performance in Thirty-Six Countries.* Pp. xiv, 351. New Haven, CT: Yale University Press. $40.00. Paperbound, $17.00.

Arend Lijphart, one of our most distinguished scholars of comparative politics, here builds directly upon his well-known exposition of two alternative models of democracy, which offer different answers to the question, Whose preferences should prevail when the people are in disagreement? The majoritarian answer offers institutions that are supposed to encourage the creation of a strong government backed by a majority of citizens. The consensus answer proposes that not merely a majority but "as many people as possible" should be brought into participation and agreement in policymaking.

This model offers institutions to share political power, encouraging compromise between representatives of greater proportions of the citizens. As in his influential 1984 book *Democracies*, Lijphart highlights the differences between these models through examining a series of features and several particular political systems (Britain and New Zealand versus Belgium and Switzerland) that exemplify the opposing approaches. He then considers each of the institutional features in turn as they operate in a large set of contemporary democratic systems.

Patterns of Democracy moves far beyond the earlier book in many important ways. Most obviously, Lijphart now covers 36 countries that have been democracies for at least 20 years since World War II. To the features considered earlier, he adds the pluralism/corporatism of interest group relations and the independence of central banks. Even for familiar institutions such as the party system, cabinet formations, and federalism, Lijphart attempts, boldly and sometimes controversially, to develop new measures to compare validly the institutional practices across countries on a majoritarian-consensus dimension, taking account, for example, of presidential systems and fractionalization within governing parties. As in the earlier work, he finds two distinct patterns in the distribution of the institutions contributing to consensus (dispersed power) democracy. Lijphart now interprets these, pleasingly, as corresponding to Robert Goodin's distinction between diffusing power through shared responsibility within institutions versus dividing power between different institutions.

Although readers may not find all measures equally persuasive, the tables and scatter diagrams provide a fascinating, plausible, and relatively accessible picture of how each country fits into the general patterns of stable democratic politics. Anyone interested in the workings of democracy should want this book on his or her shelf.

Moreover, Lijphart takes a further step in two chapters that seek to examine the consequences of adopting a majoritarian or consensus approach to democracy. In the first of these, he argues strongly that the often touted advantages of "strong" majoritarian government for economic management and controlling violence are largely illusionary. Among these relatively durable democracies, the consensus systems performed on average about as well as their majoritarian counterparts by almost all measures (significantly better in controlling inflation), after taking account of size, diversity, and economic development level. In the second chapter, he demonstrates that features of the consensus model are associated with a variety of measures of a superior "quality" of democracy, including higher voter turnout, better representation of voters and preferences, more generous welfare policies, greater representation of women in legislatures and among executives, and so forth.

Considering the overall record of equal and superior consequences, Lijphart recommends in his concluding chapter the consensus approach as "the more attractive option for countries designing their first democratic constitutions or contemplating democratic reform." Doubtless, economists, violence specialists, and policy analysts will want to explore other causal specifications, including interactions of consensual institutions with particular settings. Nor is it yet clear whether the consequences hold for unconsolidated democratic institutions. But Lijphart throws down a powerful challenge to majoritarians and other skeptics.

G. BINGHAM POWELL

University of Rochester
New York

MATTHEWS, DONALD R. and HENRY VALEN. 1999. *Parliamentary Representation: The Case of the Norwegian Storting.* Pp. xii, 211. Columbus: Ohio State University Press. $49.95. Paperbound, $23.95.

Parliamentary Representation examines how the process of democratic representation works in Norway, based largely upon the 1985 Storting representation study.

The most valuable feature of this book is the integration of many aspects of the process of representative democracy. The book begins by discussing representation in terms of the Miller-Stokes framework of mass-elite comparisons, and it rapidly moves beyond this model. The early chapters summarize the history of electoral politics in Norway, outlining the political cleavages of the nation, the parties' representation of these social interests, and the evolution of the electoral system. The next several chapters focus on the Storting. Matthews and Valen concisely describe the internal structure of the parliament and how members of parliament (MPs) are selected. In one sense, these chapters lay the groundwork for the analyses in the second half of the book. In another sense, they provide a well-presented introduction to Norwegian politics.

The second half of the book focuses on political representation. Matthews and Valen compare the congruence of mass and elite policy preferences across a range of policy issues, and further analyses examine variation in congruence. Another nice chapter analyzes MPs' perceptions of the politics and institutional structures of the Storting. The authors also frame their study in the context of party competition, using data from the Party Manifesto Project to track party positions over time. The analyses also integrate data from a survey of party activists who serve on Storting nominating committees.

This book delivers both more and less than it promises. The most valuable feature is the integration of many aspects of the political process into a study of Norwegian politics. By combining data from multiple sources, the authors offer a holistic view of the linkages within the process of representative democracy. Moreover, there is a wealth of empirical evidence available from the multiple data sources. This makes the book useful in addressing a diversity of issues, and a good introduction to Norwegian electoral politics.

One by-product of covering so much in a short book is that the discussion and analysis often could benefit from further development. Readers may frequently ask for more, either empirically or theoretically, from this study. For instance, the discussion of mass-elite congruence and the factors affecting this process could be expanded to address the depth found in other national studies that have focused on political representation. Similarly, the overview of electoral trends is quite brief. The other limitation is that the data are now over a decade and a half old; there have been significant changes in Norwegian politics since they were collected, such as those addressed in Strøm and Svåsand's recent *Challenges to Political Parties*. It would have been valuable if the mass opinion trends at least could been extended over time, using the rich Norwegian Election Study series that Valen helped to establish. Even more important, the book should have discussed its implications in light of representation theory in a more substantial concluding chapter.

Norway has always been an empirically rich, and theoretically important, case for the study of democracy. *Parliamentary Representation* confirms this tradition by showing readers how the dynamics of Norwegian electoral politics and legislative politics can bring new insights to understanding how democracy works.

RUSSELL J. DALTON

University of California
Irvine

McCHESNEY, ROBERT W. 1999. *Rich Media, Poor Democracy: Communication Politics in Dubious Times.* Pp. xii, 427. Urbana: University of Illinois Press. $32.95.

Robert McChesney is at his rhetorical best passionately describing the creation of public policy: "Public debate over the future of the media and communication has been effectively eliminated by powerful and arrogant corporate media, which metaphorically floss their teeth with politicians' underpants." But the best reason to read his latest book is the richness of his vision. In *Rich Media, Poor Democracy*, media regulation, economic logic, and our cultural paradigms for thinking about mass communication interact with each other in complex ways, and he condemns the market-based paradigm that has come to dominate our thinking about media. He calls it neoliberalism, the false equating of the marketplace with democracy. Further, even as he argues convincingly and in no uncertain terms that corporate ownership of mass communication is detrimental, his complex story acknowledges that not all of the evils others attribute to corporate media work as claimed and that advocates of public service media have made some critical errors of their own. His argument is compelling and seems intellectually honest.

The first half of the book describes the organizational structure of the current media system. In the first chapter, McChesney describes the shape of U.S. media at the turn of the millennium, ef-

fectively arguing that economic logic dictates even greater ownership consolidation and that between neoliberal political culture and mediated political campaigns, policymakers are unlikely to stem the tide. In the second chapter, he goes global, describing troubling patterns of consolidation that are concentrating the means of mass communication into the hands of a small number of transnational corporations. McChesney's view of cultural imperialism is complex. Global organizations create products empty of cultural specificity for international distribution and cultivate audiences in order to increase the kinds of cultural materials that can be globally distributed, but they also produce culturally specific content where local audiences demand it. The last chapter in this section assesses the future of the Internet in light of current organizational structures and trends. McChesney concludes that despite the technological possibilities of an infinite-channel universe, the same old players are gaining control of a crucial bottleneck, the portals people use to gain access to the Net. Here again, he paints a complex picture in which the Internet provides more variety in content, but commercialization affects both the structure of the Net and the tastes of audiences such that only the dedicated are likely to find much diversity.

In the second half of the book, McChesney traces the rise of the neoliberal model of media organization and its impacts on public service broadcasting ideals. He first revisits the central argument of his earlier work, *Telecommunications, Mass Media and Democracy.* He argues that there is nothing "natural" about a commercial media system and delves into the history of telecommunications regulation to support his point. Then he considers the current state and potential fate of public broadcasting in several nations, arguing that even the grandest public broadcaster of all, the BBC, is sacrificing its public service mission in favor of a more commercial model. In the next chapter, he critiques the current interpretation of the First Amendment as a private right of corporations, encouraging instead an interpretation of freedom of speech as a critical component of public life. The final chapter of the book argues that only the political Left can support a public interest paradigm for thinking about the mass media to oppose the neoliberal approach. Further, unless the Left makes media policy a fundamental aspect of the movement, he suggests, the Left itself will fail to flourish.

McChesney's final appeal to the Left underplays the more universal aspect of his argument: enacting changes in the media system will require changing the ways we think about mass communication as much as redistributing the means of production.

JILL A. EDY

Middle Tennessee State
   University
Murfreesboro

MITCHELL, NANCY. 1999. *The Danger of Dreams: German and American Imperialism in Latin America*. Pp. xi, 312. Chapel Hill: University of North Carolina Press. $49.95. Paperbound, $19.95.

In this study of American and German policies toward Latin America from the turn of the century to World War I, Nancy Mitchell challenges some of the most important historians who have studied the topic—Friedrich Katz and Reinhard Doerries, among others. Her argument is twofold: that there never was a serious German imperial threat to the Western Hemisphere, but that the fantasy of such a threat enabled Americans to justify to themselves their own desire for hegemony in the region.

The research that underlies Mitchell's argument is impressive. She has combed German, British, and American archives, examined a broad array of German, British, and American newspapers (which, oddly, are not listed in the bibliography), and used the relevant secondary sources in both German and English. This is true international history.

Mitchell contends that German-American relations, harmonious for most of American history, deteriorated sharply in the late nineteenth century for a variety of reasons, including trade competition and imperial ambitions. By the late nineteenth century, increasing tension had led to the drafting of war plans by the navies of both countries for a possible conflict in the Caribbean. Exacerbated by intemperate rhetoric from Kaiser Wilhelm II and American expansionists, popular spokesmen in each nation increasingly assumed the other's hostile intent.

Mitchell demonstrates persuasively, however, that all of this sound and fury signified little or nothing. War plans were never fleshed out and quickly became obsolete. Growing American strength and increasing German isolation in Europe put any German dreams of American empire out of reach. As Paul von Hintze, the German minister to Mexico, put it, "Those who can't bite shouldn't bark" (p. 210). This was excellent advice that was not always followed by Hintze himself and that was frequently ignored by Kaiser Wilhelm II. Nevertheless, Mitchell makes a powerful case for the limitations that the European situation put on German policy, and she demonstrates that on issue after issue, Berlin acted far more cautiously than it spoke. By placing German policy in its international context and by demonstrating the difference between rhetoric and action, Mitchell effectively challenges the argument that Germany pursued an imperial policy in the Western Hemisphere in the early twentieth century.

The other side of Mitchell's argument, that evoking the German threat permitted American leaders to justify to themselves their own desire for hegemony in the hemisphere, is less well developed and less persuasive. Indeed, Mitchell somewhat undercuts it herself by arguing that American leaders (as opposed to the public) did not really believe in the German menace. Her point that Americans did not want to face up to the reality that their nation was imperialist is certainly correct, but her explanation of how the mechanism of self-delusion operated lacks the sophistication and power of her interpretation of German policy.

From time to time, Mitchell's prose becomes overexuberant. My particular favorite appears on p. 208 where we learn that "a red herring" "resonates in hindsight" in "the echo chamber created by the Zimmermann telegram." Surely, an image to be cherished, as is the one on p. 22, where Wilhelm is depicted as "the hub for his dozens of splintered advisers," whose whims "trickled down" and whose personality was like "the defining fractal of a crystal."

Despite such endearing imperfections, this is a solid, important book that calls into question one of the most enduring interpretations of American foreign policy in the early twentieth century. Because, as the author herself points out, motives can never be known with certainty, the traditional view of German-American relations will not be swept away at once, but Nancy Mitchell has dealt it a severe blow.

KENDRICK A. CLEMENTS

University of South Carolina
Columbia

STEIN, KENNETH W. 1999. *Heroic Diplomacy: Sadat, Kissinger, Carter, Begin, and the Quest for Arab-Israeli Peace.* Pp. xix, 324. New York: Routledge. Paperbound, $24.99.

Kenneth Stein's book is a masterly analysis of the diplomacy and politics in one of the most significant eras of the Arab-Israeli conflict and an American-managed peace.

Stein characterizes the personalities, motivations, and diplomatic and strategic actions and orientations of the dramatis personae involved in the protracted negotiations. These men of strong will, character, and determination were Anwar Sadat, president of Egypt; Yitzhak Rabin and Menachem Begin, prime ministers of Israel; Moshe Dayan, Israeli defense minister; U.S. presidents Richard Nixon, Jimmy Carter, and Gerald Ford; and the redoubtable shuttle diplomat Henry Kissinger, Nixon national security adviser, and Nixon-Ford secretary of state.

It was indeed heroic diplomacy. There could be no more different persons (along with their ideologies, diplomatic tactics, and behavior) than the leading characters that were responsible for this remarkable achievement. Anyone familiar with at least three of them—Sadat, Carter, and Begin—would have thought it impossible that they could come to such a groundbreaking agreement.

Stein's most significant contribution to our better understanding of the Israeli-Egyptian peace process is found in the chapters dealing with the end of the 1973 war, the Kilometer 101 Talks, and the prelude to Egyptian-Israeli and Syrian-Israeli troop withdrawals. The actions of the major American, Israeli, and Egyptian negotiators deserve the book's title, *Heroic Diplomacy*. The research, considering the information available up until now, is complete.

This book, for the first time, describes and analyzes the crucial and outstanding role played by American diplomacy. Stein chronicles an evolution of American diplomacy that will enter the annals of great modern diplomatic achievements. The Camp David agreement has served subsequent Middle Eastern peace negotiations. The Israeli-Egyptian, Jordanian-Israeli, Palestinian-Israeli, and now Syrian-Israeli peace negotiations have been modeled after Camp David.

Historians who deny the role of individual history must pay greater attention to the Arab-Israeli, American-inspired, and -managed diplomacy. There is a tendency among radical international relations historians and analysts to portray events and developments as institutional and legal complexities and to claim that resolution of conflict and peace can be achieved only by complex institutional arrangements. Students of international relations who analyze the complexity of the international system via abstract models, like Marxist and liberal historians, prefer to explain human interaction according to cultural, sociological, racial, religious, and other grand cultural institutions. They must finally surrender to the fact that heroic leadership, that is, individual persistence and vision, is more significant than social-cultural, psychohistorical, and other cultural orientations.

Stein's study demonstrates that in the same culture, anthropological configuration, and historical times, there are different political leaders. Some grasp the historical opportunity and others do not. It has nothing to do with society, culture, or psychoanalysis. Stein has put together a page-turning account of events, personal differences, ideologies, and strategies. This is a result of the most extensive research, including interviews with major leaders and diplomats, military men, and analysts, directly or indirectly involved with the long road to peace.

Political scientists, Middle Eastern scholars, negotiators of conflict, and students of conflict resolution will find the book a model for subsequent events. A keen and perceptive analyst of the complexities and details of complicated negotiations, Stein has produced a benchmark in the analysis and understanding of conflict resolution negotiations. In the words of Professor Itamar Rabinovitch, former ambassador to the United States and chief Israeli delegate in the Wye Syrian-Israeli negotiations, "This masterly study offers us diplomatic history at its best."

AMOS PERLMUTTER

American University
Washington, D.C.

SULLIVAN, VICKIE B. 1996. *Machiavelli's Three Romes: Religion, Human Liberty, and Politics Reformed*. Pp. xi, 235. DeKalb: Northern Illinois University Press. No price.

Machiavelli's religious convictions have always been a subject of controversy. There are scholars who view Machiavelli as an irreverent Christian of the anti-clerical or reform-clerical variety. There are others who count him as no Christian at all because of his excoriation of Church doctrine and his description of the faith as a man-made sect. But on one point the scholars agree, that Machiavelli, whatever his relationship to Christianity, values religion—civil religion, that is—as an indispensable tool of politics. Civil religion builds solidarity between the classes and cultivates in citizens the virtues of self-sacrifice, deference to authority, and hope for the future.

Vickie Sullivan, however, is the exception to this scholarly consensus. She advances the novel proposition that Machiavelli is the enemy of all religion. Machiavelli champions political liberty, and political liberty, Sullivan argues, is imperiled by demagogues promising the moon. Since it is religion that disposes people to hope for better things to come and to trust in deliverance from travails, religion prepares people—the people—for capture by demagogues. Rome is Machiavelli's case in point. Rome never quite managed the ambition of its "princes" and in the end succumbed to the demagoguery of Caesar. Moreover, pagan Rome prepared the way for Christian Rome, which carried this practice of promise making to its ultimate conclusion—the promise of everlasting life achieved by submission to Church authority.

It is because Machiavelli is critical of the Roman republic that returning to Rome through imitation of historical exemplar is not, in Sullivan's estimation, the intention of Machiavelli. Machiavelli's intent, rather, is the founding of a new Rome using approved features of pagan and Christian Rome.

The book is divided into three parts, one part for each of these three Romes. The first part lays out Machiavelli's critique of Christianity—that it bears responsibility for the weakness of the modern world and of Italy in particular. But Christianity did triumph over paganism, and so there is strength inside of Christian weakness, which strength Machiavelli uncovers and exploits. The second part examines ancient Rome, Machiavelli's seeming ideal. But the Rome Machiavelli describes is not exactly the Rome presented by Titus Livy, Machiavelli's authority in the *Discourses*. Paying close attention to Machiavelli's departures from Livy, Sullivan detects this central defect of Roman politics: that ambitious individuals were dealt with too leniently. The secret to longevity is a harshness bordering on ingratitude. Although Rome was famous for the severity of its penalties (for example, decimation),

they were not, in Machiavelli's judgment, severe enough and were not imposed with sufficient regularity. Paradoxically, Christianity, the religion of love and forgiveness, is in some of its doctrines (for example, eternal perdition) far crueler than was pagan Rome. The third part explains Machiavelli's own project, his creation of a new Rome rid of the shortcomings of the other two. The new Rome is an irreligious republic, one that defends political life from tyrannical usurpation by multiplying the number of ambitious elite. This new Rome will endure in perpetuity and so serve as an earthly rival to Christian paradise.

Sullivan's book fits squarely within the Straussian school of analysis in that it supposes Machiavelli's main objective to be the overturning of Christian modes and orders. But the book's thesis goes beyond Leo Strauss's (*Thoughts on Machiavelli* [1958]) in contending that Machiavelli's own modes and orders consist of a republican politics free of religion. *Machiavelli's Three Romes* is an important new study, cogently argued and beautifully written.

J. PATRICK COBY

Smith College
Northampton
Massachusetts

TERRIFF, TERRY, STUART CROFT, LUCY JAMES, and PATRICK MORGAN. 1999. *Security Studies Today*. Pp. 234. Cambridge, UK: Polity Press. $59.95. Paperbound, $26.95.

For those who study and make national security policy, the world has become a confusing place. The certainties of the Cold War, with its hegemonic enemy and strategy, have given way to the uncertainties of a thousand threats—none of them a dominant one—and no strategy to speak of. Amid this new strategic environment, the field of security studies—conceived in this book as central to the discipline of international relations—has fallen on difficult times. The old verities of realism, and the newer ones of neorealism and neoliberalism, continue to dominate the field, but they are under challenge by approaches that question not only the substance of supposed threats but also the very constitutiveness of the so-called dangerous world.

The four authors of this book, three based in the United Kingdom and the fourth in the United States, have taken on the difficult task of describing the uncertainties confronting security studies, from both the theoretical and policy angles. They have accomplished the task in admirable fashion. Beginning with a discussion of the relationship between international relations and security studies, they then consider, in turn, epistemologies based in "traditional views" (realism, neorealism, and neoliberalism), peace studies, gender, and "postpositivism" (postmodernism, social constructivism, critical theory, and feminist standpoints). In two additional chapters, the authors address "nontraditional" security threats involving the environment, economics, crime, and migration. Each chapter provides a thoughtful and informative summary of competing perspectives and relevant issues and examines carefully a number of the contradictions and complexities that arise. This book is highly recommended for use in any course in which a quick and straightforward introduction to approaches to competing security theories might be useful.

At the same time, however, and in spite of their best efforts, the authors reveal something of an epistemological bias in their presentation. By far, the easiest approaches to explain are the "traditional views"—realism, neorealism, and neoliberalism. In these, the state takes pride of place and represents the ontologically prior target (or referent) of threats. These views continue to dominate both literature and policy—indeed, their acolytes are quick to dismiss all others not only as irrelevant but also as threatening to "the intellectual coherence" of security studies, as Stephen Walt once put it—and they seem, as well, to represent most closely the real world. But why not? As constructivists would point out, if you act on the social reality you have constructed, it will come to look very much as you imagine it to be.

This privileging of the traditional is not intentional in what is, after all, a fine book. Moreover, inasmuch as the nontraditional approaches are given five chapters to tradition's one, my criticism might seem churlish. But the constant invocation of (mostly) realism and neorealism as the standard against which all else is to be measured tends to diminish the fundamental challenge posed by these alternative views (especially the postpositivist ones). The seeming disorder of the field—paralleling the disorder of the real world—is here attributed not to some ontological fallacy in its constitution but to a proliferation of views and threats. That the traditional views might be flawed or privileged for reasons of power is never raised. But, then, this book is intended as a text and not a critical examination of the field of security studies itself.

RONNIE D. LIPSCHUTZ

University of California
Santa Cruz

*AFRICA, ASIA, AND
LATIN AMERICA*

BROWN, MacALISTER and JOSEPH J. ZAZLOFF. 1998. *Cambodia Confounds the Peacemakers 1979-1998.*

Pp. xviii, 317. Ithaca, NY: Cornell University Press. $39.95.

There were at least three levels to the conflict over Cambodia following the Vietnamese invasion of 1979. At the global level, the great powers—the United States, the USSR, and China—were competing for influence. At the regional level, Thailand (with support from the Association of Southeast Asian Nations) competed for influence with Vietnam. Finally, there was a struggle for power between rival Cambodian groups, the most important of which were the Vietnamese-backed Heng Samrin government and the Chinese-backed Khmer Rouge.

Brown and Zazloff provide a thorough account of the negotiations between the Cambodian contenders leading to the Paris Agreement of 1991 and of the consequences flowing from that agreement: the breakup of the alliance of the non-Communists with the Khmer Rouge, the isolation and eventual disintegration of the Khmer Rouge, the U.N.-organized elections in 1993, and the formation and disintegration of the coalition government headed by Prince Norodom Rannaridh and Hun Sen. The main text finishes rather gloomily with Cambodia's lapse back into civil war in 1997. But an epilogue dealing with the national election (which Brown and Zazloff observed firsthand) ends the book on an upbeat note.

Brown and Zazloff's narrative is generally fair, although they are unduly reverential toward Prince Sihanouk and gloss over his more dubious machinations. On how the Cambodia conflict fitted into the international politics of the late Cold War period, however, Brown and Zazloff say too little. They give the misleading impression that the United States had nothing to do with Cambodia until it arrived in the 1990s seeking to save these quarrelsome, self-destructive people from themselves.

Nor do the authors give enough consideration to the political, administrative, and military capacities of the contending Cambodian parties. They assert that Cambodia before the U.N. elections was a "failed state." The elections replaced this with a new and democratic state. Unfortunately, this also "failed" in 1997. But the 1998 election points to a turn for the better.

The reality was much simpler. Cambodia was not a democracy, but neither was it a "failed state." A "failed state" means a state that has lost almost any capacity to function, resulting in anarchy, widespread violence, economic privation, and population dislocation. That describes the situation immediately following the collapse of the Khmer Rouge regime accurately enough, but this resulted from military defeat rather than an internal process of decay.

Over the 1980s, the political, administrative, and military capabilities of the Vietnamese-backed regime increased steadily. It was weakened in the 1990s by liberalization, but, as Brown and Zazloff note, the United Nations relied on the existing administration to maintain order. Many of the problems of the post-U.N. period have reflected the power of state officials and their willingness to abuse their power for personal gain, rather than a collapsed state and anarchy.

Thus the real political history in this period of Cambodia is not the dramatic story of successes and failures of democratic governance that Brown and Zazloff tell. It is a story of an authoritarian regime that responded to pressure by incorporating former oppositionists into the political oligarchy, isolating (and on occasion destroying) those who refuse to cooperate, and legitimating the oligarchy through quasi-democratic procedures. The result was a transition from a narrowly based one-party system not to pluralist democracy but to a somewhat more inclusive dominant-party system—a story not unfamiliar elsewhere in the region.

KELVIN ROWLEY

Swinburne University
  of Technology
Hawthorn
Australia

BUCKLEY, ROGER NORMAN. 1998. *The British Army in the West Indies: Society and the Military in the Revolutionary Age.* Pp. xx, 441. Gainesville: University Press of Florida. $55.00.

Roger Buckley, a veteran historian whose valued 1979 *Slaves in Red Coats* emphasized political, military, and legal issues, now offers a descriptive "community study" of that same army. To become oriented, the reader might well start with chapter 7, which outlines the wars of 1792-1815 as they affected the West Indies, before returning to the beginning of the book. There is a good bibliography included, but nonexpert readers will need a map for this trip, for none is provided.

Unusual drawings and paintings, some of the author's own collection, are analyzed thoroughly and often insightfully. The other striking feature is lyrical descriptive passages about geography, climate, architecture, and the life of soldiers, wives, children, concubines, "King's negroes," and other civilians linked to the military. These descriptions, by a scholar and novelist very familiar with the West Indies, are always interesting but sometimes reach far beyond the surviving documents, pictures, or sites the author has studied.

The central intriguing paradox is that, in the last 14 years of the British slave trade, the imperial government bought 13,400 slaves to be soldiers in the West Indian Regiment, plus some 5000 supporting "King's negroes." This slave regiment was socially revolutionary and was resented by the local plantocracy it defended, even before some civil rights were granted to the slave soldiers. Buckley's impassioned denunciation of race and class prejudice in the military cannot fit with his claim that there were "egalitarian conditions" (p. 200) in the garrisons. He also makes the provocative suggestion that the British abolition of the slave trade was delayed because the British government desperately needed the slave soldiers. Abolition of the slave trade would have been delayed at least 7-8 years beyond 1807 if this argument had been decisive.

The most compelling descriptions concern health. Slightly more than half of the European redcoats who served in the British West Indies died in the service, most due to disease. Buckley is horrified by the fatal parsimony of local and imperial governments and by what he calls "intellectually trapped" surgeons. Here Buckley is condescending and anachronistic. He rightly applauds the advances made, especially through the use of medical statistics and routine autopsies on thousands of exiled men, yet he impatiently condemns the ignorance of those who could not yet know about germ theory or about mosquitoes as carriers of yellow fever. He is equally censorious about those who could not know that the traditional "natural" evils of slavery and the subjugation of women would not prove eternal.

Buckley disarmingly hopes his work "will one day encourage someone to write a full history of the British army in the West Indies." This will involve more than adding discussions of periods he has not covered. At least 10 times (pp. 101, 127, 136, 151, 154, 166, 208, 218, 225, 294), Buckley admits that he has not studied the surviving regimental and court martial records for the West India Regiment.

His discussions of demography, crime and punishment, and numerous aspects of the social life of the regiment are speculative where they could and should be much more accurate and convincing. This serious scholarly shortcoming, however, should not deter most readers from enjoying this well-written description of a very fascinating subject.

IAN K. STEELE

University of Western Ontario
London
Canada

LI, LINDA C. 1998. *Centre and Provinces: China 1978-1993*. Pp. xiv, 342. Oxford, UK: Clarendon Press. $85.00.

The relationship between the central authorities and the provinces in China has received much attention from scholars and commentators. In the absence of a durable constitutional arrangement, commentators have wondered about whether increasing autonomy, growing economic strength, and differences in cultural and political identity might lead China to dissolution, like the former Soviet Union.

In this scholarly treatise, Linda Li argues that the relationship between center and provinces should not be looked at in purely zero-sum terms. Just because the provinces are becoming more powerful with the reforms does not mean that the center cannot hold. After all, both the central government and the local authorities are elements of a complex state in the process of transformation. Other scholars have made similar comments before, but Li has provided the most sustained argument for a non-zero-sum approach in this attractively produced book.

The bulk of the book is a comparison of Shanghai and Guangdong's interactions with the central government in Beijing.

While Shanghai is what is known as a centrally administered municipality, Guangdong is a province known for its liberal economic policies and stellar export-oriented growth. Li focuses on how these two provincial units implemented central investment policy and on the discretionary behavior the two territorial units enjoyed until the early 1990s. She finds that while the attention of Shanghai's leaders was riveted to the central government, Guangdong became steadily more independent vis-à-vis the center during the 1980s. She suggests that the divergences were partly due to historically divergent perceptions of different roles held by local elites.

In spite of the divergent institutional contexts for the two provincial units, however, Li finds that both had substantial room for maneuver, thus blunting the reach of the central state. Indeed, Li contends that influence also flowed from the provinces to the center. The provinces did not simply implement central policies but also helped formulate central policies through advocacy. Li's emphasis on interactions thus leads her to call attention to both institutions and agency in shaping central-provincial relations. She argues that while the center and the provinces may have conflictual relations, they nevertheless need each other and will compromise out of self-interest. This is all the more so because of "the possibility that the province, as well as the national center, could become the 'central zone' of values, beliefs, and actions." She concludes that the centrist perspective of the state capacity paradigm fails to adequately explain the coexistence of central and provincial power and to anticipate circumstances of change.

While I broadly agree with Li's assessment, I believe that she underestimates the perceptions of conflict between the center and provinces by the main political actors. These evolving perceptions and the concerns they generate have driven efforts by central leaders to re-structure central-provincial relations. Unfortunately, because Li chose 1993 as the cutoff date, she was able to provide only a glimpse of the emerging trends. For example, she notes that the 1994 fiscal and tax reforms showed a trend toward a clearer demarcation of the rights and obligations of both parties in China's political economy. Such institutionalization may well serve as the shock absorbers of conflictual interests and benefit both sides in the future. Yet, ironically, central leaders pushed for such institutionalization precisely because they feared losing out to the provinces in a zero-sum game.

All in all, this is a well-crafted study and a useful contribution to the growing literature on the political economy of China.

DALI L. YANG

University of Chicago
Illinois

OKANO, KAORI and MOTONORI TSUCHIYA. 1999. *Education in Contemporary Japan: Inequality and Diversity.* Pp. xvi, 270. New York: Cambridge University Press. $64.95. Paperbound, $19.95.

English-language scholarship on Japanese education has made impressive strides over the past 10 years or so, as anyone working in this field can attest. Well, almost anyone. In trumpeting the originality of their own book, *Education in Contemporary Japan*, Okano and Tsuchiya insist that "most of those studies that are available in the English language" are "grossly incomplete" because they are preoccupied with "the roles that schools have played in the society's modernization and development." The authors need not resort to such exaggeration, however, for their valuable study can stand on its own merits, among which is its skillful incorporation of research published in English as well as in Japanese. The end result is a comprehensive, balanced, up-to-date look at the flip side of "the unprecedented 'success' of Japan's modernization," which is captured in the book's subtitle, "inequality and diversity." Structured around a flexible theoretical framework, written in unpretentious prose, backed up with pertinent statistics, and illustrated with more than 20 ethnographic case studies, it can be read profitably by specialists and non-specialists seeking a new perspective on Japanese society, as well as by students and researchers in comparative education and the sociology and anthropology of education.

The book opens with a critical discussion of contending theoretical approaches to the study of Japanese education, focusing on what Okano and Tsuchiya see as the two dominant "analytical frameworks" that have guided previous studies: "consensus theories" and "conflict theories." Notwithstanding their differences, both theories "see structural forces and the needs of the society as directly determining what occurs in schools and, in turn, regard what schools do as contributing to the maintenance of the existing society." The problem is that "what schools do and the outcomes of schooling are more diverse than either type of theory make us believe. The relations among schools, families and society are more complex, problematic, and even unpredictable." To understand how those complex relations influence the ability of schools to carry out their four main roles in modern society (transmission of knowledge; socialization and acculturation; selection and differentiation; legitimation of knowledge), the authors champion "interactionist approaches," which are based on the premise that "students, teachers, parents and others are active in attaching particular meaning to an event, and in creating their own experience" within constraints imposed by changing external factors.

Chapter 2 attempts a chronological summary of "the historical background to the present realities of schooling," commencing with the modernizing reforms instituted by the government during the Meiji period (1868-1912). While obviously no substitute for a book-length history, it succeeds in demonstrating that no matter how long the shadow cast by the organs of state control, Japanese teachers and students have never been merely passive products of their school system.

Chapters 3 and 4 combine a description of different educational tracks and institutions with a grassroots look at contemporary students' experiences of schooling, revealing "a gap between the provision of educational opportunities and the 'consumption' of them." Chapter 3 compares the experiences of diverse social groups (the middle class, girls, the poor, the privileged, correspondence school students, and rural youths from farm families), while Chapter 4 relates the experiences of different minorities in Japan (Koreans, Burakumin, and the children of recent legal and illegal foreign residents).

Chapter 5 turns to teachers' experiences of schooling, including preservice and in-service training; mandatory school transfers and interschool differences; the system of promotion; the changing fortunes of the teachers' unions; and exercising individuality in a "shared culture of teaching." Considerable attention is given to gender and generational differences between teachers and to differences between teaching in Japan and in the West.

Chapters 6 and 7 present a thoughtful analysis of the highly publicized school problems of bullying, school refusal, and physical punishment, followed by a critical assessment of the government-spon- sored reform campaigns of the 1980s and 1990s. Each chapter concludes with a useful summary and a short list of suggested readings.

MARK LINCICOME

College of the Holy Cross
Worcester
Massachusetts

EUROPE

HUGHES, MICHAEL L. 1999. *Shouldering the Burdens of Defeat: West Germany and the Reconstruction of Social Justice.* Pp. xi, 266. Chapel Hill: University of North Carolina Press. $49.95.

This book is a first-class contribution to post–World War II history. Hughes, professor of history at Wake Forest University, fills an important gap in the literature with this first analysis in English of the globally all-but-unique postwar German Equalization of Burdens (*Lastenausgleich*) legislation, which helped stabilize the war-torn society by shifting assets from property owners relatively unscathed by the war to refugees, bombing victims, and other "war-damaged" Germans. But he does far more. In contrast to the German standard work on the subject, Reinhold Schillinger's *Der Entscheidungsprozess beim Lastenausgleich, 1945-1952* (1985), which will remain the chief source for specifics on the legislation, Hughes examines the debates around the *Lastenausgleich* and its ultimate enactment in the context of post-1945 West German political culture and economic reconstruction. He is equally at home in both, and he presents both with the same pristine clarity.

In broad agreement with Volker Berghahn (especially *Industrial Relations in West Germany*, 1987) and Charles S. Maier (for example, "The Two

Postwar Eras and the Conditions for Stability in Twentieth-Century Western Europe," *American Historical Review*, 86(2):327-52 [1981]), Hughes shows effectively that, in the *Lastenausgleich* debates, Germans had learned from the past—whether due to the depth of the depression and World War II catastrophe or due to pressures from outside. What allows him to make his case so convincingly are the specific comparisons he can draw on from his earlier work on the 1922-23 inflation, *Paying for the German Inflation* (1988). The critical difference was that post–World War II German leaders understood that democracy and ultimately stability required compromise. As the Basic Principles of the most powerful postwar neoliberal economic organization, *Wirtschaftspolitische Gesellschaft von 1947*, put it: "Compromise, though much-maligned in Germany (in the past), is a valuable and indispensable tool of practical democracy." Increasingly, this moved business leaders to accept the costs of the sharing-of-burdens legislation, and the protesting groups to acknowledge the limitations, both of which were clearly buttressed by the common fear of communism.

Hughes also looks to German political cultural traditions to explain the success of the burden-sharing campaign. In the first postwar years, communalist notions deeply rooted in pre-Nazi society were especially important in bolstering the demand for a *Lastenausgleich* even among business, permitting politics to "trump economic expertise." This communalist stage, which was not unrelated to the more extreme Nazi notions of racial community, allowed the "war-damaged" to claim status as the virtuous who had sacrificed, rather than being victims, and to call for "sifting out the virtuous from among current property holders." With the triumph of the neoliberal market economy, the discourse shifted to the right of individual restitution of property

and professional or social status, which had more "restorationist" implications. The key to the success not only of the *Lastenausgleich* campaign but also of the stabilization and remarkable democratization of West German society was ultimately that "the war-damaged leadership sought to be accepted into, not overthrow the Federal Republic"—and that Adenauer Germany rewarded that acceptance. This phenomenon, which James Diehl showed dramatically for the post–World War II German veterans in *Thanks to the Fatherland* (1993), was critical for the German "political miracle" of democratization. Hughes adds an important amendment to this: "The West German economy was successful enough to legitimate the social-market economy and finance a meaningful *Lastenausgleich*— but weak enough to justify limits on any *Lastenausgleich*"—and thereby prevent the collapse of the "economic miracle" that financed all the stabilization and democratization.

DIETHELM PROWE

Carleton College
Northfield
Minnesota

UNITED STATES

BILLINGSLEY, WILLIAM J. 1999. *Communists on Campus: Race, Politics, and the Public University in Sixties North Carolina.* Pp. xvi, 308. Athens: University of Georgia Press. $29.95.

Nearly a decade after McCarthyism appeared to have played itself out in American higher education, the North Carolina General Assembly passed a law to prevent Communists or anyone who had invoked the Fifth Amendment before a federal or state investigative panel from speaking on a public college or university campus. Although there had been no known Communist activity in North Carolina for a decade prior to the enactment of this legislation, a number of opinion makers and rural lawmakers seemed convinced that public higher education was being exploited by subversives. Not many of those less convinced were eager to publicly challenge the demagogues. In large part, this occurred because (contrary to the general misperception spread about by V. O. Key, Jr., and others) liberalism was not a vital force in North Carolina. The state's cultural values were, and today remain, "distinctly agrarian, traditional, and southern." Jesse Helms was a force in promoting this attack on public higher education in 1963; he was elected to the United States Senate in 1972, and in 2001 he still represents North Carolina there.

William J. Billingsley's *Communists on Campus* is a sober and detailed account of the causes and consequences of the Act to Regulate Visiting Speakers, which was in force in North Carolina between 1963 and 1966. As Billingsley sees it, the law was doomed to fail not only because it was an infringement on the authority of the system's governing board in violation of what was permissible by the national higher education establishment—importantly, the Southern Association of Colleges and Schools threatened to withdraw accreditation—but also because the state's ruling elite were concerned that the prestige and prospects of the research university at Chapel Hill would be irrevocably harmed if ultimate power was not directly returned to the trustees. If not, the law would have had a long-term negative impact on the state's economy. Moreover, academic administrators, faculty, and students at Chapel Hill and around the state were overwhelmingly anti-Communist, and outside pressure was hardly necessary to impose political conformity. After some of the bite was taken from the speaker ban by 1966, the demands on higher educa-

tion took other forms—for example, there was more than the usual vigorous campaign to rid campuses of those deemed disorderly or disruptive—in the second half of the decade. Finally, in 1968, a federal court found the statutes "facially unconstitutional because of vagueness" and ruled them "null and void."

Billingsley makes a compelling case that the Cold War—Soviet expansionism or the newer threat from the People's Republic of China—was not the only driving force behind the speaker ban and the subsequent sniping. Another motivation was to derail or at least slow down the civil rights movement. As Jim Crow began to unravel, white conservatives reacted by embracing the politics of anti-Communism. Of course, some believed that the hand of Communism was behind any effort to end racial segregation.

As many politicians saw it, the Chapel Hill campus (the oldest state-supported university in the country, having been created in 1776, its first students arriving in 1795) was too leftward leaning and dangerous, and they were convinced that it was imperative to hem in some of its faculty and students. The administration was aware "that the absence of CP [Communist Party] members was insufficient to placate critics," that the critics were not primarily interested in "the removal of nonexistent CP members but surveillance of dissidents and insurgents—including civil rights activists—whose views fell beyond the acceptable parameters of the state's political culture."

Still, there is not much of a story here. During the period that the posturing and skirmishing were being played out in the media and across the state, no one was convicted of any crime and only the contracts of an unlucky graduate student and an instructor of social work were not renewed, the latter after the law had been declared unconstitutional. Even when it was in effect, the law actually carried no criminal penalty for violation;

it only mandated that academic administrators in public institutions of higher learning enforce it. For the most part, they were eager to oblige. When they felt it necessary to act cowardly or duplicitously, they preached, as they often do, the gospel of "the greater good."

In the end, the reputation of the campus at Chapel Hill as one of America's better universities remained untarnished. The reputation of academic administrators remained unchanged.

LIONEL S. LEWIS

State University of New York
Buffalo

CASPER, SCOTT E. 1999. *Constructing American Lives: Biography and Culture in Nineteenth-Century America.* Pp. xii, 439. Chapel Hill: University of North Carolina Press. $49.95. Paperbound, $19.95.

Scott Casper's *Constructing American Lives* is a cultural history of biography and ideas about biography in America from the 1790s to the turn of the twentieth century. Casper believes that nineteenth-century biography has much to tell us if the right questions are asked: How did nineteenth-century biographies work? What were their purposes and means of achieving these purposes? Finally, how did Americans understand, discuss, debate, and reshape the meanings of biography during this period? As a cultural historian, Casper reconstructs the American experience of biography, taken "on its own terms." A cultural history of biography should expand the logic, method, purpose, and subject matter of its inquiry beyond mere notions of genre or text, author or reader, into the space of a complexly interactive formation both constitutive and reflective of that cul-

ture. Casper succeeds impressively in doing this.

The author's historical narrative, which this brief review can recount only in much-condensed summary, unfolds in four parts: (1) postrevolutionary and early Republic biography (1790-1820), one strand emphasizing civic character and character formation for the new nation, the other emphasizing Samuel Johnson's notion of "domestic privacies"; (2) early to mid-century biography (1820-60), shaped by didactic and nation-building values and focusing on representative great men and women, yet also beginning to diverge into sectional biography; (3) mid-century reevaluation of biographical didacticism, literary reconception of the biographer's task, and distinction between "high" realms of literary biography and "middle" realms of didactic biography (1850-80); and (4) end-of-century divergence between the biographical pantheons created by literary publishers in the Northeast and subscription firms in the Midwest and West, this phenomenon occurring in the midst of academic historians' questioning the very value of biography (1880-1900). By century's end, biography, or at least high-culture biography, had been redefined as literature, a redefinition that, in turn, effaced much nineteenth-century biography, which seemed no longer worthy of the name.

Casper's study resourcefully allies methods of new historicism (reading texts in relevant contexts) with those of history of the book (archival gathering of data regarding production and distribution)—methods often pursued separately—in his examination of many different kinds of materials. Those materials include, among others, biographies of "great men," campaign biographies, "mug books," biographical series, lives of women and minorities, reviews of and writings about biography, documents relating to publishing and distribution, letters, and diaries.

The book's five main chapters of historical narrative alternate with brief sections that Casper calls "interludes," "designed to capture moments in Americans' biographical experience." These interludes focus on individual biographers and readers: Parson Weems, Nathaniel Hawthorne, Jared Sparks, James Garfield, and two "ordinary" readers of the 1830s and 1840s, Michael Floy and Julia Parker. They complement the main chapters' large, weightily documented story of nineteenth-century biography by entering the reading and writing lives of individuals. Thus Casper's book enacts, in its manifold approach to the subjects, makers, and readers of biography, one of the defining dramas and challenging cruxes of this form, namely, how to understand life as both individual and social, as particular yet related to other people and to the web of culture, all of these elements being neither monolithic nor purely theorizable before the fact.

Constructing American Lives, one may infer from dates given in the acknowledgments, took the better part of a decade to complete, including six years during which it was "sustained" by the author's department (History) at the University of Nevada, Reno. Such a substantial investment of time and the correlates nourished by time—curiosity, patience, scholarly endurance, and judgment applied to a large and worthwhile project—are to be valued and praised especially in our contemporary academic atmosphere of the rush to publish. The powerfully good results of this investment are apparent on every page. They account for how and why the book has much to say to a broad and diverse audience of readers: not only those interested in nineteenth-century American biography, history, and culture but also anyone interested in our contemporary culture of

biography and in what might be called the scholarship of time travel wherein we may, while remaining consciously within and aware of our own historical moment, move somewhat toward the experience of a real past, inhabited by real people, whose real experience in their culture is thrillingly worth the effort and time it takes to discover.

CATHERINE PARKE

University of Missouri
Columbia

CHALOUPKA, WILLIAM. 1999. *Everybody Knows: Cynicism in America*. Pp. xviii, 241. Minneapolis: University of Minnesota Press. $25.95.

An advance blurb to William Chaloupka's *Everybody Knows* announces that it is "the best book on American politics in quite a while." Accustomed to public relations hype, one would normally treat such pronouncements with a generous dollop of skepticism, if not downright cynicism. We do not want to be disappointed, because our hopes have been dashed before. Once burned, twice shy. We have become cynics. Everybody knows that publicists use inflated rhetoric, just as everybody knows that politicians lie through their teeth. Chaloupka's book is about that very subject, our pervasive cynicism about everything, especially public matters.

Sometimes in life, however, one can be surprised. *Everybody Knows* just may be the best book on American politics in quite a while. Indeed, Chaloupka has written a superb book. Offering an insightful analysis that has far-reaching implications while presented in a lively format that manages to be neither depressing nor romantic, *Everybody Knows* explores a seemingly intractable American tendency toward political cynicism. To be sure, Chaloupka is not the first to observe that Americans are a cynical bunch. Numerous others have opined that Americans have lost faith in their political system. From Watergate to Monicagate, from Roger Ailes to Dick Morris, from Rush Limbaugh to Cokie Roberts, we have learned to abandon our credulity along with our hope. As E. J. Dionne has told us, Americans now hate politics.

But Chaloupka is the first to resist the temptation to call for some restored national sense of sincerity or civility as antidote. Numerous public commentators in recent years have lamented our collective drift toward disbelief and, in turn, have prescribed various initiatives toward recuperating our lost allegiance. We have heeded calls for more virtues, more values, more trust, more community, more citizenship, more civility, more soulfulness, more decency, more republicanism, more social capital, more meaning, more deliberation, and so on. Most recently, young Jedediah Purdy has jumped into the fray with his unironic plea for "common things." Chaloupka successfully puts all of these civic appeals into perspective. Preaching against cynicism will not undo it and probably will compound it, creating even more cynical backlash when promises inevitably fall short. Alas, these do-gooding people are setting us up to be suckers once again, and we know it.

Cynicism in America is more entrenched than our civilitarians seem to realize. Chaloupka warns that there is no easy way or any 12-step program out of the self-fulfilling syndrome of cynicism. Instead, we need to learn how to distinguish between different cynical modes. Some homegrown varieties of cynicism are angry, hateful, and lethal. Ruling or rich cynics are more powerful than sideline cynics. Some cynicism is, however, healthy and attractive. Drawing upon Peter Sloterdijk's *Critique of Cynical Rea-*

son (1983), Chaloupka cautiously recommends a reconsideration of Diogenes' classical kynicism as a possible antidote to our modern discontent. The ancient kynic poked fun at the pompous, and such sportiveness might be able to tease our current cynics back into cheeky encounters with politics.

Chaloupka is nobody's fool, and he is not floating a balloon for us simply to burst. Still, one suspects that his application of kynicism to the American context may be too generous. Diogenes mocked power by urinating, masturbating, spitting, and farting in the public sphere. Howard Stern better exemplifies Sloterdijk's "cheeky" kynic than baby-boomer humorist Dave Barry. Hegel's critique of Diogenes' public perversity may come into play here, too. Diogenes repudiated Socrates' eroticism by publicly masturbating, albeit in a tub. Such cheeky displays are liable to isolate, claims Hegel, rather than to "invite people back into the public realm with both high purpose and good spirits," as Chaloupka entertains. The reader does not, however, need to cast all such doubts aside in order to appreciate this wise and wonderfully written book.

JOHN SEERY

Pomona College
Claremont
California

EPSTEIN, WILLIAM M. 1999. *Children Who Could Have Been: The Legacy of Child Welfare in Wealthy America*. Pp. vii, 155. Madison: University of Wisconsin Press. $22.95.

Children Who Could Have Been is a somewhat shocking and angry account of the child welfare system in America. It is Epstein's view that that social need and society's response to it are driven by what is termed social efficiency, defined as society's expectation that essential social goals for children can be achieved in the poorly planned and poorly funded programs that the child welfare system comprises. Epstein does a sensitive job of discussing two cases that languished long term in the child welfare system. In this discussion, he presents compelling accounts of the harm to these two children resulting from badly conceptualized and executed interventions to deal with the child maltreatment that characterized the two cases. The cases also speak to the pathetic efforts of a system that has historically not done a great job of providing adequate and timely services to children, to re-create and self-regulate itself in providing sound services for the children who must use it. More generally, Epstein posits that, in many instances, services offered through the child welfare system have not helped children but may have actually harmed them. He suggests that were it not for some native resilience of the children placed in the child welfare system, they would have been much worse off after their interface with it.

Epstein thoroughly reviewed child welfare evaluation and outcome studies that have been conducted over the past three decades. Major child welfare studies cited in his review were used as supporting documentation for the Adoption Assistance and Child Welfare Act of 1980. Under the provisions of this act, the possibility was created that service improvement would occur beginning at intake, through the treatment phase, and would result in better placements for children. Epstein believes that most of the efforts to implement system changes through the act of 1980 have had little effect on the life chances of the children served by the child welfare system. He claims that it is "pernicious liberals," those who research and run child welfare services and claim liberal values and politics, who have colluded with conservative politicians who have no real interest

in improving the situation of poor, neglected, multiple-need children. In his scathing analysis of major child welfare studies, he contends that "pernicious liberals," many of whom are academicians, have done sloppy research. With all but a few exceptions, Epstein finds the studies he reviewed to be conceptually unclear and methodologically flawed; in addition, researchers either ignored their findings that raised questions about program effectiveness or used weak trend data to support their claims of program effectiveness. This furthers his claim that researchers and administrators of child welfare programs are not guided by what is known to be good for children in the shaping of services; rather, they are guided by political considerations in claiming program effectiveness. He asserts that the "pernicious liberals" are satisfied that a modicum of success has been achieved through less-than-authentic efforts to help endangered and troubled children, and political conservatives are happy that whatever is provided for children caught in the child welfare system be provided as cheaply as possible.

Although he claims that the research about child welfare programs and policy is less than credible, as are the programs created and supported by "pernicious liberals," Epstein offers little in the way of solutions. He does suggest that honest experimentation be conducted with well-thought-out, well-funded, and well-evaluated congregate models of service such as Boys Town. Although a broad-brush approach such as Boys Town to children in need will be very costly, it was just that type of intervention that gave hope to the two cases he reviewed.

Although Epstein raises considerable questions about the extant research and the persons who do it, and he lays much of the blame for the failure of the child welfare system at the feet of those who, over time, looked at ways to improve it, this book is a must read for child welfare policymakers, scholars, and administrators.

PETER B. VAUGHAN

University of Pennsylvania
Philadelphia

GJERDE, JON. 1999. *The Minds of the West: Ethnocultural Evolution in the Rural Middle West, 1830-1917*. Pp. xiii, 426. Chapel Hill: University of North Carolina Press. $39.95. Paperbound, $19.95.

This well-received book earned the 1997 Theodore Saloutos Memorial Book Award from both the Immigration History Society and the Agricultural History Society. It has recently been issued in a paperbound edition. Gjerde undertakes a sweeping analysis of the acculturation process experienced by the major ethnic groups settling the upper Middle West. He focuses mainly on German Catholics and Norwegian Lutherans in Iowa and Minnesota, but he also incorporates those such as German Lutherans and Irish Catholics in the region including Illinois, Iowa, Minnesota, Wisconsin, and the Dakotas. He contrasts the "minds" that organized the cultural and social patterns of northern European immigrants and native-born northeastern internal migrants. The European mind emphasized hierarchical authoritarianism, conservatism, and collective institutions—the family, the church, and the community—to maintain the moral order. In contrast, the American mind, derived from native Puritanism, emphasized individualism, liberalism, and democracy as fundamental to achieving economic growth and progress. From the mid-nineteenth century until World War I, immigrant groups maintained distinct and insular communities united internally by language and culture, plucking from the wider society only those bits valued—rights to land, freedom of religion, individualism, and citizenship. Gjerde draws heavily from ethnic presses, dairies, and religious publications and synthesizes the rich body of historical and anthropological studies of ethnicity of the region. In addition, major novels of the period add rich human detail.

In four parts, Gjerde describes the cultural interactions of the two minds that shaped regional social and political patterns. Part 1, "The Region," covers the West as an idea and a context. For Europeans, the abundance of land and freedom allowed them to simultaneously preserve cultural patterns while paradoxically cementing loyalty to their new country. Yankees, for the same reasons, were suspicious of the region's potential to fragment the Union. In "The Community," part 2 and the heart of the book, Gjerde shows a chain migration process that fostered tightly knit homogeneous communities that, unlike Europe, were voluntary and thus more fluid. The diverse cultural landscape meant that boundaries between communities were maintained, but theological conflicts, in particular, simmered within. In part 3 "The Family," Gjerde shows how cultural differences were reproduced. Because agriculture was carried out by the household, and land use was shaped by inheritance, ethnic distinctions continued due to the conservative tendencies of the family. Europeans maintained a patriarchal authority that subordinated women and children to the preservation of a corporate lineage linked to land. Yankees, however, treated inheritance, land, and working relationships more democratically, and relationships as more contractual and voluntary. Finally, in part 4, "The Society," Gjerde shows that the family as the fundamental building block of society shaped perspectives toward politics at the community and regional level.

Political party participation and attitudes toward nineteenth-century concerns such as temperance and women's suffrage reflected the theological and social divide between the groups.

Gjerde's impressive argument about cultural evolution informs another clash of minds in the rural Midwest. Three or four generations later, small towns, long accustomed to people's leaving, face a wave of new immigration. Rather than abundant land, the attraction for Mexican and Asian immigrants is work in the meatpacking plants in such places as Storm Lake and Marshalltown, Iowa, or Garden City, Kansas. First recruited by the meatpacking companies because of labor shortages (like the railroads' recruitment of nineteenth-century immigrants), these ethnic groups soon formed migration chains that continually replenish the local workforce and, again, foster distinct ethnic settlements. As Gjerde described a period a century earlier, clashes have emerged between those who think migrants should become Americans and speak English, and those who want to celebrate inclusiveness. History, of course, shows that the past is repeated, but the lesson does not make accommodation any easier.

SONYA SALAMON

University of Illinois
Urbana

REAGAN, MICHAEL D. 1999. *The Accidental System: Health Care Policy in America*. Pp. xiv, 176. Boulder, CO: Westview Press. $55.00. Paperbound, $15.95.

There is no doubt where Michael Reagan stands on the main issues in health care. He has written a highly readable, if somewhat polemical, book on the many ailments of the American health care "system." His presentation veers toward the introductory level, but the book contains a lot of information and is a good review of how we got to where we are.

The main argument of the book is a nonstarter in any other advanced industrial country: that government has a mandate to provide health care coverage as a right of citizenship. Only in the United States is the ideal of universal access based on need contradicted by a preference for market-based choices over government intervention. Other countries have introduced a number of market mechanisms to control spiraling costs and instill competition and choice into health care, but these all operate within the framework of fundamental government regulations. The American contradiction has resulted in what Reagan calls an "accidental system"—"it has not been purposely created but inadvertently developed . . . from ideological preferences[s] . . . and decision[s,] with absolutely no thought" to their future impact.

Reagan takes us through the history and politics of health care policy in the twentieth century and elaborates our major public programs (Medicare and Medicaid), legislative initiatives, delivery systems (now dominated by managed care), and the sorry state of the uninsured. He presents some important observations. For example, after the debacle of the Clinton plan, a curious turnaround in the attitude of the public and legislators toward government intervention ushered in a host of new bills that increased micromanagement of health care. These included the Newborn and Mothers' Health Protection Act, an expansion of the Children's Health Insurance Program, and the introduction of Medicare + Choice at the national level and, at the state level, mandates on coverage in employers' plans and "pushing" (Reagan's word throughout) Medicaid recipients into health maintenance organizations (HMOs). Reagan does not explain this about-face beyond saying that "being anti-Washington does not mean being antigovernment in the new state activism," which leaves us wondering about his main argument.

Reagan's solution to the problems of American health care is to universalize Medicare. Medicare is one program that apparently modifies antigovernment sentiment. But several reforms are making it more market-based and selective. For example, Medicare + Choice allows wealthier recipients to choose plans that retain many fee-for-service features but at a higher cost. Those who cannot afford these costs opt for basic HMO plans that are fully paid by Medicare. Reagan acknowledges that the "trilemma" he sets up is irresolvable—optimizing any two of the ideals of high-quality care, maximum access, and low cost undermines the third. He does not explain how increasing the number of Medicare recipients would affect the "trilemma." Nor is he, therefore, convincing about why this solution is better than any of the alternatives being tested. For example, several states are achieving near-universal coverage by cutting costs in the Medicaid program and using the savings to cover the uninsured. While arguable, the measures all recognize that health care has limits (rationing in Oregon, managed care elsewhere). To be sure, state initiatives create an even more unsystematic system, but might they be more politically feasible than trying to emulate other countries? We all recognize that something has to give. What we need is sound argumentation for why.

In the end, Reagan does not provide the kind of sound argumentation that would advance our debate on health care. His book reads like a compilation of undergraduate lecture notes, asides included (he seems to enjoy sarcasms). I prefer a more sophisticated, reasoned approach for my students, and a book with more references for information that is clearly derivative.

MARY RUGGIE

Columbia University
New York City

RILEY, RUSSELL L. 1999. *The Presidency and the Politics of Racial Inequality: Nation-Keeping from 1831-1965*. Pp. xiv, 373. New York: Columbia University Press. $49.50. Paperbound, $22.50.

In 1990, Derrick Bell wrote a chilling essay entitled "The Space Traders." It is set in the near future: America is in danger of collapse due to decades of fiscal and environmental mismanagement, and a party of aliens from an unknown planet arrives with a proposition. They offer to fix all these problems, and, in return, they want every African American delivered to a designated area for immediate emigration. Even though no one knows the fate of these citizens, the fictional president of the United States, without any apparent hesitation, engineers the trade. He sets in motion the legal precedents, orchestrates public support, and even suppresses dissent. On 15 January (Martin Luther King, Jr.'s birthday), the trade is completed as millions of African Americans are transported aboard space ships. Bell's essay raises the question of the extent to which African Americans are welcomed as an integral part of American culture. Russell L. Riley's *Presidency and the Politics of Racial Inequality* does not employ Bell's dystopian format, but it does raise this related question: to what extent is the presidency historically an office that is complicit in sustaining racial inequality?

According to Riley, occupants of the presidency are driven exclusively by the institution's "nation-keeping" mandate set out in the Constitution. Explained by Hamilton in the *Federalist Papers*, "energy" in the executive was primarily designed to protect the nation against both foreign and domestic threats. The suppression of the Whiskey Insurrection by Washington and the Alien and Sedition Acts under Adams were early exercises of this presidential nation-keeping power. Placed in the context of racial conflict, however, the nation-keeping power took on new and tragic dimensions. Incentive structures in the Constitution as well as racism in the political culture at large ensured that no president would be elected to take on the mammoth project of racial equality in the first place, and, once in office, no president would invest his power in such an uncertain endeavor.

Riley presents an extensive historical analysis to establish his thesis that no president has acted to promote racial equality until social movements independent of the office grew to such proportions that a president was forced to act in order to secure national stability. Beginning with the Jackson presidency and the "thirty years 'war' " against slavery, and extending through the New Deal and the Truman, Eisenhower, Kennedy, and Johnson administrations, Riley concludes that even those presidents deemed most heroic in regard to civil rights "embraced transformational change when they were convinced that in the fashion of Luther, they could do no other."

This historical narrative is a rich and powerful one that ranges from sustained presidential neglect of civil rights (FDR) to overt suppression (Jackson and the abolitionist mail controversy). Riley is particularly adept at unpacking Lincoln's complex strategies in regard to slavery, war goals, and reconstruction plans. In some areas, his analysis is less convincing. For example, in his review of Lyndon Johnson's record on civil rights, Riley contends that Johnson's goals were designed only to "sign on" African Americans as "footsoldiers in the war on poverty" and to seek their help in "steering black organizational skills into party building enterprises." But these conclusions overlook both Johnson's intricate psychological and political relationship with the Kennedys as well as his high-risk strategy in regard to the 1964 and 1965 Civil Rights Acts, both of which are only loosely tethered to a nation-keeping role.

Riley's theoretical assessment that the presidency has been grossly overrated as a "monumental" institution poised to intervene in moments of national crisis is probably itself overstated. Overlooked is the question of what impact past heroic presidencies, mythic though they may be, have on current occupants of the office as well as on public expectations. Nevertheless, Riley does engage in such a thoughtful and provocative exercise that *The Presidency and the Politics of Racial Inequality* should become a standard work on the subject.

PHILIP ABBOTT

Wayne State University
Detroit
Michigan

SCHIEBER, SYLVESTER J. and JOHN B. SHOVEN. 1999. *The Real Deal: The History and Future of Social Security*. Pp. xix, 450. New Haven, CT: Yale University Press. $45.00. Paperbound, $18.95.

Multidisciplinarity is in vogue, but few scholars (including Social Security commentators) seem comfortable—much less competent—crossing disciplinary domains. Policy analysts and economists do not waste time in archives; historians rarely get to discuss future options. *The Real Deal* is an exception, happily, to this generalization. Sylvester Schieber, a Beltway veteran now with a major pension consulting firm, and Stanford economist John Shoven offer us a balanced account of how the nation's largest social insurance program evolved. In the last part of the book, the pair consider ways of ensuring that Social Security will have sufficient funds; much of their analysis builds on ideas that the senior author proposed while serving on the latest (1994-96) advisory council.

The first half of *The Real Deal* appropriately builds on firsthand accounts by such program stalwarts as Arthur Altmeyer, Robert Ball, and Robert Myers, as well as Martha Derthick's *Policymaking for Social Security* (1979) and historians. To this literature, Schieber and Shoven add some archival gems of their own, using language by turns witty and provocative. For instance, they seize on an allusion to "Frogdom" that appeared in an article Altmeyer received in 1937. The analogy of frogs slowly boiling to death as water heats becomes the authors' way of explaining how Social Security's financing became more problematic as the ratio between workers and beneficiaries altered in a pay-as-you-go system.

Schieber and Shoven take the past seriously. The pair agree with other scholars about the importance of the 1939, 1950, 1965, and 1972 amendments to Social Security. More convincingly than other overviews, *The Real Deal* identifies a disconnect between financing and principles. Fights in 1937-38 over how to finance the program, claim the authors, were never resolved. "It is amazing what religious zeal can do if it's backed by a little esthetic logic," note the authors. New cohorts of experts and rising generations of workers no longer share the faith in Social Security evinced by the program's architects. Despite its past successes, pundits and analysts disagreed funda-

mentally about whether Social Security could continue to provide "adequate" support for low-income workers while guaranteeing an "equitable" return to future beneficiaries. The 1983 compromises were intended to fix technical flaws, but recent developments show that there were neither easy votes nor clever ways to patch over fundamental disagreements.

To my mind, the weakest section of *The Real Deal* is the discussion of deliberations of the 1994-96 Advisory Council. Schieber's impressions of fellow members and his goals ensure the account's value as a primary reference. But the broader picture gets lost in details. I question the authors' assertion that "no prior council had focused on the issue of fairness across generations to the extent that this one did," given the rhetoric of the council report and legislative debate in 1939. I may have been persuaded had Schieber and Shoven referred to the generational-equity debate that raged in the 1980s and the series of public opinion polls and journal articles that fan voters' anxieties.

In the last section, Schieber and Shoven make the case for a two-tier program that features mandatory private savings accounts. Even critics will appreciate the lucid manner in which the proposal is set forth. *The Real Deal* is indispensable for libraries and class use.

W. ANDREW ACHENBAUM

University of Houston
Texas

WYCKOFF, WILLIAM. 1999. *Creating Colorado: The Making of a Western American Landscape, 1860-1940.* Pp. xi, 352. New Haven, CT: Yale University Press. $30.00.

Creating Colorado is a fine example of the "new regional geography." Cultural-historical geographer William Wyckoff situates Colorado metaphorically and physically at the heart of the mountain West of the United States. All of the West's economic systems are represented in the state: extractive industries, manufacturing, service industries, tourism, dryland farming, irrigated farming, and ranching. Colorado has also had a substantial Hispanic population and a considerable range of European immigrants. For the West, labor unions were remarkably strong because of highly capitalized, deep mining. Wyckoff is thus able to convincingly demonstrate that Colorado is not one state but many and thus a metaphor for all varieties of the American West. Colorado's rivers drain east and west of the continental divide, and Colorado perforce has become home to some of the most ambitious federally funded and managed river basin management projects in the country. Much of the state's complexity, of course, comes from the tyranny of the rectangular survey system, forcing unnatural ecological boundaries onto political units.

Wyckoff's book is structured around five themes: the formative impact of first effective settlement; the development of Colorado as a unique meeting place (but not a melting pot) of cultures; the intersection of capitalist and liberal individualist social and economic structuring mechanisms; the fragility of the Western ecology; and the close interaction of human geographies and political institutions.

As Wyckoff rightly reminds us, as late as 1893 the West was still "a colonized periphery that had little control over its resources." This central fact has much to do with the development of political institutions in the region. For good or ill, the West was a ward of the federal government, and the manipulation of that government by Eastern interests had much to do with Colorado's early development. As time wore on, the region's development would be increasingly guided by lo-

cal elites, but those elites, like the Eastern elites before them, worked through the federal government. Wyckoff summarizes this theme nicely when he says that, "contrary to frontier myths, the federal government often led rather than followed the course of settlement. . . . the colonial nature of the relationship between Washington, D.C., and the West was clear." Once American political control of the region was secured from the claims of both indigenous peoples and other European states, "the phalanx of essentially private entrepreneurial capital was complemented and assisted by sympathetic territorial, state, and national governments." One of the most effective ways Colorado was able to control its own destiny was by the creation of an unusually comprehensive narrow-gauge rail transportation system at the hands of such local entrepreneurs as General William J. Palmer and Otto Mears.

In the chapter "Mountain Geographies," Wyckoff does a fine job of indicating how the birth of the national environmental movement in the late nineteenth century can be traced to the serious problems posed by the fragile ecosystem of Colorado's mountain region. Because of the intensity and complexity of settlement here, and because of the evocation of the aesthetics of tourism in the mountains from Alfred Bierstadt onward, these problems were encountered and thus resolved in Colorado before anywhere else in the mountain West. As Wyckoff puts it, "The impulse toward conservation was apparent in the state's 1876 constitutional convention." This impulse strengthened over time, with the state's elites usually being ahead of the federal government in their desire to use governmental power to protect their fragile mountain ecosystem, although usually in such a way as to allow recreational development of these resources. This early, elite, aesthetic impulse to preservation matured into a more general economic impulse, in particular when it was realized how ecologically fragile the major agricultural production systems of the state could be.

Wyckoff is to be commended for a fine volume that should be of interest to social scientists interested in how events work themselves out in real places and how the particular character of places can modify those events. I, for one, hope that he will now turn his attention to the working out of those themes in other parts of the American West.

PETER J. HUGILL

Texas A & M University
College Station

SOCIOLOGY

COLLINS, PATRICIA HILL. 1998. *Fighting Words: Black Women and the Search for Justice.* Pp. vii, 312. Minneapolis: University of Minnesota Press. No price.

When assigned to teach the unit on community to poor black second-graders in the early 1970s, Patricia Hill Collins, as well as her pupils, knew that the experiences of the white children in their texts did not mirror their own. She encouraged her pupils to talk about their own lives. Afterward, they returned to the book with fresh eyes and reworked its ideas into the context of their own experiences. This was a catalyst in Collins's growing recognition of the place of ideas in the legitimated curriculum produced by the elites (read: whites) in hierarchical power relations. Moreover, theory in the academy, says Collins, operates very much like curricula elsewhere. In either case, theory and curriculum appear hegemonic yet spark rebellion in the form of oppositional knowledge (read: fighting words) and generate unanticipated results.

The creation of theories apart from those legitimized by the academy is central to Patricia Hill Collins's arguments in *Fighting Words: Black Women and the Search for Justice.* It explores the questions "What epistemological criteria best evaluate critical social theories that aim to oppose oppression?" and "What standards might be used to determine how effectively a critical social theory confronts injustice?" *Fighting Words* builds upon Collins's *Black Feminist Thought* (1990) but supersedes it by focusing upon political realities; examining the intersection of race, gender, and science; evaluating the politics of postmodernism; assessing the gendered content of Afrocentrism; and suggesting an epistemology for empowerment. Collins confines these matters to three questions and delves into a multiplicity of sources across disciplines to forge a "sociology of knowledge" to ground her answers and pithy analyses.

Part 1's question, "What issues does Black feminist thought confront as critical social theory?", permits Collins to revisit her "outsider-within" theory. To be sure, the outsider (read: nonwhite, nonmale, non-elite) inside mainstream operations produces oppositional knowledge that serves to redefine concepts of marginality and to reclaim strength. Despite these advantages, black women insiders face the politics of containment, according to Collins. Even more poignant is the urgency to thwart ongoing surveillance, or control measures, and break out of the designated "place." Chapter 1, "The More Things Change, the More They Stay the Same," reflects their dilemma. Collins suggests that black feminist thought must formulate new strategies to confront reconfigured discrimination. However, she admits that coming to voice publicly carries little weight against racism without possessing attendant powers in social institutions.

The second part of *Fighting Words* concerns itself with the question "What issues does Black feminist thought raise for critical social theory?" Answers emerge from an extensive critique of sociology, postmodernism, and Afrocentrism. Collins is at her best in the structural organization of this argument. Readers will appreciate her treatment of sociologist Joyce Ladner's path-breaking *Tomorrow's Tomorrow* (1972; 1995). That seminal study emphasized race, gender, and class within a framework bolstered by "qualitative research grounded in positivist science." Much of what black women accrued from the race-gender-class focus slips away in the deconstruction and decentering of knowledge through postmodern lenses. Finally, the contested terrain between women and men within Afrocentrism suggests that their debate is far from settled.

In Part 3, Collins asks, "What contributions can Black feminist thought make to critical social theory?" The author moves beyond critique and toward an epistemology of empowerment. Sojourner Truth serves as a model, and Collins argues that spirituality is important to contemporary black women's conceptualization of critical social theory. Ultimately, the solution to injustice is through moral authority.

Readers may find this conclusion less thought provoking than others in *Fighting Words*, yet it will not detract from Collins's sophisticated theoretical and creative contribution to the literature.

WILMA KING

University of Missouri
Columbia

DILLON, MICHELLE, 1999. *Catholic Identity: Balancing Reason, Faith,*
and Power. Pp. x, 289. New York: Cambridge University Press. $45.99. Paperbound, $19.95.

In *Slouching to Gomorrah*, Robert Bork laments the fragmentation of our society and the rejection by many of God, reason, the laws of history, and moral or natural law. Communitarian sociologists such as Amitai Etzioni think the remedy for this social anarchy is a return to core values. But others including Michelle Dillon find the recovery of such "universalism" unrealistic. However, the advent of cultural diversity need not, she thinks, mean the proliferation of subcultural groupings disconnected from a broadly shared tradition. As an instance of this possibility, she offers this study of pro-change Catholics. She shows how they have managed to craft their own identity while remaining connected to the broad Catholic tradition. This construction of their own proper identity by pro-change Catholics, she maintains, involves a "critical, reflexive, and collectively contested activity whereby the plurality of symbols and traditions within Catholicism are appropriated and reinterpreted in multiple ways."

One of the pro-change Catholic groups she highlights in this study is Dignity, the association of gay and lesbian Catholics. Acquainting herself with the Boston chapter by interviews and attendance at their liturgies, she notes their strong attachment to the Mass and the symbols of Catholicism. But their view of church beliefs as socially constructed enables them to reinterpret the church's teaching on sexuality. Also, their creation of a gay and lesbian Catholicism engaged them in systematically linking faith and sexuality and publicly affirming the boundlessness between them.

The case of gay Catholics she finds especially interesting since their very lifestyle is pathologized by the Church. The pain of this experience is brought out in a number of stories. One man in his late forties told how easy it was as an adolescent in a parochial school to contemplate suicide.

For many, the question naturally arises, Why bother? Why this attachment to a tradition when that same tradition is used by the Church authority to denounce their sexuality? Various reasons are given. A college-educated woman in her mid-thirties says, "It's like a gene thing. . . . I want to stay connected to that spirituality and also this social justice stuff. . . . and there's a way in which ritual . . . touches different parts of me. . . . [Church] is a place to go to celebrate that spirituality. [But] I feel incredibly disconnected . . . from the hierarchy of our church." Others note their feeling for the universality of the Church and its continuity over 2000 years and how its collective historical memory is inscribed in their personal memories.

Pro-change Catholics, Dillon notes, are committed to remodeling the Church as a more inclusive and pluralistic community while at the same time they want to retain solidarity with the larger Catholic community. Putting this in a broader perspective, she sees this effort of pro-change Catholics as an emancipatory model for those seeking to free themselves from inegalitarian structures and traditions.

Among other interesting observations, she notes that what pro-change Catholics are doing in an organized way other dissenting Catholics are doing in a less deliberate way. Moreover, when she sampled the views of 20 Catholic theologians drawn at random from the faculties of two major centers of Catholic theology (admittedly renowned for their academic liberalism), she found they agreed to a large extent with the understanding of Catholicism held by pro-change Catholics.

This book is altogether a thoughtful study and grist for the mills of pro-change Catholics. But how many swallows does it take to make a spring?

THOMAS BOKENKOTTER

Xavier University
Cincinnati
Ohio

HALLAM, ELIZABETH, JENNY HOCKEY, and GLENNYS HOWARTH. 1999. *Beyond the Body: Death and Social Identity.* Pp. xi, 232. New York: Routledge. $85.00. Paperbound, $25.99.

Whether an individual's identity is so tied up with the physical body as to be lost when that body ceases functioning is an issue that has been of concern for several millennia at least. Many, perhaps most, cultures have postulated the existence of a soul which continues after the death of the body, a soul, moreover, which continues to interact with others even after death. This book considers such interactions for a variety of situations.

The authors are Elizabeth Hallam, director of cultural history at the University of Aberdeen; Jenny Hockey, senior lecturer in health studies at the University of Hull; and Glennys Howarth, at the time of publication associate professor of sociology at the University of Sydney and currently at the Department of Social and Political Sciences, University of Bath, England. As might be expected from these affiliations, the book shows a preference for British academic research.

The authors posit a Western sharp dichotomy between life and death and argue instead for a blurring of the line with an emphasis on the social context. As they note on the first page, "Not all bodies are synonymous with a self and not all selves have an embodied corporeal presence." The first chapter is essentially an annotated review of the literature on the body in its social setting. This is followed by a discussion of how the dying and dead body is depicted in the visual arts, and the changes in these representations from the medieval period to the present. Contemporaneous viewing of the body, the use of such materials as photographs in remembering the deceased, and artistic depictions all serve to bring out the complex agendas involved in the social context of death, with an emphasis on how they reflect on the nature of power and social relationships. This is followed by a discussion of the "old" body—such questions as how people perceive and deal with the aging body, and the concept of social death, where the body remains alive but social interactions are reduced almost to nothing. This leads into a discussion of the concept of when death occurs and the impact of technological advances on the medical definition of death, focusing on stillbirths and persistent vegetative states as examples. Coroner's courts, dealing with cases of sudden death, aim to define the causes of the end of life and, in doing so, define a retrospective biography, largely social, of the individual. An identity is imposed on the individual, possibly in contradiction to known previous identities when secrets are revealed. Church courts in the sixteenth and seventeenth centuries, devoted to resolving testamentary questions, again had to consider the individual's biography in order to determine his intentions, but disposition also depended on gender, moral, and cultural contexts. Returning to the present, the authors consider the role of the mortician in arranging the body to be lifelike, to accord with the survivor's memories. The remaining three chapters (other than the conclusion) all deal with the continuing presence of the dead individual, either as subsumed in the selves of the survivors; as physical manifestations, such as ghosts; or as mediated through spiritualists and clairvoyants.

I found the book to contain a number of interesting and illuminating insights, making it a worthwhile read, though I was often put off by an apparent need of the authors to seem properly academic, detracting from the points they were making. In some portions, the book represents a work in progress, as, for example, the chapter on ghosts and the like, which is based on a single extended interview with one Christian English minister. The bibliography, though extensive, is far from definitive. I commend the authors, however, for being willing to include such currently nonrespectable topics as spiritualism in dealing with how real people view death and the continuing presence of the deceased. They carry their point, that there is a rather fuzzy line, rather than a sharp dichotomy, between life and death.

SAM SILVERMAN

Lexington
Massachusetts

NORMAN, DONALD A. 1999. *The Invisible Computer: Why Good Products Can Fail, the Personal Computer Is So Complex, and Information Appliances Are the Solution.* Pp. xii, 302. Cambridge: MIT Press. Paperbound, $13.95.

The theme of this book is that the personal computer is unduly complex because of its heritage, which it has failed to outgrow. Most new technological products, early in their life cycle, are technology based, and technical advance is the main basis of competition. This business strategy works satisfactorily because the early adopters are technologically sophisticated and the technological basis for the product is undergoing continuous change. But eventually, usually within a few years, the mass market of consumers begins adopting the product. Now the main strategy for diffusing the product must become customer driven, and the buyers demand convenience and pleasure from using the product. Now the basis of business competition shifts to price, appearance, and user friendliness. What the product provides must now match consumer needs.

But this transition has not occurred for personal computers in the United States, despite the fact that approximately 37 percent of U.S. households have now adopted them. Computer companies continue to pursue technological advance, advertising that their products are faster and more powerful, despite the fact that personal computers are used mainly for such relatively simple tasks as word processing and e-mail communication. This disconnect is explored at length in this book, and its reasons are traced mainly to the history of computer development and to the training and mind-set of computer entrepreneurs.

The author, Donald Norman, is professor emeritus of cognitive science at the University of California, San Diego, and a cofounder of the Nielson Norman Group, an executive consulting company. Norman is especially known for his 1990 book, *The Design of Everyday Things*. He suggests three axioms of design: simplicity, versatility, and pleasurability. Norman analyzes the case of the phonograph to show that being first and best with a technology is not good enough for business success. Thomas Edison invented the phonograph, but consumers preferred a competing product, the Victrola, which won the marketplace.

Norman's advice to technologists? Listen to the consumer, especially the mass majority who adopt a new idea after the innovators and early adopters. Norman predicts that the personal computer will eventually be replaced by various specialized applications that will not be identifiable as computers per se. Examples are home information centers, weather displays, and computerized shopping lists.

Norman's arguments are well illustrated with photographs and graphics, and the writing is clear. The main theme deserves attention, more than it has received to date.

EVERETT M. ROGERS

University of New Mexico
Albuquerque

WILK, RICHARD R. 1997. *Household Ecology: Economic Change and Domestic Life Among the Kekchi Maya in Belize*. Pp. xxxii, 280. DeKalb: Northern Illinois Press. Paperbound, $20.00.

This is a paperback reprint of Wilk's book, first published in 1991; the basic text is unchanged but Wilk has added a new preface that discusses the reception of his work. In both his dissertation and the original volume, Wilk shows that the Kekchi Maya are relatively recent immigrants into what has become Belize. Because of this, government officials have used his work to claim that the Kekchi do not deserve any special treatment as indigenous people. Wilk raises the issue of the anthropologist's ethical responsibilities to the people he studies and draws attention to the problem of other people's using one's work to the detriment of the people studied and the difficulties in foreseeing how one's work will be used.

Wilk begins his analysis of Kekchi households with a critical review of the literature that purports to explain the current conditions in Indian communities by saying that the people are "traditional" and do not want to change or that they are victims of larger political economic forces. He rejects both reasons and argues instead that Indian communities and their "traditions" are creations of specific historical conditions, that these traditions reflect responses to changing conditions, and that Indians are not passive victims but active creators of local adaptations that respond to changing political and economic conditions. For Wilk, households are the places where these adaptations emerge.

Wilk organizes his discussion of households around his larger theoretical focus on cultural ecology. Culture provides the conceptual structures that organize labor, social units, access to resources, reproduction, and ideology. These resources and the ways in which people use them allow societies to adapt to particular social, political, economic, and physical environments. Cultural organizations are an adaptive response, but they also become part of the environment that has to be taken into account when circumstances change.

To make his argument, Wilk turns to a detailed discussion of the Kekchi in Belize. He relies on data from his year of fieldwork in the community of Aguacate and comparative surveys he did in two other communities. For comparative material, he also uses data from other Kekchi communities in different areas.

Wilk organizes his materials to build his ecological argument. He describes the range of environmental constraints: historical, political, economic, and physical. Having provided the larger context, he turns to the resources available for Kekchi livelihood and discusses land tenure, crops, domestic and wild animals, and gathered resources. Given these resources and constraints, Wilk then discusses labor requirements of the assorted crops, labor bottlenecks, and ways of organizing labor groups. Finally, Wilk returns to his discussion of households as adaptive groups.

Wilk's argument about households as the point of mediation between larger political economic units and local environments is a reasonable one. However, his reliance on cultural ecology gets in the way of his household analysis. The ecological approach has considerable difficulty in integrating outside analytical perspectives with people's perceptions, values, and beliefs. As a consequence, there is curiously little about what households actually do, what their goals are, or the ways in which they organize themselves to utilize their available labor and resources.

Overall, the book is disappointing. The initial critical reviews of development, evolutionary theory, and household analyses are interesting but ultimately do not connect with the Kekchi ethnography. The ethnography itself is neither a detailed statistical account of Kekchi household economies nor a general ethnography of how Kekchi householders utilize their resources to make their living in a complex and changing environment.

NICOLA TANNENBAUM

Lehigh University
Bethlehem
Pennsylvania

ECONOMICS

BRADY, ROSE. 1999. *Kapitalizm: Russia's Struggle to Free Its Economy*. Pp. xxvii, 289. New Haven, CT: Yale University Press. $30.00.

Rose Brady, the Moscow bureau chief for *Business Week* from 1989 to 1993, relies on dozens of interviews to chronicle the impact, on the previously stagnant and autarchic Russian economy, of rapid privatization, ruinous inflation, and mass unemployment. Her account of the major reforms and crises of the past decade brings into focus the peculiarities of the new Russian capitalism, which include the rapid enrichment of new entrepreneurs, many from the former Soviet elite; asset stripping and deindustrialization; massive exports of capital (estimated, on p. 100, at between $5 billion and $50 billion in 1993) to such safe havens as Switzerland and Cyprus; and ineffective fiscal and monetary policies that transformed Russia into "a patchwork of many different local and regional economies, all loosely sewn together."

Particularly painful are Brady's accounts of key episodes that led the Russian economy to its sorry state in 2000. Under the partial (and therefore flawed) "shock therapy" of 1992, prices were liberalized without adequate monetary controls, so that inflation soared to 2509 percent that year and the ruble lost more than 97 percent of its value, in dollar terms, between January 1991 and January 1997. By the middle of the decade, entrepreneurs whom Brady calls the "ruble barons" had created huge financial, energy, and industrial conglomerates that dominated the economy. Their positive television coverage of President Boris Yeltsin and their illegal contributions of money to his campaign allowed him to win reelection as president in 1996 despite his serious illness. In August 1998, a new economic crisis wiped out the modest gains of 1997, forced the state to repudiate its debt, and caused a collapse of the ruble from 6:1 to the dollar in July 1998 to 23:1 in January 1999 and 27:1 a year later.

Brady's narrative strategy is especially effective in two case studies, one of hope, the other of despair. The first case has to do with the Vladimir Tractor Factory. By 1997, the factory had undergone a massive restructuring at the hands of a young manager, elected by the workers, whose Harvard M.B.A. proved less useful than his ability to survive political chaos. The second case is a vivid supplement to Stephen Handelman's fine study of organized crime in Russia (also published by Yale University Press). In this supplement, Brady sketches a portrait of "Victor," a young thug who nonchalantly describes the various forms of extortion used by organized crime. He reports the going rate, in 1994, of a contract murder: $5000.

Twelve statistical tables reiterate the well-known trends of rampant inflation, mass unemployment, and negative industrial growth (until 1997), but equally striking are the 28 photographs that illustrate the new appearance of Russia in the 1990s, especially Alexei Rogov's images of peddlers in impromptu street markets, pro-Communist demonstrators, bewildered workers in obsolescent machinery factories, and beggars in the snow. A chronology of major events helps to place the drama of economic change in the context of political crises that reflect authoritarian and xenophobic attitudes inherited from the czarist and Soviet cultural traditions. To the list of recommended readings in the bibliography I would add the books of Marshall Goodman, who analyzes Yeltsin's Russia from the perspective of an expert on the Soviet economy; the sociological studies of attitudes toward economic reform, with special attention to workers, pensioners, and other losers in the liberalization process, by Lynn Nelson and Irina Kuzes and by Bertram Silverman and Murray Yanowitch; and Alfred Kokh's memoir of the privatization campaign, probably the largest transfer of property in human history.

THOMAS C. OWEN

Louisiana State University
Baton Rouge

OTHER BOOKS

ENTMAN, ROBERT M. and ANDREW ROJECKI. 2000. *The Black Image in the White Mind: Media and Race in America.* Pp. xix, 305. Chicago: University of Chicago Press. $26.00.

ERICKSON, JOHN. 1983. *The Road to Berlin: Stalin's War with Germany.* Pp. xiii, 877. New Haven, CT: Yale University Press. Paperbound, no price.

————. 1999. *The Road to Stalingrad: Stalin's War with Germany.* Pp. x, 594. New Haven, CT: Yale University Press. Paperbound, $19.95.

ESAIASSON, PETER and KNUT HEIDEAR, eds. 2000. *Beyond Westminster and Congress: The Nordic Experience.* Pp. xii, 506. Columbus: Ohio State University Press. $65.00. Paperbound, $29.95.

EVANS, GEOFFREY, ed. 1999. *The End of Class Politics? Class Voting in Comparative Context.* Pp. xv, 364. New York: Oxford University Press. $35.00.

FALK, RICHARD. 1995. *On Humane Governance: Toward a New Global Politics.* Pp. xvi, 288. University Park: Pennsylvania State University Press. $45.00. Paperbound, $16.95.

FALOLA, TOYIN. 1999. *The History of Nigeria.* Pp. xviii, 269. Westport, CT: Greenwood Press. $35.00.

FARKAS, GEORGE. 1996. *Human Capital or Cultural Capital? Ethnicity and Poverty Groups in an Urban School District.* Pp. xiv, 216. Hawthorne, NY: Aldine de Gruyter. No price.

FESTENSTEIN, MATTHEW. 1998. *Pragmatism and Political Theory: From Dewey to Rorty.* Pp. viii, 237. Chicago: University of Chicago Press. $50.00. Paperbound, $19.00.

FIELD, HERMANN and KATE FIELD. 2000. *Trapped in the Cold War: The Ordeal of an American Family.* Pp. 451. Stanford, CA: Stanford University Press. $45.00.

GREVEN, MICHAEL T. and LOUIS W. PAULY. 2000. *Democracy Beyond the State? The European Dilemma and the Emerging Global Order.* Pp. vii, 191. Lanham, MD: Rowman & Littlefield. $65.00. Paperbound, $24.95.

GRIFFITH, IVELAW LLOYD. 1997. *Drugs and Security in the Caribbean: Sovereignty Under Siege.* Pp. xix, 295. University Park: Pennsylvania State University Press. $35.00. Paperbound, $16.95.

HABIBULLAH, MUZAFAR SHAH. 1999. *Divisia Monetary Aggregates and Economic Activities in Asian Developing Economies.* Pp. xiii, 196. Brookfield, VT: Ashgate. $69.95.

HALEY, JOHN OWEN. 1998. *The Spirit of Japanese Law.* Pp. xx, 251. Athens: University of Georgia Press. No price.

HARDING, JENNIFER. 1998. *Sex Acts: Practices of Femininity and Masculinity.* Pp. vi, 154. Thousand Oaks, CA: Sage. $69.95. Paperbound, $22.95.

HARDT, HANNO. 1999. *In the Company of Media: Cultural Constructions of Communication, 1920s-1930s.* Pp. xii, 186. Boulder, CO: Westview Press. $60.00.

HARGROVE, ERWIN C. 1998. *The President as Leader: Appealing to the Better Angels of Our Nature.* Pp. ix, 229. Lawrence: University Press of Kansas. $25.00.

HART, DAVID M. 1998. *Forged Consensus: Science, Technology, and Economic Policy in the United States, 1921-1953.* Pp. xiv, 267. Princeton, NJ: Princeton University Press. $39.95.

HAYS, SHARON. 1996. *The Cultural Contradictions of Motherhood.* Pp. xv, 252. New Haven, CT: Yale University Press. Paperbound, $25.00.

HAYWARD, JACK, BRIAN BARRY, and ARCHIE BROWN, eds. 2000. *The British Study of Politics in the Twentieth Century.* Pp. xv, 511. New York: Oxford University Press. $60.00.

JUDSON, KATHARINE B., ed. 2000. *Native American Legends of the Great Lakes and the Mississippi Valley.* Pp. 204. DeKalb: Northern Illinois University Press. $38.00. Paperbound, $18.00.

JUMONVILLE, NEIL. 1999. *Henry Steele Commager: Midcentury Liberalism and the History of the Present.* Pp. xviii, 328. Chapel Hill: University of North Carolina Press. $49.95.

KALMAN, LAURA. 1996. *The Strange Career of Legal Liberalism.* Pp. viii, 375. New Haven, CT: Yale University Press. $40.00.

KANE, STEPHANIE. 1998. *AIDS Alibis: Sex, Drugs and Crime in the Americas.* Pp. ix, 222. Philadelphia: Temple University Press. No price.

KAPLAN, ALICE. 2000. *The Collaborator: The Trial and Execution of Robert Brasillach.* Pp. xvi, 308. Chicago: University of Chicago Press. $25.00.

KATZENSTEIN, MARY FAINSOD. 1998. *Faithful and Fearless: Moving Feminist Protest Inside the Church and Military.* Pp. xiii, 270. Princeton, NJ: Princeton University Press. $24.95.

KEKES, JOHN. 1997. *Against Liberalism.* Pp. xi, 244. Ithaca, NY: Cornell University Press. $42.50. Paperbound, $16.95.

KESSLER, HERBERT L. and JOHANNA ZACHARIAS. 2000. *Rome 1300: On the Path of the Pilgrim.* Pp. ix, 237. New Haven, CT: Yale University Press. $35.00.

KHOURY, DINA RIZK. 1997. *State and Provincial Society in the Ottoman Empire: Mosul, 1540-1834.* Pp. xviii, 253. New York: Cambridge University Press. No price.

KIRBY-SMITH, H. T. 2000. *The Celestial Twins: Poetry and Music Through the Ages.* Pp. xi, 328. Amherst: University of Massachusetts Press. $40.00.

KIRK, DONALD. 2000. *Korean Crisis: Unraveling of the Miracle in the IMF Era.* Pp. xii, 386. New York: St. Martin's Press. $55.00.

MASTNY, VOJTECH. 1996. *The Cold War and Soviet Insecurity: The Stalin Years.* Pp. xi, 285. New York: Oxford University Press. $30.00.

MATHIAS, FRANK F. 2000. *The GI Generation: A Memoir.* Pp. xiii, 267. Lexington: University Press of Kentucky. $25.00.

MATUSOW, ALLEN J. 1998. *Nixon's Economy: Booms, Busts, Dollars, and Votes.* Pp. xii, 323. Lawrence: University Press of Kansas. $35.00.

MAYER, KENNETH R. and DAVID T. CANON. 1999. *The Dysfunctional Congress? The Individual Roots of an Institutional Dilemma.* Pp. xii, 195. Boulder, CO: Westview Press. $55.00. Paperbound, $15.95.

McCAFFRAY, SUSAN P. 1996. *The Politics of Industrialization in Tsarist Russia: The Association of Southern Coal and Steel Producers, 1874-1914.* Pp. xxii, 299. DeKalb: Northern Illinois University Press. No price.

McCLINTOCK, CYNTHIA. 1998. *Revolutionary Movements in Latin America: El Salvador's FMLN and Peru's Shining Path.* Pp. xix, 491. Washington, DC: United States Institute of Peace Press. $37.50.

McKENNA, TERESA. 1997. *Migrant Song: Politics and Process in Contemporary Chicano Literature.* Pp. xii, 158. Austin: University of Texas Press. $27.50. Paperbound, $12.95.

MEILAENDER, GILBERT. 2000. *Things That Count.* Pp. 393. Wilmington, DE: ISI Books. $24.95.

MELONE, ALBERT P. 1998. *Creating Parliamentary Government: The Transition to Democracy in Bulgaria.* Pp. xxi, 323. Columbus: Ohio State University Press. $45.95. Paperbound, $20.95.

MENDOZA, PLINIO APULEYO, CARLOS ALBERTO MONTANER, and ALVARO VARGAS LLOSA. 2000.

Guide to the Perfect Latin American Idiot. Pp. xvii, 219. New York: Madison Books. $24.95.

NINO, CARLOS SANTIAGO. 1996. *Radical Evil on Trial.* Pp. xii, 220. New Haven, CT: Yale University Press. Paperbound, no price.

NOHLEN, DIETER, MICHAEL KRENNERICH, and BERNHARD THIBAUT, eds. 1999. *Elections in Africa.* Pp. xvi, 984. New York: Oxford University Press. $140.00.

OAKES, GUY and ARTHUR J. VIDICH. 1999. *Collaboration, Reputation, and Ethics in American Academic Life: Hans H. Gerth and C. Wright Mills.* Pp. viii, 188. Champaign: University of Illinois Press. $34.95. Paperbound, $14.95.

O'CADIZ, PILAR, PIA LINQUIST WONG, and CARLOS ALBERTO TORRES. 1998. *Education and Democracy: Paulo Freire, Social Movements, and Educational Reform in Sao Paulo.* Pp. xv, 270. Boulder, CO: Westview Press. $60.00.

OH, KIE-CHANG JOHN. 1999. *Korean Politics.* Pp. xii, 255. Ithaca, NY: Cornell University Press. $45.00. Paperbound, $16.95.

OH, KONGDAN, ed. 2000. *Korea Briefing, 1997-1999: Challenges and Change at the Turn of the Century.* Pp. ix, 243. Armonk, NY: M. E. Sharpe. $64.95. Paperbound, $24.95.

O'MALLEY, PADRAIG, ed. 1999. *Southern Africa: The People's Voices: Perspectives on Democracy.* Pp. x, 217. Parktown, South Africa: National Democratic Institute for International Affairs. Paperbound, no price.

OULD-ABDALLAH, AHMEDOU. 2000. *Burundi on the Brink, 1993-95: A United Nations Special Envoy Reflects on Preventive Diplomacy.* Pp. xxv, 169. Washington, DC: United States Institute of Peace Press. Paperbound, no price.

PAGDEN, ANTHONY. 1998. *Lords of All the World: Ideologies of Empire in Spain, Britain and France c. 1500-c. 1800.* Pp. ix, 244. New Haven, CT: Yale University Press. $40.00. Paperbound, $18.00.

POLLACK, JONATHAN D. and CHUNG MIN LEE. 1999. *Preparing for Korean Unification: Scenarios and Implications.* Pp. xx, 98. Santa Monica, CA: RAND. Paperbound, $15.00.

PORKET, J. L. 1998. *Modern Economic Systems and Their Transformation.* Pp. xvii, 318. New York: St. Martin's Press. $79.95.

POTTS, MALCOLM and ROGER SHORT. 1999. *Ever Since Adam and Eve: The Evolution of Human Sexuality.* Pp. x, 358. New York: Cambridge University Press. No price.

PRZEWORSKI, ADAM, SUSAN C. STOKES, and BERNARD MANIN, eds. 1999. *Democracy, Accountability, and Representation.* Pp. ix, 351. New York: Cambridge University Press. $59.95. Paperbound, $22.95.

PYCIOR, JULIE LEININGER. 1997. *LBJ and Mexican Americans: The Paradox of Power.* Pp. xvi, 329. Austin: University of Texas Press. $45.00. Paperbound, $19.95.

RABINOVICH, ITAMAR. 1998. *The Brink of Peace: The Israeli-Syrian Negotiations.* Pp. xv, 283. Princeton, NJ: Princeton University Press. No price.

RANCIERE, JACQUES. 1999. *Disagreement: Politics and Philosophy.* Pp. xiii, 150. Minneapolis: University of Minnesota Press. No price.

RAUSCH, JANE M. 1999. *Colombia: Territorial Rule and the Llanos Frontier.* Pp. xi, 285. Gainesville: University Press of Florida. No price.

REID, ANNA. 1999. *Borderland: A Journey Through the History of Ukraine.* Pp. xiii, 258. Boulder, CO: Westview Press. $25.00.

RESCHER, NICHOLAS. 1999. *The Limits of Science*. Rev. ed. Pp. xii, 282. Pittsburgh, PA: University of Pittsburgh Press. Paperbound, $19.95.

ROY, RAMASHRAY and PAUL WALLACE, eds. 1999. *Indian Politics and the 1998 Election: Regionalism, Hindutva and State Politics*. Pp. 375. New Delhi, India: Sage. $49.95.

ROZELL, MARK J. and CLYDE WILCOX, eds. 2000. *The Clinton Scandal and the Future of American Government*. Pp. xxii, 269. Washington, DC: Georgetown University Press. $55.00. Paperbound, $18.95.

RUSSELL, RICHARD B. and LYNDON B. JOHNSON. 1998. *Colleagues*. Pp. xxi, 243. Macon, GA: Mercer University Press. Paperbound, $17.95.

SAGGERS, SHERRY and DENNIS GRAY. 1998. *Dealing with Alcohol: Indigenous Usage in Australia, New Zealand and Canada*. Pp. vii, 240. New York: Cambridge University Press. No price.

SAINSBURY, DIANE, ed. 2000. *Gender and Welfare State Regimes*. Pp. xiv, 293. New York: Oxford University Press. $74.00. Paperbound, $29.95.

SAITO, LELAND T. 1998. *Race and Politics: Asian Americans, Latinos, and Whites in a Los Angeles Suburb*. Pp. xiii, 250. Champaign: University of Illinois Press. $49.95. Paperbound, $21.95.

SAMPSON, GARY P. 2000. *Trade, Environment, and the WTO: The Post-Seattle Agenda*. Pp. xi, 154. Washington, DC: Overseas Development Council. Distributed by Johns Hopkins University Press, Baltimore, MD. Paperbound, $13.95.

SANDER, KATHLEEN WATERS. 1998. *The Business of Charity: The Woman's Exchange Movement, 1832-1900*. Pp. xi, 165. Champaign: University of Illinois Press. $39.95. Paperbound, $16.95.

SANDLER, STANLEY. 1999. *The Korean War: No Victors, No Vanquished*. Pp. xiv, 330. Lexington: University Press of Kentucky. $42.00. Paperbound, $19.00.

SMITH, MARK J. 1999. *Ecologism*. Pp. viii, 107. Minneapolis: University of Minnesota Press. $37.95. Paperbound, $14.95.

SMITH, W. RAND. 1998. *The Left's Dirty Job: The Politics of Industrial Restructuring in France and Spain*. Pp. xiii, 294. Pittsburgh, PA: University of Pittsburgh Press. $50.00 Paperbound, $22.95.

SOLINGEN, ETEL. 1998. *Regional Orders at Century's Dawn: Global and Domestic Influences on Grand Strategy*. Pp. xiii, 334. Princeton, NJ: Princeton University Press. $60.00. Paperbound, $18.95.

SOLOMON, RICHARD H. 2000. *Exiting Indochina: United States Leadership of the Cambodia Settlement and Normalization with Vietnam*. Pp. xix, 113. Washington, DC: United States Institute of Peace Press. Paperbound, $12.50.

SOMERVILLE, JOHN. 2000. *The Communist Trials and the American Tradition*. Pp. viii, 269. New York: International. Paperbound, $12.95.

SPINOSA, CHARLES, FERNANDO FLORES, and HUBERT L. DREYFUS. 1999. *Disclosing New Worlds: Entrepreneurship, Democratic Action, and the Cultivation of Solidarity*. Pp. x, 222. Cambridge: MIT Press. Paperbound, $15.00.

SPRITZER, LORRAINE NELSON and JEAN B. BERGMARK. 1997. *Grace Towns Hamilton and the Politics of Southern Change*. Pp. xv, 266. Athens: University of Georgia Press. Paperbound, no price.

SREMAC, DANIELLE S. 1999. *War of Words: Washington Tackles the Yugoslav Conflict*. Pp. xi, 284. Westport, CT: Praeger. $39.95.

SRINIVASAN, T. N. 1998. *Developing Countries and the Multilateral Trading System: From the GATT to the Uruguay Round and the Future.* Pp. x, 140. Boulder, CO: Westview Press. $35.00.

STAFFORD, BARBARA MARIA. 1998. *Good Looking: Essays on the Virtue of Images.* Pp. xv, 259. Cambridge: MIT Press. Paperbound, $15.00.

STAM, HENDERIKUS J., ed. 1998. *The Body and Psychology.* Pp. ix, 240. Thousand Oaks, CA: Sage. $66.00. Paperbound, $24.95.

INDEX